*A Companion to Australian*

M000273398

Camden House Companion Volumes

The Camden House Companions provide well-informed and up-to-date critical commentary on the most significant aspects of major works, periods, or literary figures. The Companions may be read profitably by the reader with a general interest in the subject. For the benefit of student and scholar, quotations are provided in the original language.

# A Companion to Australian Aboriginal Literature

Edited by
Belinda Wheeler

CAMDEN HOUSE

Rochester, New York

First published 2013 by Camden House
Reprinted in paperback 2015

Camden House is an imprint of Boydell & Brewer Inc.
668 Mt. Hope Avenue, Rochester, NY 14620, USA
www.camden-house.com
and of Boydell & Brewer Limited
PO Box 9, Woodbridge, Suffolk IP12 3DF, UK
www.boydellandbrewer.com

Paperback ISBN-13: 978-1-57113-938-2
Paperback ISBN-10: 1-57113-938-9
Hardcover ISBN-13: 978-1-57113-521-6
Hardcover ISBN-10: 1-57113-521-6

**Library of Congress Cataloging-in-Publication Data**

A companion to Australian Aboriginal literature / edited by Belinda Wheeler.
    pages cm.
Includes bibliographical references and index.
ISBN-13: 978-1-57113-521-6 (hardcover : acid-free paper) —
ISBN-10: 1-57113-521-9 (hardcover : acid-free paper)
    1. Australian literature—Aboriginal Australian authors—History and criticism. I. Wheeler, Belinda, 1974– editor of compilation.

PR9608.2.A96C66 2013
820.9'89915—dc23

2013010308

This publication is printed on acid-free paper.
Printed in the United States of America.

# Contents

# Foreword

ABORIGINAL LITERATURE MAY BE a new field in academic study, yet the term designates a set of creative and communicative practices that reach into deep time, "time immemorial" as Aboriginal people sometime call it, while also having a vital and diverse presence in contemporary culture. At the start of the twenty-first century, Indigenous Australian writers are prominent practitioners in the major literary genres of fiction and nonfiction, poetry, drama, and writing for young people. They regularly receive awards and accolades for their work. Alexis Wright won the prestigious Miles Franklin Literary Award for her novel *Carpentaria* in 2007, and Kim Scott won jointly for his novel *Benang: From the Heart* in 2000 and for his novel *That Deadman Dance* in 2010. Australian Indigenous writers are also leading innovators in collaborative expression across the generations, across art forms, in life writing, storytelling, film, performance, and video art, taking power in their responsibility for custodianship and transmission of culture. There are many reasons, then, why Aboriginal literature is an exciting area of creative achievement, worthy of attention, celebration, and scholarly inquiry. This new companion makes an important contribution to the work in the field, extending and deepening our understanding.

The term *Aboriginal literature* has a relatively recent currency. Writer-scholars Anita Heiss and Peter Minter used it for the title of their 2008 anthology where, in an introductory essay under that heading, they wrote, "This anthology presents, for the first time in a single volume, the range and depth of Aboriginal writing in English from the late eighteenth-century to the present day" (1). Almost all that material then appeared interwoven with other Australian writing from across the same period in the *Macquarie PEN Anthology of Australian Literature* and *The Literature of Australia*. Both were published in 2009 as different editions of the same work, and both were accompanied by another version of Heiss and Minter's defining essay, "Australian Literature," giving the term wide circulation and authority. The authors are careful to qualify the extent of inclusion, tacitly acknowledging that the field is larger than the scope of their anthology. It can encompass oral, visual, and performative expression, including in Indigenous languages where song and story, lore and law connect with living traditions from times long before the British arrived. More problematically it might reach to transcription, translation, and appropriation by outsiders. Heiss and

Minter's project establishes a lineage for Australian Aboriginal writing. In their words their anthology "records the history" of the "transformation in the human condition of all Aboriginal peoples" as it was "witnessed in writing ranging from the journalism, petitions and political letters of the nineteenth and early twentieth centuries, to the works of poetry and prose that are recognized widely today as significant contributions to the literature of the world" (1).

In identifying that lineage, they draw on important recent scholarship and critical discussion by Indigenous and non-Indigenous researchers alike, including earlier anthologies edited by Kevin Gilbert in 1988, Jack Davis, Mudrooroo (Colin Johnson), Stephen Muecke, and Adam Shoemaker in 1990; the contributors to *Blacklines: Contemporary Critical Writing by Indigenous Australians* (2003), edited by Michele Grossman; the work of Penny van Toorn in *Writing Never Arrives Naked: Early Aboriginal Cultures of Writing in Australia* (2006), and many others. *A Companion to Australian Aboriginal Literature* adds to this body of material.

Aboriginal literature has its own traditions, modes, and rhetoric, and it is almost always charged with political commitment. It asks to be respected and valued on its own terms. As Mick Dodson writes in his foreword to Heiss and Minter's anthology, "This is a cultural product as much as it is a literary text. . . . Much of that creativity and effort [of recent Indigenous publishing] has been understandably linked to the politics of Aboriginal Australia" (xiii). It therefore calls for different kinds of response and engagement, with the recognition that it is a distinct and separate expression of the Indigenous cultural world. At the same time, it connects with and even permeates the wider Australian current in so many ways that it needs to be interpreted in that larger context too: as dialogue, incursion, counterpoint. How many non-Indigenous Australian writers have used Aboriginal experience or culture in their work, in an often one-sided imaginative response? Aboriginal writing is the necessary answer. One of the most attractive and powerful aspects of Aboriginal creative expression is its capacity to cross boundaries, to give proper protocols, and to share its making communally, entering into exchanges with others. That is part of the transformative quality that enables work to reach out and travel, to connect with other indigenous cultures around the world, and to respond to the intense interest shown internationally. Several contributors to the current volume explore these interactions, investigating the collaborative interfaces in editing, life writing, translation, and transformation from one form or medium into another, in what constitutes a new turn in the field.

That is part of a consideration of how Aboriginal literature has the potential to change received understandings, not only of Australian literature but of literature itself, in the largest possible sense. The *Longman Anthology of World Literature* (2008) represents Australian writing with two pieces, both Indigenous, as if recognizing that Australian literature must begin there. In a "worldly" reassignment of priority, no other Australian literature is given a place. The two works, connected by title, suggest a story of disappearance followed by return: "We Are Going," the famous poem by Oodgeroo Noonuccal (1920–93), and "Going Home," a story by Archie Weller (1957–). That is a way of asking a radical question about what a truly Australian literature would actually be and offering an uncompromising answer. Ironically, though, Weller's Aboriginality subsequently came into question itself, though that need not reflect on the literary quality of his work. It shows, however, that any discussion of Aboriginal literature leads to searching inquiry.

Aboriginal literature asks us to think again about what is literature at its furthest limits and horizon. In the past, anthropologists rather than literary scholars discussed the cultural expression of Aboriginal Australians, often with little regard to individual authorship. The richness of song and drama was recognized by advocates of Aboriginal art, but the term *literature* has not always been applied in oral cultures without writing as conventionally defined. The challenge to those conventions in the course of the twentieth century, however, and the philosophical skepticism directed at hierarchical notions of the literary have encouraged alternative interpretive approaches and a more generous or fluid understanding of where literature begins and ends. In this companion, for example, contributors explore drama, film, music, writing for children and young adults, humor, and the gothic under the rubric of Aboriginal literature, as a newly conceived canon develops. Boundaries recede, and the potential to reach out and to reorient is embraced. As curator and author Philip Jones writes in relation to the contemporary art of central Australia, specifically that of Emily Kame Kngwarreye, whose work has ravished the world, "these paintings are fragments of a great, rambling literature" (14). The same is true of writing. Each work can be read and appreciated in itself, but it is also part of something larger, both an Indigenous record and a participant in a larger process of communication, not limited to Australia's borders.

*A Companion to Australian Aboriginal Literature*, edited by Belinda Wheeler, acknowledges both international interest in and the open and changing character of the field. It is a significant milestone on the journey for recognition, appreciation, and esteem, and it points the way to a discussion that connects beyond itself to parallels in other fields, becoming increasingly expansive, nuanced, and multilateral. It is always necessary to pay tribute to the teacher. This companion incorporates a new set of teaching voices to guide and challenge us on the way, as we read David

Unaipon, Oodgeroo Noonuccal, Vivienne Cleven, Sally Morgan, Lionel Fogarty, Alexis Wright, Kim Scott, Melissa Lucashenko, and many more. Students, scholars, and interested readers can be grateful.

Nicholas Jose
Professor of English and Creative Writing
The University of Adelaide

## Works Cited

Heiss, Anita, and Peter Minter. *Anthology of Australian Aboriginal Literature.* Montreal: McGill-Queen's University Press, 2008.
Jones, Philip. "Colours Fade to Black." *Australian Literary Review,* September 7, 2011, 14.

# Acknowledgments

I WOULD LIKE TO THANK the contributors and Camden House for supporting this important project. Numerous other Australian and Australian Aboriginal literature scholars also assisted me in various ways throughout the project. The number of people is much too long to list here, but please know that your advice was greatly appreciated. Thanks must also go to Jen, who believed in this book from day one. This book is dedicated to all Australian Aboriginals.

Belinda Wheeler
November 2012

# Chronology

THIS CHRONOLOGY is not intended to be comprehensive. Rather, it serves to give a brief overview of Australian Aboriginal history.

| | |
|---|---|
| 68,000 years ago (approximately) | Aboriginal Australians first settled in Australia. |
| 58,000 years ago (approximately) | Aboriginals living near Lake Mungo (in New South Wales). Human remains from this time period have been located at this ancient site. |
| 55,000 years ago (approximately) | Aboriginals living in the Northern Territory. Recent archaeological evidence supports this fact. |
| 45,000 years ago (approximately) | Aboriginals created petroglyphs in South Australia. (These are the first dated petroglyphs on record in Australia.) |
| 1401 | Chinese sailors explore parts of the Northern Territory. A fifteenth-century Ming statuette remains. |
| 1450 | (approximately) Indonesian fisherman fish the coast of Northern Australia, and Indonesian traders begin trading with Australian Aboriginals. |
| 1606 | While exploring the western coast of Cape York Peninsula, Willem Jansz (Dutch) and his *Duyfluen* crew are the first Europeans to come into contact with Australian Aboriginals. |
| 1770 | (August 22) Lt. James Cook (English) claims possession of Australia's east coast for Britain. |
| 1788 | (January 26) The First Fleet (led by Cpt. Arthur Phillip [later Governor Phillip] and comprised of convicts and naval officers and their families) establishes the first European colony in Sydney, Australia. Aboriginal resistance occurs within days of the settlers arriving.[1] |

---

[1] There were countless conflicts between European settlers and Australian Aboriginals that resulted in the loss of life. For the purposes of this brief chronology only some of the most significant conflicts are listed.

1789 Governor Phillip's men capture several Aboriginals, including Bennelong (ca. 1764–1813). Bennelong is introduced to English culture—language, dress, food—and reportedly helps Governor Phillip communicate with the Indigenous population.

1790 Bennelong travels with Governor Phillip to England for the first time, and he meets King George III. Bennelong later returns to Australia.

1796 Bennelong's letter to Mr. Philips, Lord Sydney's steward, is the first known text (to date) written in English by an Australian Aboriginal.

The Darug (native people of Sydney) begin a twelve-year resistance to the settlers' "invasion."

1800s Queensland "killing wars" occur throughout the 1800s and kill more than ten thousand Aboriginals. (Current historians are still gathering information about these fatalities.)

1803 Tasmania (then called Van Diemen's Land) is "settled" by colonists and used as a penal colony.

1810 Aboriginals begin to be moved into mission stations where they are taught European beliefs and trained in various forms of menial labor. Though many missions close, they remain a constant fixture throughout the nation for more than 150 years.

1813 Settlers cross the Blue Mountains (in New South Wales) and begin expanding further west.

1828 (approximately) The Black Wars of Tasmania (war between Aboriginals and settlers) begin. The conflict lasts until 1832. Thousands of Aboriginals are killed.

1831 Aboriginals in Western Australia, led by Yagan, begin a three-year resistance against settlers.

1833 Yagan is killed and beheaded. His head is transported to England, where it is displayed in an English museum.

1836 A seventeen-year war between Aboriginals from the Victoria region and settlers begins. Thousands of Aboriginals are killed.

1837 A British select committee investigates the treatment of Aboriginals and recommends the appointment of "Protectors of Aborigines." The policy of protection for Aboriginals marks the Catholic Church's new involvement in missionary work and schools for Aboriginal children.

1838    The Myall Creek Massacre in northern New South Wales. Approximately thirty Aboriginals (Wirrayaraay) are killed by twelve settlers (including convicts). Originally no charges are laid, but later seven settlers are tried, convicted, and hanged for their crimes.

1848    The Board of National Education decrees that it is impractical to provide Indigenous children with any form of education.

1868    The first Australian cricket team, consisting of all Aboriginals, tours England.

1869    Victoria implements an Aboriginal Protection Act giving authorities extended power over the Aboriginal population, including regulating marriages, residence, and employment.

1870    The Kalkadoon Wars (1870–90) between Aboriginals and settlers begin in Queensland. Close to one thousand Kalkadoons are killed.

1876    Trugernannar, reportedly the last "full-blood" Tasmanian Aboriginal dies.

1886    Victoria and Western Australia pass Half-Caste Acts that allow authorities to forcibly remove half-caste children from their families and assimilate them into white society.[2]

1888    It is reported that the Aboriginal population stands at approximately 80,000, which is 220,000 less than earlier estimates.

1901    The Commonwealth of Australia is established. The Immigration Restriction Act formally puts White Australia Policy into law.

1905    Aborigines Act of 1905 implemented in Western Australia. The act assigns a Chief Protector of Aborigines who serves as a legal guardian of all Aboriginal children, including half-castes, in Western Australia. The chief protector is given various powers that enable him to separate children under the age of sixteen from their families and move them to settlements.

---

[2] The term *half-caste* was given to Aboriginal children who were deemed to have more than 25 percent Aboriginal blood. Half-caste children, in particular, were removed from their families because the government believed they were more likely to assimilate into white society. For the sake of brevity I will only list several notable examples of legislation that disrupted Aboriginal children and their families, but it should be noted that government legislation between 1885 and 1970 led to more than a hundred thousand Aboriginal children being forcibly removed from their families and placed into various types of government or religious facilities.

1914    Aboriginals begin serving in the First World War despite the Defense Act 1909 preventing their involvement.

1920    The Aboriginal population is estimated to be between sixty and seventy thousand—the lowest ever.

1929    David Unaipon's (1872–1967) collection of myths, *Native Legends*, is published. It is considered (to date) the first book published by an Australian Aboriginal. The book's publisher, Angus and Robertson, sells the book's copyright to William Ramsay Smith without Unaipon's permission.

1930    William Ramsay Smith's *Myths and Legends of the Australian Aborigines* is published in London without acknowledgment of David Unaipon as the original author.

1937    A federal conference in Canberra supports a new assimilation policy.

1938    The Aboriginal Progressive Association declares January 26 to be a national Day of Mourning. This day marks the 150-year anniversary of European settlement in Australia.

1939    Approximately three thousand Aboriginals serve in the Second World War.

1948    All Aboriginals are now considered Australian citizens and British subjects under the Commonwealth and Citizen Act.

        Harold Blair, Australia's first classically trained Aboriginal tenor, makes his operatic debut at Melbourne's Princess Theater. Though Blair's singing career was short lived, he became a prominent Aboriginal activist.

1951    "An Aboriginal Moomba: Out of the Dark" is performed on the streets of Melbourne. This original carnival-style show featuring an all-Indigenous cast later prompts an annual Moomba festival which is still in existence today.

1956    Aboriginal musician Jimmy Little signs with Columbia Records helping to establish him as Australia's first Indigenous pop star.

1960    Musician Jimmy Little secures a role in the Hollywood film, *Shadow of the Boomerang*. Little stars as an Indigenous Christian worker fighting for justice against an American cowboy.

1961    The Australian Institute of Aboriginal and Torres Strait Islander Studies Center (AIATSIS) opens in Canberra with an interim council.

1962    Aboriginals are able to vote for the first time under an amended Commonwealth Electoral Act.

Aboriginal singer Georgia Lee records the first blues record by an Indigenous artist, *Georgia Lee Sings the Blues Down Under*.

1963    Jimmy Little's gospel song "Royal Telephone" rockets up the Australian music charts selling more than seventy-five thousand copies and solidifying Little as one of the country's most popular artists.

1964    Oodgeroo Noonuccal (formerly Kath Walker) (1920–93) publishes *We Are Going*, the first book of poetry by an Aboriginal author.

The federal government formerly establishes an academic council and foundational members at AIATSIS. Aboriginal Studies Press is established as the publishing arm of the organization. The press originally publishes books by non-Indigenous writers about Australian Aboriginals.

Yagan's remains are buried in an unmarked grave in Liverpool, England.

1965    Inspired by the US Freedom Riders, Australian Freedom Riders (led by Aboriginal university student Charles Perkins) travel throughout New South Wales and a small portion of Queensland to protest Aboriginal discrimination and segregation.

1967    A national referendum vote of 92 percent permits the counting of Australian Aboriginals in the national census.

1968    Lionel Rose (1948–2011), boxer, is the first Australian Aboriginal to receive the Australian of the Year Award, an annual award given on January 26 (Australia Day) for the outstanding achievements made by an Australian. The first Australian of the Year Award was presented in 1960.

1970s    The Institute for Aboriginal Development Incorporated (IAD) Press, in Alice Springs, is established to publish work by Aboriginals and Torres Strait Islanders.

1970    Oodgeroo Noonuccal (then known as Kath Walker) is appointed a Member of the Order of the British Empire (MBE) in recognition of her contribution to social justice, equality, and education.

1971    The Aboriginal flag, designed by Luritja artist Harold Thomas, is flown for the first time in Adelaide.

Neville Bonner (1922–99) is elected as the first Aboriginal member of Federal Parliament. He serves as the senator for Queensland from 1971 to 1983.

Evonne Cawley (1951–), Aboriginal tennis player, winner of seven Grand Slam women's titles, including Wimbledon, the Australian Open, and the French Open, is named Australian of the Year.

1972     The Aboriginal Tent Embassy is erected on the grounds of Parliament House in Canberra as a protest for Aboriginal land rights. The Tent Embassy remains in existence today.

1973     Formal end of White Australia Policy.

1975     Racial Discrimination Act is passed in the federal government.

1976     Pat O'Shane is the first Aboriginal person to be admitted to the bar.

1977     After being in existence for thirteen years, the Aboriginal Studies Press publishes its first book authored by an Aboriginal, Jimmie Barker's *The Two Worlds of Jimmie Barker: The Life of an Australian Aboriginal, 1900–1972.*

1978     Galarrwuy Yunupingu (1948–), Yolngu leader, is named Australian of the Year (jointly with businessman Alan Bond).

1979     Neville Bonner, politician, is named Australian of the Year (jointly with naturalist Harry Butler).

1982     Aboriginal elder Eddie Mabo begins legal proceedings for the right of native title in Australia's High Court.

Mark Ella (1959–), Aboriginal rugby union player, is named Australian of the Year.

1983     The First National Conference of Aboriginal Writers takes place at Murdoch University in Perth, Western Australia.

1984     Several protection acts previously enforced in Queensland to "protect" Aboriginals end.

Lowitja O'Donoghue (1932–), Aboriginal nurse and public administrator, is named Australian of the Year.

Warumpi Band, a band comprised of Aboriginal and non-Aboriginal musicians, releases the first Aboriginal-language song for a mainstream audience called "Jailanguru Pakarnu" ("Out from Jail").

1985     Warumpi Band and Midnight Oil (a prolific internationally recognized Australian band with a strong social conscious) join forces for their "Blackfella-Whitefella" tour. The tour travels around the country, including remote Aboriginal settlements.

1987 Sally Morgan's (1952–) autobiographical novel, *My Place*, is published. The book is a national and international success, bringing Aboriginal writers and Aboriginal rights to a wider audience.

Oodgeroo Noonuccal renounces her given name (Kath Walker) and adopts her Indigenous name. Noonuccal also returns her MBE in protest against the upcoming 1988 Bicentenary celebrations.

A royal commission into Aboriginal deaths in custody begins in response to the large number of Aboriginal incarcerations and deaths.

Magabala Books, then the publishing arm of the Kimberly Aboriginal Law and Culture Center (in Western Australia), publishes its first title, Merrilee Lands' *Mayi—Some Bushfruits of the West Kimberly*, with the assistance of federal government funds.

Former Freedom Rider and prominent Aboriginal activist Charles Perkins receives the Officer of the Order of Australia award for service to Aboriginal welfare. The Order of Australia is awarded by Queen Elizabeth II to recognize the achievements of Australian citizens.

1988 On January 26 (Australia Day) tens of thousands of Aboriginals and Torres Strait Islanders march through Sydney streets protesting two hundred years of white rule and celebrating their survival. The day is renamed Survival Day by the Indigenous community. Protests continue throughout the year-long bicentenary celebration.

The first anthology of Australian Aboriginal poetry, *Inside Black Australia: An Anthology of Aboriginal Poetry*, edited by Aboriginal poet, playwright, artist, printmaker Kevin Gilbert, is published by Penguin Australia.

1989 Aboriginal and Torres Strait Commission (ATSIC) is established as the main Commonwealth agency for Indigenous affairs.

The University of Queensland Press grants the first national David Unaipon Award for an unpublished Indigenous writer to Graeme Dixon (1955–) for his poetry collection, *Holocaust Island*. The award is one of the few available for unpublished Indigenous authors. As part of the Unaipon Award, recipients receive a monetary prize (currently $20,000) and their work is guaranteed publication with the press.

1990    Magabala Books becomes an independent Indigenous publishing house.

The University of Queensland Press establishes a Black Australian Writers series.

The first comprehensive anthology of Australian Aboriginal writing, *Paperbark*, is published by the University of Queensland Press. The anthology's editors are Jack Davis, Stephen Muecke, Adam Shoemaker, and Mudrooroo Narogin (Colin Johnson).

Doris Pilkington Garimara (1937–) wins the David Unaipon Award for *Caprice: A Stockman's Daughter.*

Aboriginal film director Tracey Moffatt has her first film, *Night Cries: A Rural Tragedy* (1989), selected for official competition at the 1990 Cannes Film Festival.

1991    The Royal Commission into Aboriginal Deaths in Custody releases its report and makes numerous recommendations. Most notably, the report finds that, of the ninety-nine deaths it investigated, close to half of the people who died had been forcibly removed from their families when they were children.

The Council for Aboriginal Reconciliation is established to create a formal process for reconciliation between non-Indigenous and Indigenous Australians.

Bill Dodd (1965–) wins the David Unaipon Award for *Broken Dreams.*

The Aboriginal band Yothu Yindi releases its song "Treaty," cowritten with Australian singer-songwriter Paul Kelly. The song is the first by an all-Aboriginal band to chart on the Australian music charts. The song also sells well internationally, peaking at no. 6 on the American Billboard Music Charts' Club Play Singles.

1992    Eddie Mabo High Court decision, otherwise known as the *Mabo* case, formally recognizes native title rights for Australian Aboriginals and invalidates the long-held claim that Australia was *terra nullius* prior to European settlement.

Mandawuy Yunupingu (1956–), leader of the Aboriginal band Yothu Yindi, is named Australian of the Year.

Philip McLaren (1943–) wins the David Unaipon Award for *Sweet Water.*

1993    International Year of the World's Indigenous People.

John Muk Muk Burke (1946–) wins the David Unaipon Award for *Bridge of Triangles*.

1994     Native Title Act 1993 becomes law.

Valda Gee and her sister, Rosalie Medcraft, win the David Unaipon Award for *The Sausage Tree*.

1995     Warrigal Anderson (1948–) wins the David Unaipon Award for *Warrigal's Way*.

The Deadlys Awards are first held. The awards, which celebrate artistic achievement by Aboriginal and Torres Strait Islanders in several areas including music, become an annual event that still runs today.

1996     *Wik peoples v. The State of Queensland*, otherwise known as the *Wik* decision, formally states that native title rights can coexist with existing pastoral leases.

Steven McCarthy (1960–) wins the David Unaipon Award for *Black Angels Red Blood*.

Controversy surrounds formerly praised Indigenous author Mudrooroo Narogin (Colin Johnson) following revelations that he is not Indigenous. Genealogical records show that the novelist and literary critic is of Irish and African American heritage. Johnson retires from public life following the controversy.

1997     The Australian Human Rights and Equal Opportunity Commission (HREOC) releases its report, *Bringing Them Home: Report of the National Inquiry into the Separation of Aboriginal and Torres Strait Islander Children from Their Families*. The commission makes numerous recommendations to the federal government.

John Bodey (1941–) wins the David Unaipon Award for *When Darkness Falls*.

1998     The Sorry Books campaign is launched by Australians for Native Title in response to the federal government's refusal to formally apologize to members of the Stolen Generation. The book campaign allows Australians to write their individual apologies to members of the Stolen Generation.

The first National Sorry Day held on May 26, one year after the tabling of the *Bringing Them Home* report.

Ruth Hegarty (1929–) wins the David Unaipon Award for *Is That You Ruthie?*

Cathy Freeman (1973–), athlete, named Australian of the Year.

1999    Samuel Wagan Watson (1972–) wins the David Unaipon Award for *Of Muse, Meandering and Midnight*.

2000    The United Nations Committee on the Elimination of Racial Discrimination criticizes the Australian government's inadequate response to the recommendations made by the HREOC's *Bringing Them Home* report.

Corroboree 2000 is held at Sydney Opera House to commemorate ten years of reconciliation.

Kim Scott (1957–) wins the Miles Franklin Literary Award for his novel *Benang*. The award, which is arguably the most prestigious literary award for an Australian play or novel, was established in 1957. Scott is the first Indigenous writer to receive the award.

Vivienne Cleven (1968–) wins the David Unaipon Award for *Bitin' Back*.

2001    Robert Lowe (1947–) wins the David Unaipon Award for *The Mish*.

Aboriginal film director and writer Rachel Perkins wins the New York International Independent Film and Video Festival's genre award for Best Feature Film—Musical for *One Night the Moon* (2001).

2002    Larissa Behrendt (1969–) wins the David Unaipon Award for *Home*.

2003    Fiona Doyle (1969–) wins the David Unaipon Award for *Whispers of This Wik Woman*.

2004    Tara June Winch (1983–) wins the David Unaipon Award for *Dust on Waterglass* (published as *Swallow the Air*).

Musician Jimmy Little is awarded the Officer of the Order of Australia for service to the entertainment industry and his reconciliation work.

2005    ATSIC is dismantled by the federal government (then led by Prime Minister John Howard) and replaced by a Commonwealth-appointed advisory board. The Indigenous community is strongly against these changes.

Yvette Holt (1971–) wins the David Unaipon Award for *Anonymous Premonition*.

2006    Gayle Kennedy wins the David Unaipon Award for *Me, Antman and Fleabag.*

2007    Northern Territory "intervention" takes place under the recommendation of then–Prime Minister John Howard and the Indigenous Affairs Minister Mal Brough. The intervention mandates several actions including quarantining 50 percent of welfare payments to Aboriginals and abolishing Community Development Employment Projects in the region.

Prime Minister John Howard loses the federal election. Newly elected Prime Minister Kevin Rudd announces his intentions to apologize to the members of the Stolen Generation and create closer links between the government and Aboriginals.

Alexis Wright (1950–) wins the Miles Franklin Literary Award for her novel *Carpentaria.*

Elizabeth Eileen Hodgson (1956–) wins the David Unaipon Award for *Skin Painting.*

2008    On February 13, the Australian Parliament (under Prime Minister Kevin Rudd) formally apologizes to the Stolen Generations.

Marie Munkara wins the David Unaipon Award for *Every Secret Thing.*

Anita Heiss and Peter Minter's *Anthology of Australian Aboriginal Literature* is published. This anthology is the first to be released simultaneously in Australian and overseas markets.

2009    Mick Dodson (1950–), law professor, is named Australian of the Year.

Nicole Watson wins the David Unaipon Award for *The Boundary.*

2010    Indigenous academic Megan Davis is named on the United Nations (UN) Permanent Forum on Indigenous Issues. She is the first Australian Indigenous woman to be appointed to a UN body.

Yagan's remains (previously interred in Liverpool, England in 1964) are officially laid to rest near Perth, Western Australia, following a traditional Noongar ceremony.

Jeanine Leane (1961–) wins the David Unaipon Award for *Purple Threads.*

2011    The Australian Electoral Commission registers the first Indigenous political party, First Nations Political Party (FNPP).

The first Australian national institute for Aboriginal and Torres Strait Islander health research, the Lowitja Institute, opens in Melbourne.

Kim Scott wins the Miles Franklin Literary Award a second time for his novel *That Deadman Dance*.

Dylan Coleman wins the David Unaipon Award for *'Mazin' Grace*.

2012    (January 26) The Aboriginal Tent Embassy celebrates its forty-year anniversary.

# Introduction: The Emerging Canon

*Belinda Wheeler*

Australian Aboriginal literature has come a long way. Achievements by Australian Aboriginal authors, poets, film directors, musicians, and playwrights are being increasingly recognized around the world. However, as recently as the early 1970s Australian Aboriginal artists were a marginalized voice in Australian literary studies and mainstream Australian culture. With the exception of praised works such as those by writers David Unaipon and Sally Morgan, poets Oodgeroo Noonuccal (formerly Kath Walker) and Lionel Fogarty, musicians Jimmy Little and the members of Yothu Yindi, and playwrights Kevin Gilbert and Jack Davis, there were few "celebrated" Australian Aboriginal artists in the mid- to late twentieth century. Though Aboriginal literature existed well before the first book by an Australian Aboriginal was published—Unaipon's collection of myths, *Native Legends* (1929)—there was no market for material by Aboriginals in mainstream Australian society. Although the success attained in the face of colonial pressure by these few exceptional Aboriginal artists motivated other Aboriginals to share their work, it was arguably not until the lead-up to the 1988 Australian bicentennial celebrations that the wider Australian public showed genuine interest in Australian Aboriginals, their culture, and their literature. For the first time a large portion of Australia's non-Aboriginal community wanted to explore literature written or performed by Australian Aboriginals. This resulted in an explosion of Aboriginal literature in various genres including life writing, fiction, poetry, film, drama, and music. This book chronicles many of the literary achievements by Australian Aboriginals from before the bicentenary through today.

Creative work by Australian Aboriginals is making a decisive impression across the Australian literary landscape. The critical success of individual works—particularly those "published" since 1987, such as Sally Morgan's *My Place* (1987), Yothu Yindi's "Treaty" (1992), Jack Davis' *Wahngin Country* (1992), Doris Pilkington Garimara's *Follow the Rabbit-Proof Fence* (1996), Alexis Wright's *Plains of Promise* (1997) and *Carpentaria* (2006), Rachel Perkins' *Radiance* (1998), Kim Scott's *Benang* (2000), Tara June Winch's *Swallow the Air* (2006), and Anita Heiss's *Not Meeting Mr. Right* (2007)—and anthologies published for an Australian audience, such as *Inside Black Australia: An Anthology of Aboriginal Poetry* (1989), edited by Kevin Gilbert, and *Paperbark: A Collection of Black Australian Writings* (1990), edited by Jack Davis, Stephen Muecke, Adam Shoemaker, and Mudrooroo Narogin (Colin Johnson) have significantly contributed to the increased number of texts created by contemporary Australian Aboriginals. In addition to this newer material, scholars and publishers have also begun recovering previously unpublished works written by Australian Aboriginals and reissuing texts that had fallen out of print.

This critical success is also spreading to other parts of the world as Australian Aboriginal authors are successfully marketing their work abroad. Countries such as Germany, Italy, and Denmark are among the largest consumers of translated Aboriginal texts, and countries such as Canada and the United States are importing Australian editions of these works. On a small number of occasions, publishers in the United States have republished several Aboriginal-authored texts for American audiences. Miramax, for example, published Doris Pilkington Garimara's *Follow the Rabbit-Proof Fence* under a slightly modified title, *Rabbit-Proof Fence* (2002), following the success of Phillip Noyce's film of the same name. Australian and international literary communities have noted the growing worldwide interest in Australian Aboriginal writing by welcoming two highly praised anthologies published in both the Oceania and North American markets, *Anthology of Australian Aboriginal Literature* (2008; edited by Anita Heiss and Peter Minter and published simultaneously in Canada and Australia), which is devoted exclusively to Australian Aboriginal literature, and *The Literature of Australia* (2009; edited by Nicholas Jose and published in the United States and Australia), which contains an extensive selection of material by Australian Aboriginals. Australian Aboriginal literature is being increasingly recognized for its depth and breadth, but until now there has been no companion volume that summarizes and contextualizes the canon for scholars, researchers, and general readers. The present companion fills this void with a collection of essays by an international group of scholars that focus on various genres within Australian Aboriginal literature.

To begin to fill this void, it is necessary to trace Australian Aboriginal literature from its beginnings. Australian Aboriginals have been producing oral texts in their native languages for thousands of years. As with other indigenous cultures, such as Africans, Native Americans, and First Nations, Australian Aboriginals passed down their histories from generation to generation through their rich oral traditions. These oral traditions, tribal rituals, and artwork served Australian Aboriginals well and promoted a kinship within their culture that survived for tens of thousands of years. As has been seen in the Australian Aboriginal community and other indigenous cultures around the world, the moment when European and indigenous cultures come together has been a mixed blessing. European cultures have decimated numerous indigenous cultures in various ways including unspeakable genocides. History has taught us that European cultures still have a long way to go if they are going to atone for their forebears' actions and offer the indigenous every opportunity that their European counterparts have. And while much more still needs to be done in the way of reconciliation, European involvement with the indigenous has enabled current generations from every corner of the globe the chance to read, see, or listen to creative material authored by the indigenous.

Contemporary audiences' appreciation of indigenous literature or literature from marginalized voices has hastened the recovery of "lost" literary voices. Only fairly recently, in 1983, did noted African American literary scholar and critic Henry Louis Gates Jr. discover Harriet E. Wilson's *Our Nig* (1859), which was later identified as the first novel written by an African American woman in the United States. In 2002, Gates recovered another lost literary masterpiece, Hannah Crafts's *The Bondwoman's Narrative* (ca. 1850s). Though the exact date of composition is unknown and there is little information available on Crafts, her slave narrative was a best seller in 2002. Across the globe, scholars have also recently recovered Australian Aboriginal texts. A notable example being the first document written in English by an Australian Aboriginal— Bennelong's 1796 letter to Mr. Philips. Surprisingly, the discovery did not involve a scholar coming across an original manuscript and verifying the details, as Gates did. Instead, Bennelong's letter was rediscovered in a rare printing of an 1801 edition of the German book, *Monatliche correspondenz zur beförderung der erd- und himmels-kunde*, volume 4. In his 1796 letter to Philips, Bennelong thanked Philips and his wife, his patrons, for all they had done for him, and he requested basic clothing items. The power differential between Philips and Bennelong is clear, and Bennelong is careful to balance words of praise with his request. The short space of time between Australia's colonization (eight years prior, 1788), Bennelong's capture (in 1789), and the composition of Bennelong's letter is proof that while many European settlers and early anthropologists, such as Charles Staniland Wake, saw Aboriginals as "the most uncilvilised [*sic*] of the races of mankind," they were capable of quickly learning the ways of the Europeans (cv–cvi). The recent discoveries or rediscoveries of work by Indigenous or marginalized authors who had no formal education suggest the likely existence of a remarkable number of "lost" texts still waiting to be recovered.

Scholars are actively seeking to recover lost works in English by Aboriginals so they can fill many of the literary gaps in Australian Aboriginal literature. In Heiss and Minter's *Anthology*, for example, only eight Aboriginal authors are listed between Bennelong's 1796 letter (the first entry) and David Unaipon's early 1920s contributions. Though

Heiss and Minter do not contend that their anthology is comprehensive, this number is telling. Furthermore, all the works included prior to Unaipon's were in the form of letters, news articles, or petitions. The reasons for the limited number and genres of texts available to us today tell us a great deal about Australia's history. Widespread access to education for Aboriginals was unheard of in the early days of European settlement. Although it is highly likely that some Aboriginals taught themselves to read and write, some learned to read and write from family or friends, and some were taught basic reading and writing skills by European settlers. Even if they produced such texts, they would have been hampered by further obstacles including a lack of interest in Indigenous writings by a non-Indigenous public, limited access to quality writing materials, and the unwillingness of non-Indigenous audiences to accept an Indigenous person as a credible author.

The ability of Indigenous authors to successfully prove authorship was unquestionably a large obstacle to overcome. African native Phillis Wheatley, the first African American to publish a book, had to endure various tests by Europeans to prove she indeed authored *Poems on Various Subjects, Religious and Moral by Phillis Wheatley, Negro Servant to Mr. John Wheatley, of Boston, in New England* (1773). Even after she passed all these tests, the first few pages of her book contained letters by "respected" white men in the community certifying her authorship. Australian Aboriginal writers also endured the same scrutiny. David Unaipon's authorship was questioned by some when he released his collection of myths and legends, *Native Legends*, and even Sally Morgan's authorship of *My Place* was scrutinized by non-Aboriginals and Aboriginals. For every published Indigenous author who successfully withstood scrutiny and secured a publisher, there were likely countless others who did not. While most contemporary Aboriginal authors have withstood scrutiny, others such as Colin Johnson (formerly known as Mudrooroo) and Archie Weller were unable to validate their lineage, and they were subsequently ostracized from the Indigenous community. The legitimate Indigenous voices from the past need to be recovered to fill the large gaps in Australian Aboriginal literary history of future anthologies like Heiss and Minter's.

From the late 1920s onward, there has been an increasing, albeit gradual, interest in Australian Aboriginal literature. Works by Aboriginal writers such as Unaipon and Noonuccal began receiving national attention, and their literary success slowly built a market for other Aboriginal writers. The historical events of the 1960s and 1970s also brought Australian Aboriginals more recognition for their role in Australia's history: in 1962 Australian Aboriginals were permitted to vote for the first time; in 1965 a small group of Australian Freedom Riders (Aboriginals and non-Aboriginals), modeled on the successful US Freedom Riders, travelled throughout parts of New South Wales and Queensland to assess Aboriginal discrimination in rural areas; and, in a 1967 national referendum, the overwhelming majority of voters agreed that Australian Aboriginals should be included in the national census. During this period many Aboriginals, including sports figures Lionel Rose and Evonne Cowley, author Noonuccal, and members of the public service Pat O'Shane and Neville Bonner, were awarded various honors, including the prestigious Australian of the Year award, in recognition of outstanding achievements to the community.

Despite the aforementioned progress, it would be naïve to say that reconciliation between the Aboriginal and non-Aboriginal community had been achieved. As these developments took place, unspeakable discrimination, neglect, and abuse were still occurring in Aboriginal communities nationwide. Up until the early 1970s, the practice by the government to systematically remove Aboriginal children, particularly half-castes (children deemed to have at least 25 percent Aboriginal blood), from their families and relocate them to various government-run facilities or religious-run missions to acculturate them into white society continued. These children were forcibly removed from their homes and forbidden to speak their native language or practice their tribal rituals, and most were kept away from their families until they were eighteen years of age. As a result, many "Stolen" children had difficulty reconnecting with their family members, their heritage, or their oral histories later in life. The forced removal of close to a hundred thousand Aboriginal children between the early 1900s and the 1970s had a devastating effect on the Indigenous populace. Little had been said publicly about this blight on Australia's history, but the "celebration" of European settlement would change this forever.

With preparations for the 1988 Australian bicentenary underway, the public's attention focused increasingly on Australian Aboriginals: their history, culture, and literature. This was a pivotal moment for Aboriginal authors. As scholar Kay Schaffer notes, "it was not until the late 1970s . . . that Indigenous people in Australia were able to find a public forum for their writings, and a non-Indigenous audience willing to listen" (5). Although many Indigenous texts were published prior to the release of Morgan's *My Place*, the critical acclaim this work received nationally and internationally was arguably the defining moment in Australian Aboriginal literature. In the American edition of Morgan's text, Pulitzer Prize–winning author Alice Walker reviewed Morgan's work stating, "Sad and wise and funny . . . unbelievably and unexpectedly moving, Sally Morgan's love for her own spiritual and racial roots and her struggle to uncover them reveals a new Australia (the old) and a new way to embrace the elders and the young of all our peoples, wherever (and whoever) they might be. A book with heart." Morgan's work—a mixture of autobiography and fiction—was one of the first to mention children being stolen away from their parents, and it would prompt a deluge of writing by authors detailing their life histories (life writing). The increased interest in Aboriginal writing and access to mainstream publishers opened the door for Aboriginal authors outside of the life-writing genre. In the twenty-five years since Morgan's canonical work was published, the number of texts published by Aboriginal writers in various genres has risen rapidly.

While numerous themes resonate throughout Australian Aboriginal literature, the most dominant is the Stolen Generation. The loss of identity that was the consequence of legislation enacted by Australia's federal and state governments has haunted numerous Australian Aboriginals, and many have chosen writing as a vehicle to overcome past injustices and start the healing process. Aboriginals had been recording and sharing their life histories within their culture for countless years, but, until they were recognized as citizens, there were few public forums in which they could speak out against their forced removal and correct the many history books that failed to accurately document what really happened. Furthermore, the upcoming bicentenary celebrations prompted many Australians to reflect on the nation's two-hundred-year history, providing many Aboriginal authors with an unprecedented opportunity to share their creative work with a larger audience. Some notable publications that discussed the Stolen Generations include the aforementioned Morgan's *My Place*, Doris Pilkington Garimara's *Caprice: A Stockman's Daughter* (1990), and John Muk Muk Burke's *Bridge of Triangles* (1994).

It should be noted that while countless life-writing publications were produced at the time of the bicentennial celebrations, many of the texts were only printed once and quickly became very scarce. Despite limited print runs, the overall volume of material produced in recent decades cements Australian Aboriginal literature's status as an emerging canon in its own right. This canon has inspired this companion volume and guided its depth and organization. In the *Anthology of Australian Aboriginal Literature*, eighty authors are listed, and of those eighty approximately sixty wrote for a wide audience, while the remaining authors (mostly from the 1800s and early 1920s) wrote a small number of personal letters, petitions, or short news articles for a limited readership. Because the Australian Aboriginal literary canon is still emerging, each contributor to this companion primarily focuses on a representative sample of authors in each genre to contextualize the genre for readers. Some contributors have also chosen to focus on a small number of authors within a particular genre because these authors do something unique from their counterparts. This may make a chapter less comprehensive, but it does make the discussion more rewarding. It is also important to note that many contributors have limited their discussions to materials that are readily available to a worldwide audience and not just the Australian market. As mentioned earlier, many Australian Aboriginal texts are often only published once with a limited print run, and few are distributed outside the country. The more readers from around the world seek out Australian Aboriginal texts, the greater their accessibility will become. Also, technological advances, such as e-readers, are starting to increase accessibility worldwide. This limited accessibility to material authored by Australian Aboriginals has, in some ways, constrained the scope of the first edition of this companion, but it is this editor's hope that later editions of this book and other companions will grow as worldwide interest in Australian Aboriginal literature develops and as older and newer Aboriginal authored texts are made readily available for consumers.

In addition to depth, this companion's organization reflects dominant genres within the emerging canon. For example, although the genre of life writing appeared in Australian Aboriginal literature much later than many other genres—such as myths (ca. 1929 with David Unaipon's collection, *Native Legends*) and poetry (ca. 1964 with Kath Walker's book of poems, *We Are Going*)—the companion opens with life writing because of its widespread national and international acclaim and because of its strong connection with the oral tradition. Because they use first- and secondhand accounts, life writers have been able to close many of the gaps in Australia's history. These works preserve the few remaining oral histories from years past, and their accounts regularly promote healing between groups inside and outside of the Aboriginal community.[1]

Though life writing is recognized as a legitimate genre today, its beginnings were originally tenuous. Michael R. Griffiths's essay begins the companion with a detailed examination of the genre's complicated past. Griffiths notes, "The irreducible value of works of life writing as speech acts of political self-assertion" and the restoration of kinship in the community "have paradoxically been the basis of life writing's disavowal as nonliterary" by various critics. Life writing's ability to simultaneously restore and rearticulate kinship in the face of colonial history originally challenged the typical concept of genres in the Western tradition, argues Griffiths, but that new way of thinking is largely why Aboriginal life writing has ultimately been accepted into the Australian literary canon. Griffiths examines several well-known texts from the West Australian region to illustrate the importance of region for many writers; he uses firsthand interviews with Aboriginal life writers, and, to show how fluid Australian Aboriginal life writing is as a genre, he makes the case for the inclusion of Angus Wallam's children's book, *Corroboree* (2004), as an example of life writing.

---

[1] It is a documented fact that many ancient Aboriginal rituals, languages, and so on have been forever lost because of various government acts and legislation that prevented family members from passing down their oral histories and rituals to the next generation.

Another significant obstacle for Aboriginal writers, particularly life writers, has been editorial control. Many of the original life writers were not formally educated, and they had to hand over a lot of control to their publishers in order to have their stories published. The amount of control publishers and editors exercised over these works distorted the authors' original intentions. Some were so heavily edited that it was hard to determine whether the published texts were "written" by the Aboriginal authors or their editors. Other publishers mishandled Aboriginal authors' works for their own benefit. For example, the rights to David Unaipon's *Native Legends* were later sold by his publisher without his consent, and the book was republished in England without acknowledging Unaipon as the original author. Historically, in the area of life writing, the number of cases in which editors distorted writers' words was alarmingly high. Whether the amount of editorial control was seen as a way to "assist" often first-time authors is questionable. The results were harmful, and in many cases they caused a further rift been the Indigenous and non-Indigenous community.

Jennifer Jones's essay examines the oral tradition to find several notable instances where Aboriginal authors' intentions were heavily distorted by editors for their own ends. She provides readers with an excellent summary of many of these life-writing texts before she leads into a full-length discussion of Ella Simon's autobiography, *Through My Eyes* (1978). As part of her research, Jones delved deeply into the archive to review various versions of Simon's "text." In her essay she includes an original dictation of Simon orally transcribing her life story to her non-Indigenous editor. Jones's analysis of what Simon said and what was eventually published in her book clearly highlights just some of the liberties her non-Indigenous editors and publishers took as they assembled and later represented Simon's "original" life story. The distortion between an author's intention and the editor-approved publication will be surprising to many readers of the companion, but it is necessary for readers to understand much of the justified mistrust that Aboriginal authors had for non-Indigenous editors. For readers of the companion who are aware of this contentious relationship, Jones' essay demonstrates that we can still gain much from the archive that can strengthen our understanding of Australian Aboriginal literature and potentially lead to newer, more accurate editions of an Aboriginal author's life story.

Contemporary Aboriginal writers have learned from the early publishing experiences of their elders, leading many to seek more control of their work. Some contemporary Australian Aboriginal writers, for example, have elected to circumvent the Indigenous/non-Indigenous editorial relationship by working with members of their own communities, particularly their relatives, as they prepare their texts. Martina Horakova's essay explores these intergenerational collaborations that combine oral family histories with life writing, and she examines how the assisting relatives openly signify their editorial hand. In particular, Horakova's research shows that, of all the intergenerational collaborations in the life-writing genre published to date, including many of the texts that she briefly summarizes at the beginning of her essay, two works, Rita and Jackie Huggins' *Auntie Rita* (1994) and Kim Scott and Hazel Brown's *Kayang and Me* (2005), stand out formally and poetically from the others and indicate the varied directions intergenerational collaborations have taken. They are both double-voiced narratives presenting two equally authoritative narrative voices, voices that are formally delineated by different fonts, thus signaling a clear shift in subjectivity. Horakova's discussion marks a significant discovery within the life-writing genre that will be of significant interest to both readers well versed in the genre and those acquainting themselves with the genre for the first time.

As Jones's and Horakova's essays show, the process of translating spoken English and various Aboriginal languages or specific phrases into written English can be problematic. The process is further complicated when already "translated" texts (vis-à-vis editorial control) are translated again into other languages. Because of the increased interest in Australian Aboriginal literature worldwide, particularly in the European markets of Germany, Italy, the Netherlands, and Slovenia, there is an increasing need for these texts to be translated for non-English speakers. Danica Čerče and Oliver Haag's study of German, Italian, Dutch, and Slovene translations of two texts and their systematic comparison of these texts with the original Australian editions shows the vital need for translators to work more closely with authors, editors, and publishing houses to provide consumers with texts that closely resemble the original published versions or the authors' original intentions. If they do not work together, as Čerče and Haag show, the translated editions can have dramatic implications for the text, the author, the reader, the genre, and the way Aboriginal literature and culture are understood by the global community. Čerče and Haag focus on two groundbreaking books on the international stage, the Miramax publication of Doris Pilkington Garimara's *Rabbit-Proof Fence* (2002) and Sally Morgan's *My Place*. Though Čerče and Haag examine texts in the life-writing genre, their systematic evaluation of specific words and phrases in the text, rather than plot summary, character analysis, and so on, provides audiences with an absorbing discussion applicable to all the genres in which Aboriginal authored texts have been, or are going to be, translated. Čerče and Haag's essay reminds all consumers of Australian Aboriginal literature, whether novices or specialists, to always seek the truest representation of an author's work regardless of the genre.

Poetry is another genre in which Australian Aboriginal writers have been highly active. Despite increased scholarly interest in this genre, notes Stuart Cooke, literary critics have neglected a critical aspect of Aboriginal poetry: its close connection to the oral tradition. In his essay Cooke traces the strong relationship between traditional forms of songpoetry and contemporary Aboriginal poetry by highlighting the connections between the voice of the poet and the written word. After discussing some of the general characteristics of Aboriginal songpoetry, Cooke examines Paddy Roe's *Gularabulu* (1983) and explains how it exemplifies Aboriginal poetics merging with written literatures. He concludes with an analysis of Lionel Fogarty's poetry: how it extends the poetic boundaries of the English language and demonstrates how contemporary works can be traced back to their historic songpoetry roots. Without a systematic study of the connection between the oral poetic tradition and today's poets, Cooke argues, students and scholars have missed out on a vital cultural tradition that showcases "the progressive nature of the present moment, with an end to reveal dynamic, moving environments." Cooke's fresh perspective on this genre will interest established Aboriginal literature scholars and poetry enthusiasts who are reading Aboriginal poetry for the first time.

Following Cooke's essay, the companion moves on to fiction, specifically young adult fiction, adult Aboriginal fiction, and the Gothic. Like many life-writing authors who share their histories as a way to reconnect with their families, their communities, and their country, characters in many works of young adult literature, adult fiction, and the Gothic also wrestle with identity construction. An award-winning writer of young adult fiction in her own right, Jeanine Leane discusses the way many protagonists in Aboriginal young adult novels seek to reestablish connections with their families and their homeland as a means of crossing borders and transforming themselves, their rite of passage. In particular, Leane's essay covers three award-winning texts in detail: John Muk Muk Burke's *Bridge of Triangles*, Melissa Lucashenko's *Steam Pigs* (1997), and Tara June Winch's *Swallow the Air* (2006). The historical progression of these novels—Burke's text is set in the early post–Second World War years, Lucashenko's in early 1990s Australia amid growing discussion about possible reconciliation and a formal apology by the federal government to Australian Aboriginals for former injustices, and Winch's during the late 1990s and 2000s—combine to illustrate just a few of the tumultuous times Australia faced from the mid-1940s until the 2010s. It is this historical progression juxtaposed with the protagonists' journeys as they seek to reconnect with their past and their homeland in the face of outside forces, such as the government, that makes Leane's essay an intriguing read for all who are interested in the young adult fiction genre.

Following Leane, Paula Anca Farca focuses on the increasingly significant theme of humor in contemporary Aboriginal adult fiction. The humor presented in many works of adult fiction, argues Farca, serves as a literary device to approach a range of controversial issues inside and outside the Aboriginal community, including sexuality, racial discrimination, proselytism, and the government's mistreatment of the Aboriginal community. Farca covers a diverse range of texts, Vivienne Cleven's *Bitin' Back* (2001), Marie Munkara's *Every Secret Thing* (2009), Gayle Kennedy's *Me, Antman and Fleabag* (2007), and Anita Heiss' *Not Meeting Mr. Right*, several of which have received the prestigious David Unaipon Award for an unpublished Indigenous writer. Farca's careful selection of texts highlights Aboriginal individuals or communities from different walks of life, including those who live in the country and those who live in the city, those who are educated and those who are not, and those who are financially secure and those who are not. The diversity represented in these texts reminds us that the controversial issues of the day are not isolated to one type or class of people but affect various populations. The use of humor in these contemporary works "bites back" at audiences to educate them about these issues and to challenge many outdated opinions.

Just as humor in adult fiction can be used to challenge and educate audiences, so too can the Gothic. In her essay on the Gothic in Aboriginal literature, Katrin Althans provides readers with an overview of the controversial genre and the Gothic's place in literary and cultural history. She then launches into a larger discussion about how Aboriginal writers have successfully combined elements of Aboriginal tradition and culture with the original European Gothic to negotiate issues of Aboriginal cultural strength and identity. Althans surveys a wide variety of Aboriginal authors who either focus specifically on the Gothic in their writing or who use it periodically in their work. Notable authors Althans discusses include David Unaipon, Sam and Nicole Watson, Alexis Wright, Kim Scott, Melissa Lucashenko, and Philip McLaren. Several novels by Mudrooroo (Colin Johnson) are also discussed because although his heritage has since been successfully questioned, his books had, and continue to have, a significant impact on the genre. In her essay, Althans also further highlights the Gothic's influence in Aboriginal literature by discussing material beyond the traditional novel—websites and television.

From Althans' discussion of the Gothic in various types of "literature" including television drama, the companion transitions into drama on the stage. Maryrose Casey explains how performance has been a "crucial point of cross-cultural exchange from the first European colonial settlements." The long-established tradition of performance in Aboriginal culture, since even before Europeans settled in Australia, provides Casey with a rich canvas on which to survey a variety of Australian Aboriginal plays from various periods. Casey recalls some of the earliest recordings by Europeans about Aboriginal performances they had witnessed before discussing some of the first acclaimed Aboriginal playwrights, including Kevin Gilbert, Robert Merritt, Gerry Bostock, Jack Charles, Gary Foley, and Jack Davis. Casey moves through the decades, critiquing many plays by additional playwrights including Jimmy Chi, John Harding, Eva

Johnson, Jane Harrison, Noel Tovey, David Page, and Wesley Enoch. Many of these plays highlight a continuing theme in many Aboriginal genres—"the pain and injuries of colonization and racism." Thus, companion readers see that, just as life writing has been used to affirm life experiences by Aboriginal Australians, so too have many of the works within drama.

Just as theater directors masterfully prepare their performance for the stage, so do film directors. Films, whether short or feature length, are a powerful vehicle for directors to share their work with a diverse audience. For many, films are the first genre that introduces audiences to Australian Aboriginal literature or culture. In his essay, Theodore Sheckels briefly lists a selection of feature films by non-Aboriginal directors about Aboriginals, such as non-Aboriginal director Phillip Noyce's award-winning *Rabbit-Proof Fence* and Baz Luhrman's less successful film, *Australia*, before turning his attention to Aboriginal writer-directors. Sheckels explains that while there is a public keen to watch films that depict Australian Aboriginal literature and culture, the opportunities for many Australian Aboriginal directors to present this material has been limited. Even with these challenges, however, Sheckels shows that films produced by Australian Aboriginal directors about Aboriginal life, particularly the Stolen Generations, are far more effective than those by their non-Indigenous counterparts. Rachel Perkins and Tracey Moffatt are two Aboriginal writer-directors, in particular, who have overcome various obstacles to succeed nationally and internationally. Films by Perkins and Moffatt about the Stolen Generations, Sheckels argues, are more effective than the works by non-Indigenous directors because of their indirection—their ability to focus on one subject yet also (under the surface) refer to another potentially more powerful subject. The range of films Sheckels discusses demonstrates to readers that although the number of Aboriginal directors may still be quite small, they are having a far-reaching impact on national and international audiences.

Another genre in which Australian Aboriginals have excelled is music. Andrew King traces popular Indigenous music from its beginnings until today. King divides the history of Australian Aboriginal music into four phases to detail a wide array of individual artists and bands who achieved, or continue to achieve, national and international success. Notable artists King includes in his essay include groundbreaking artists from the 1950s and 1960s Georgia Lee, Harold Blair, and Jimmy Little; Aboriginal bands No Fixed Address, Yothu Yindi, Shakaya, and Local Knowledge; and contemporary singers Archie Roach, Christine Anu, Troy Cassar-Daley, and MC Wire. King also devotes a portion of his essay to lyrics in Indigenous songs to demonstrate the strong connection of Native Australians to their heritage and their desire for continued reconciliation efforts between the Indigenous and non-Indigenous. King's eclectic discussion of various periods and genres within the music industry, as well as his examination of various concert venues and award ceremonies that focus on Indigenous music, makes his essay a valuable contribution to the companion.

Australian Aboriginal literature has become an integral component of Australian literature and a recognized canon in its own right. This is despite a number of historical atrocities and a government infrastructure and a white majority's "way of life" that continues to oppress many Australian Aboriginals. Much of the literature produced by Australian Aboriginals refers to the Stolen Generations specifically or to other injustices that have occurred or continue to occur. Yet much of this material does not blame current generations, and many Australian Aboriginals have a genuine interest in continuing to promote reconciliation between the Indigenous and non-Indigenous. Twenty-eight years ago Marnie Kennedy (1919–85) wrote in the preface to her autobiography, *Born a Half-Caste* (1985), "This story was written with the hope that white people will know and understand the plight of my people. . . . There is hope also that young white Australians will help to heal the damage the government did over a hundred years [ago]" (1). Kennedy's sentiment continues to be repeated by many other Aboriginal writers and artists, as well as many non-Aboriginals who wish to build strong connections between the two communities. Many nonindigenous and indigenous communities from around the world are increasingly noticing the work of Australian Aboriginal writers and artists, and it is the continued conversation between these groups and an acknowledgement of the past that will continue to promote reconciliation and continue to strengthen this significant canon.

# Works Cited

Kennedy, Marnie. *Born a Half-Caste*. Canberra: Australian Institute of Aboriginal Studies, 1985.

Schaffer, Kay. "Stolen Generation Narratives in Local and Global Contexts." *Antipodes* 16, no. 1 (2002): 5–10.

Wake, Charles Staniland. "On the Antiquity of Man and Comparative Geology." *Journal of the Anthropological Society of London* 5 (1867): cv–cxvii.

Walker, Alice. Review of *My Place* by Sally Morgan (book jacket). New York: Little Brown, 1993.

# 1: Indigenous Life Writing: Rethinking Poetics and Practice

*Michael R. Griffiths*

> *Write of life*
> *the pious said*
> *forget the past*
> *the past is dead.*
> *But all I*
> *see in front of me*
> *is a concrete floor*
> *a cell door*
> *and John Pat.*
>
> —Jack Davis[1]

WHAT DOES IT MEAN to "write of life"? And how does Aboriginal writing position itself in relation to the politics of life itself? The opening stanza to Jack Davis's poem about sixteen-year-old John Pat, brutally beaten by police in 1983, troubles the relation between the Aboriginal custom of not speaking the name of the dead and the necessary task of memorializing such trauma. One way to read the stanza is to identify the pious as a double category: the pious may be those whites who insist Davis "forget the past"; yet, paradoxically, the pious may equally refer to those voices of tradition from within the Aboriginal community that insist upon maintaining the taboo against speaking the name of the dead. John Pat's death is a tragedy, like that of so many Aboriginal victims of Australia's (post)colonial inheritance of trauma and continued structural violence and systematic dispossession.[2] Speaking Pat's name is not only

---

[1] *Epigraph:* Jack Davis, "John Pat," in *John Pat and Other Poems* (Melbourne: Dent, 1988), 2–3.

[2] I have argued elsewhere that despite their gaining independence from the imperial metropole, Indigenous peoples in Australia continue to be colonized. I therefore employ parentheses around "post," questioning whether we have in fact moved beyond colonialsm. See my "Settler Colonial Biopolitics and Postcolonial Iterability in Kim Scott's *Benang*," in *Postcolonial Issues in Australian Literature*, ed. Nathanael O'Reilly (Amherst, NY: Cambria, 2010), 157–84. Chadwick

tragic because of his death in police custody, on "a concrete floor / a cell door," but also because of Davis's necessary compulsion to continue to speak his name and thereby break a traditional taboo.

Aboriginal life writing, like many forms of Indigenous aesthetics in (post)colonial Australia, is a syncretic practice: bound to a postcolonial structure of mourning and trauma while also deeply engaged with tradition and its restoration. This double condition of tradition and continuance has been a consistent problem in the Indigenous paradigm of writing and of life writing particularly. To write of life, it is often necessary to break with precolonial Indigenous tradition: at the very least (since one is writing), the traditional positioning of self and kinship within the complexity of oral culture. In order to undertake the necessary task of memorializing past injustices, it is necessary that tradition shift on uneven sands. Syncretic rethinking of Aboriginal tradition is at once an act of preservation and transformation—and, as Davis's poem attests, preservation of tradition can involve the rearticulation of cultural forms.[3] To turn to life writing proper, one can note that Doris Pilkington Garimara foregrounds this tension in naming from the earliest pages of her *Follow the Rabbit-Proof Fence* (1996), noting that her mother and aunt, whose stories she compiles from interviews, refer to their deceased sister in a different manner than that which she chooses to preserve in her writing of their narrative: "they refer to their sister Gracie in the interviews simply as 'the sister we lose 'em in Geraldton,' or 'your Aunty'" (xi). This, Pilkington Garimara notes, "is the custom in traditional Aboriginal communities where the name of a person is never mentioned after their death" (xi).

---

Allen makes a similar case about Aotearoa New Zealand and the United States. Chadwick Allen, *Blood Narrative: Indigenous Identity in American Indian and Maori Literary and Activist Texts* (Durham, NC: Duke University Press, 2002), 8, 28–36.

[3] It should be noted, however, that the taboo on speaking the names of the dead varies among Aboriginal groups and depends much on context. Among Pilkington Garamara's people, the Gududjara, the taboo remains commonplace and thus the tension at the heart of naming practices in life writing is central to her work. Yet many southern groups that have experienced more extensive and sustained colonial contact do not maintain the taboo on naming the dead. Noongar people, for instance, often believe in commemorating the dead through their very names. Kim Scott, in naming collaborators who passed away before the completion of a recent language project, insists explicitly that this is done with "no disrespect to other Australian Aboriginal groups for whom names of the deceased are taboo" (Scott and Roberts ii). Noongar people are typically highly respectful of the taboos of Yamatji (north Western Australian) and Wongai (east Western Australian) Aboriginal peoples. When a Ngaanyatjarra elder died in a police van in 2008, Noongar justice campaigners prominent in the Deaths in Custody Watch Committee referred to him in their public statements only as Mr. Ward, avoiding his given name.

Yet Pilkington Garimara nonetheless writes Gracie, name and all, into her story. In this sense, the inscription of true accounts of people's real lives is a double problem that is insurmountably a part of Aboriginal life writing. Among the most central tasks of life writing, then, is that of the restoration of community and kinship connections, what the Noongar novelist and life writer Kim Scott has called "regeneration, continuity, and going back to go forward" (quoted in "Mixed Blood"). In simultaneously returning to Aboriginal tradition and narrating its dispossession and disruption by the colonizing process, life story does not simply reproduce a narrative of a static cultural form but rather forms a part of a complex regenerative process. This essay is a consideration of the generic conditions of Australian Aboriginal life writing; it reads Australian Aboriginal life writing as such a process of simultaneously restoring and rearticulating kinship in the face of a history of ongoing dispossession and colonization. As a non-Indigenous Australian academic working in the United States, I have become acutely aware that efforts by outsiders like me to group such Indigenous literary practices into imaginary coherent genres risks occluding the cultural differences of a broad corpus of writing based on lived experience. However, I would argue that there is much to be gained in attempting to vigorously conceive, promote, and disseminate the literary value of Aboriginal life writing as a way of avowing its serious literary and political import—of interest internationally.[4] In thinking about such literary categories as genre in the context of Aboriginal life writing, ironically it is necessary to think beyond the bounds of the text—beyond the conditions of writing as a form of intellectual production separate from lived experience. This is not a typical way of thinking about genre or the literary in the Western tradition from which such classificatory moves are typically inherited. *Poēsis*, after all, has in the Western tradition since Aristotle been opposed to *praxis*, ways of acting in the world and in a community have been supposed to be separate from those of *making* art. As for life, as Giorgio Agamben notes, the Greeks had two words for life: on the one hand *bios*, meaning forms of socially conditioned, collective, and individuated life, and on the other hand *zoē*, meaning the mere fact of living (1). I contend that precisely such divisions as this *poēsis/praxis* binary

---

[4] Some have argued that Aboriginal community and kinship is ultimately not a space *for* the settler-Australian or international reader. This caveat is significant given that life writing, particularly after this 1980s renaissance, was precisely invested in revealing to a wide audience the experiences of Aboriginal people and communities. As Scott puts it, "Indigenous communities have had too much intervention and interference. Preserving a gap between these communities and the 'white' community can promote healing and help consolidate a heritage" (Scott and Brown, 191). The ethics of teaching Aboriginal literature may arise in the always tense balance between doing justice to a multiple tradition and knowing the limits of one's speaking position.

obscure and delegitimize a truly critical avowal of the political possibilities of Aboriginal life writing. Aboriginal life writings often engage processes of meaningful community *bios* from a form of collective and individual life that has been consistently subject to disruption and assimilation; it is a poetic practice of making life from and through community connections so often fragmented by colonization. Life writers are not only literary figures engaged in a literary task of craft and composition. They are also active agents of community building, kinship restoration, the (re) construction of knowledge about region and community, and the critique of colonialism. They engage living elders, conduct interviews, reconnect with family members, and craft these experiences into story. It is in this relation between community and construction that Aboriginal life writing finds its particular specificity.

This mention of ancient Greek concepts is not an attempt to produce some artificial continuity between the Western canon and Aboriginal life writing but exactly the opposite: it is an attempt to show how such concepts surreptitiously destabilize the reception of Aboriginal poetic productions. By noting the Greek inheritance of concepts of life and making, I want to highlight some of the ways that Aboriginal writing has been hindered from the recognition it deserves. It is necessary to say in advance that this hindrance is without justification. As Walter Mignolo argues, "With and in each language comes different concepts of . . . life which [lead] to philosophical practices that cannot be dependent on Greek canonical dictums in matters of thought" (456). As Aileen Moreton-Robinson similarly notes, "Indigenous intellectual production might be inspired by a different understanding of the human subject" than that which conceals the hegemonic aims of whiteness within the neutral category of the "Western" or "European" as the privileged place of epistemology ("Whiteness," 85). In light of the Western schism between praxis and poetics, one can see the way in which Aboriginal life writing, in blurring the lines between the two, has risked being refused the recognition of having genuinely literary value. As Kim Scott notes, "I have looked in bookshops for my own books and, failing to find them in the Australian Literature section, finally located them under 'Australiana'" (Scott and Brown, 202). I would contend that, rather than go along with this refusal, it is necessary to impress upon students and others in the academy that Aboriginal life writing is personal *and* political, community focused *and* the poetic triumph of voice; it is because Aboriginal life writing refuses to be either *praxis* or *poēsis* that it challenges that age-old binary itself. The irreducible value of works of life writing as speech acts of political self-assertion and kinship restoration have paradoxically been the basis of life writing's disavowal as nonliterary. This question of the literary generic conditions of life writing has been crucial from the beginning of the academic reception of indigenous life writing globally. The influential critic of Native American literature Arnold Krupat has noted that indigenous North American autobiography had "been almost entirely ignored by students of American literature—who have, otherwise, been quite interested in autobiography as literature" (28). This same evasion can be identified in the treatment of Australian Aboriginal biography and autobiography as a distinct and influential strand of Aboriginal literature—as reflected in Scott's remark about the marketing of his work in Australian bookstores. I note this dismissal of life writing here at the outset, even as one can be optimistic that it may be on its way out. Nonetheless, deeper structural dimensions to the poetics of Western thought may provide some reason as to the upward battle which life writing has faced in its struggle for literary acceptance. Even as their stories are often meticulously crafted literary narratives, Aboriginal life writers, biographers, and autobiographers often position questions of literary value as having equal importance alongside the political, kin-based, and cultural praxes that their craft engages. This question of poetics, practice, and the cross-cultural concept of life itself bears contextualization.

The inherent syncretism of Aboriginal knowledge must be recognized as emerging from a (post)colonial history in which its traditions and indeed its people have often suffered.[5] As I have elsewhere suggested, assimilation must be read as a biopolitical process, which is to say, an example of colonial manipulation of race, eugenics, and the destruction of kinship through population management.[6] Delineating biopolitics in Australia, Morgan Brigg argues, "Western traditions emphasize speech and the written word to establish a politics focused through *life*, whereas Australian Aboriginal traditions emphasize land and ancestors to establish a politics organized through Country" (404). Life, as Brigg notes, is often thought of in a European post-Enlightenment sense as being based on speech and writing as it pertains to narratives of an enclosed individual self, rather than to a self continuous with kinship and country. Restoring kinship and belonging in life writing also means problematizing the Western biopolitical notion of life as it pertains to the management of colonized populations. By drawing together and restoring kinship and community with self and individual Aboriginal lived experience, Aboriginal life writing challenges the

---

[5] Agency as well as victimhood, however, must be emphasized, as A. Dirk Moses argues in "Time, Indigeneity, and Peoplehood: The Postcolony in Australia," *Postcolonial Studies* 13, no. 1 (2010): 9–24.

[6] I have elsewhere written about what I call "settler colonial biopolitics" and the way many metafictive texts also challenge this paradigm. See my "Settler Colonial Biopolitics." See also my "Biopolitical Correspondences: Settler Nationalism, Thanatopolitics, and the Perils of Hybridity," *Australian Literary Studies* 26, no. 2 (2011): 20–42.

colonial biopolitical notion of life and insists on a the maintenance of a concept of kinship and belonging vested in country.

This essay offers a brief and necessarily partial survey of the bounds of life writing. It frames an approach to life writing that I have already begun to limn: the tension between the preservation of tradition, the critique of colonialism, and the restorative poetic praxis that emerges in interlacing the two. As the partial survey conducted here proceeds, I will focus increasingly on a more defined regional space, moving westward and then south to Noongar country. Such regionally specific nonfiction productions affect a *poēsis* of imaginary content in relation to stories that refer to individual and collective histories and ultimately reconfigure the colonized meaning of life or *bios*. After surveying broadly the work of significant figures such as Pilkington Garimara and Jackie Huggins, I will turn to consider Kim Scott and Hazel Brown's *Kayang and Me* (2005) and the work of Sally Morgan, as well as a lesser-known children's story by Noongar writer and community leader Angus Wallam, *Corroboree* (2004). These writers use community, country, and self as entwined to disarticulate the false dichotomy between *poēsis* and *praxis* and redefine Aboriginal life. They do so through a regenerative process, drawing in both Indigenous tradition and a critique of colonialism. Against the Western myth of art as the solitary production of an individual genius, much of the Indigenous praxis of life writing involves collaboration.

Aboriginal life writing can be positioned both against and in relation to a long tradition of settler writing about Aboriginal people. As such, Aboriginal life writing, biography, and autobiography each form separate but related strands in a corpus of enunciations of truth about Aboriginal society and individual subjectivity.[7] There is a long tradition of ethnographic writing about Aboriginal people that affects an authentic speaking position. One early example of such ethnobiography, as Gillian Whitlock terms it, is Douglas Lockwood's *I, the Aboriginal* (1962) (241). This strand is indeed the least authentic within this broad corpus, but situating Aboriginal life writing in relation to ethnobiography may be pedagogically useful in allowing students to observe the tradition against which much Aboriginal life writing sets itself. Certainly, it is not adequate to conflate such ethnobiography with the practice of life writing by Aboriginal people. The latter phenomenon can be seen to extend back as far as the writings of David Unaipon. Unaipon's collection from the 1920s, *Legendary*

---

[7] Anne Brewster takes into account a wide range of texts in her *Reading Aboriginal Women's Autobiography* (Sydney: Sydney University Press, 1996); Gillian Whitlock considers the place of Aboriginal autobiographical writings in her "From Biography to Autobiography," in *The Cambridge Companion to Australian Literature*, ed. Elizabeth Webby (Cambridge: Cambridge University Press, 2000), 232–57.

*Tales of the Australian Aborigines*, is both ethnographic and invested in storytelling. More recently one could cite such overtly autobiographical accounts as Dick Roughsey's *Moon and Rainbow: The Autobiography of an Aboriginal* (1971) and Jack Mirritji's *My People's Life: An Aboriginal's Own Story* (1976) as significant early texts for any syllabus on Aboriginal life writing, autobiography, or Aboriginal writing generally. Roughsey's and Mirritji's texts asserted their authenticity through the fact that they were written by initiated men from remote communities. As the foreword to Roughsey's text puts it, *Moon and Rainbow* can be received as "maybe the most important book ever to be written on the Australian Aborigines," because "it is the first genuine book by a full-blood Aboriginal seeking a better understanding of his people by white Australians" (9). The foreword also predicts that Roughsey's text "may be the catalyst which will trigger a great outflow of writing and self-expression by other Aborigines" (9). Where books like Roughsey's and Mirritji's were presented for public consumption as texts of great authenticity and arising from autodidactic "full-blood" and "tribalized" Aborigines (as the colonialist rhetoric of the time had it), the emergence of a strong tradition of Aboriginal autobiography in the following decades was not so much based on such appeals to authenticity. Perhaps the most significant literary moment for Aboriginal life writing was the emergence in the 1980s of a richly proliferating field of texts by significant autobiographical and life writers as Sally Morgan, *My Place* (1987) and Ruby Langford Ginibi, *Don't Take Your Love to Town* (1987). These texts were later followed in the 1990s and beyond with works such as Doris Pilkington Garimara's *Follow the Rabbit-Proof Fence* (1996) and *Under the Wintamarra Tree* (2003). Where the occasional autobiographies of the 1970s had been marketed through the "authentic" access to traditional Aboriginal life given by their authors, this 1980s field of women's autobiography was more politically engaged as it responded to the revelation of the Stolen Generations.

So, while prior to Morgan's and Langford Ginibi's seminal texts, a sporadic series of texts by Aboriginal men emerged, after the 1980s a group of predominantly women writers effectively carved out a space for autobiographical and other life accounts on the literary scene. Tracey Bunda has even designated this sphere as an enunciatory site of the "black sovereign woman," and the presence of such a critical voice indicates that the role of non-Indigenous academics in positioning such cultural production will recede in centrality (75–85, esp. 75). While this chronology is important to note, it is also useful to make several caveats. While filmmaking must remain an unfortunate omission, outside the scope of this brief essay, it would do to at least remark on and recommend Essie Coffey's exceptional 1978 film *My Survival as an Aboriginal*. Coffey's film dramatizes the structural discrimination experienced by Aboriginal people in western New South Wales, the efforts of Aboriginal legal

services to alleviate this discrimination, and the importance and centrality of traditional knowledge in the lives of its subjects. Coffey's film also
deploys subtle and savvy cinematic techniques to draw out the spatial-
ized and mediated erasure of Aboriginal people from western New South
Wales. Similarly, the Warlpiri Media Association has been experimenting
with local content in Yuendumu since the early 1980s. Televisual media
and film have had a strong role in the self-expression of Aboriginal individuals and communities for almost as long as life writing, interrupting a
narrative that aims to see the (nonetheless remarkable) achievements of
Morgan and Huggins as an easily delineated "first" or "renaissance."

Another caveat arises when we recognize that while seminal texts
in this 1980s renaissance in Aboriginal life writing were predominantly
penned by women, they embraced kinship relations crossing the entire
community, encompassing the voices of men, and particularly elder men.
After the success of *My Place*, Morgan turned in *Wanamurraganya: The
Story of Jack McPhee* (1989) to chronicle the life of its titular figure, a
man central to Morgan's efforts to reconnect with her Palyku extended
family in the Pilbara region of Western Australia. Seen at a metatextual
level, Morgan's text recalls the idea of the initiated man predominant in
earlier life stories such as Roughsey's and Mirritji's. However, this text
does not take the "traditional Aboriginal man" as a static subject, but
rather refracts this figure through a careful consideration of the interrup-
tion of tradition by colonialism. While McPhee is described by Morgan as
a "male who had been through the Law," her presentation of his story,
while embracing his knowledge of tradition, also takes seriously his tactical adoption of European practices, his mobility within settler spheres,
and the discriminatory exclusion he experienced at the margins of these
spheres (16).[8] McPhee's story reveals the harassment and surveillance
experienced by Aboriginal people in possession of exemptions from legislation governing Natives. "Why," the diegetic McPhee wonders at one
point, "did I need an exemption certificate just because I was a different colour?" (126). McPhee also lucidly reveals the double bind facing so many Aboriginal people prior to 1967: attempting to obtain the
provisional citizenship granted by exemption was conditional on aban-
doning (at least outwardly) the commitment to extended family that in
no small way defines Aboriginal society (156–69). Morgan's telling of
Jack McPhee's story establishes life story as a genre vested in the tension between the endurance of Aboriginal tradition and the recognition
of its attempted destruction by settler colonizing practices of governance.
McPhee's story, then, functions both as an authentic expression of the
reflections of "Wanamurraganya, the son of a tribal Aborigine," and

---

[8] Jack's experience of initiation as a Garimara man is recounted in the chapter "A
Man in the Mulba Way" (51–60).

those of "a man who is fighting with being black and white. A man who chooses not to live in the tribal way, but who can't live the whiteman's way because the government won't let him" (17).

As Morgan's telling of Jack McPhee's story shows, collaboration is a significant part of life writing. Morgan's introduction can, in many ways, be seen as a poetics and methodology for life writers. Morgan distinguishes between writer and teller, an important distinction, implying the active agency of the teller beyond an antiquated understanding of the ethnographic informant. As Morgan insists, the writer of another's story must dialogically relate to the teller. The teller must retain editorial control through a sustained process of consultancy: "There may be things which the writer like to include but which the teller objects to. In this case the final decision always belongs to the teller" (15). Archival work can also assist in this process, but, as Morgan points out, the status of the written archive should not supplant the recollection of the teller. As Morgan notes with humor, one report on McPhee's marriage in his Native Affairs file remarks on the chief protector's having interviewed him at Moore River Native Settlement. McPhee, instead, recalls that the chief protector merely spoke to the superintendent of Moore River Native Settlement and never sought to address McPhee directly: "there are times when an oral account is far more reliable than a written one" (16). Texts such as *Wanamurraganya* reveal that Aboriginal life writing, though often the province of women writers, has embraced a complex restoration of kin and community.

Collaboration may also take place between Aboriginal and non-Aboriginal writers. Notable among the latter are the collaborations between Nyikina man Paddy Roe and Anglo-Australian poststructuralist academic Steven Muecke; these include *Gularabulu* (1983) and *Reading the Country* (with artist Kim Benterrak, 1984). Where traditional ethnobiography often foreclosed the active presence of Aboriginal voice, Roe and Muecke's work was an ongoing collaboration. Aboriginal collaborations across generations have also produced writings that exceed not only biography but even the literary. Jackie Huggins used a paradigm of placing her own voice adjacent to that of her mother Rita Huggins in their collaboration *Auntie Rita* (1994). Jackie's narration both reflects biographically on Rita's assertions while commenting on political and literary questions. Influencing such collaborations as that of Kim Scott with his *kayang* (elder woman, aunty), Hazel Brown, *Auntie Rita* provides a political lens on Aboriginal experience as Jackie theorizes experiences of racism and colonialism narratively described by her mother. Indeed, as we will see with Morgan's, Scott and Brown's, and Wallam's texts, collaborations between Aboriginal people across generations have been a significant part of the construction of life writing, and various forms of such collaboration have inscribed a specific praxis. Before turning to these case studies, however, it is necessary to position some of the theoretical, methodological, and reception issues that have informed Indigenous life writing.

Life writing draws from nonfiction sources, it is often written and edited collaboratively, and its value exceeds its status as text and draws from its dissemination in the Aboriginal and non-Aboriginal Australian circuits of reception. As such, life writing should be considered simultaneously a poetic craft and a praxis of restoring kinship and community in the face of the biopolitical disruption of the Stolen Generations.

As we have seen, the romance of the literary as an act of pure *poēsis* has led to the unfortunate risk of dismissal attendant upon life writing. This is surprising since texts like *Auntie Rita* and *Kayang and Me* are hardly uncomplicated in their presentation of voice. For instance, Scott weaves through his text sensitive orthographic renderings of Hazel Brown's remembrances from Noongar country alongside his own metatextual reflections on the meaning of Aboriginal identity, community, literature, and the concept of home. From his "very regional perspective," Scott reflects on the meaning of Aboriginal identity, particularly for descendants of the Stolen Generations like himself (Scott and Brown, 238). As with Rita and Jackie Huggins's collaboration, the interwoven voices of Kim and Hazel deploy connections between past and present that both trouble and inform Aboriginal identity within a specific region: the southwest, and Wilomin Noongar country in particular.[9]

Even voices from the Indigenous literary scene have positioned Indigenous biography and autobiography as incommensurable with received standards of literary generic categorization. Colin Johnson—known as Mudrooroo until his claim to be an Aboriginal was refuted conclusively—attacked the apparent eschewal of "activist literature" that he saw resulting from the predominance of Indigenous "life story" (*Indigenous*, 15–16). He worried that, with the publication of Sally Morgan's *My Place*, a new "Period of Reconciliation" had begun, which was "heavily edited literature written and revised in conjunction with a European and its message is one of understanding and tolerance," and "[a]s such, it is not concerned with the future aims and aspirations of Indigenous people" (16). Mudrooroo's statements did not entirely disavow life writing but frequently implied that both the use of editing and the project of narrating Indigenous lives to a white audience aimed more at the making of a multicultural society than the activist aims that he emphasized. He states, in conversation with other writers, that "I've always had reservations about autobiography and biography as a genre. [Elsie R.] Labumore's work is not really autobiography or biography;

---

[9] I use the spelling of *Wilomin* employed by Scott in that text. In more recent collaborative efforts, Scott has moved to spelling the clan name *Wirlomin*.

it's a story of a whole community, rather than self. Sally Morgan's is a prime example of writing about self and so that's more autobiography. But I think the shift in men's writing is towards the novel" (*Indigenous Literature*, 200). Mudrooroo here appears to emplace a hierarchy wherein writing about the self is autobiographical, apolitical, and panders to white literary demand for the authentic. Work like Labumore's is presented as preferable since it "is not really autobiography or biography; it's a story of a whole community, rather than self" (200). But, finally, men's writings of creative invention and "Maban reality" such as that of his own or that of Sam Watson are positioned by Mudrooroo as truly political Indigenous writings (199).[10] Writing about the self, for Mudrooroo, is implicitly seen as void of both political content and poetic invention. The inextricability of the genre from political self-assertion should, rather, be understood as primary since, as I have noted, writing of life means writing against the biopolitical history of colonization. As Aileen Moreton-Robinson notes, "Mudrooroo's critique is spurious because he separates Indigenous women's lives from the Indigenous struggle. He relies on a white patriarchal definition of what it is to be political, thus denying subjectivity as a site of resistance. . . . Indigenous women's life writings make visible dimensions of the hidden history and colonial legacy of this country through their gaze as subject" (*Talking Up*, 2–3). For Moreton-Robinson, life writing is political on the merit of this revelation of the colonial past. Mudrooroo's characterization of Morgan's life story as merely about "self" is a misrepresentation. The categorical assertion that writing about self is separate from writing about community is problematic; as such, Mudrooroo's categorization of Aboriginal writing cannot be maintained on its own terms. Moreton-Robinson's claim that Aboriginal life writing reveals "the hidden history and colonial legacy of this country" further challenges the settler colonial construction of "life" (*Talking Up*, 2–3). Such a legacy draws in the biopolitical management of Aboriginality with its disruption of traditional conceptions and supplantation by colonized ways of living. As I have begun to address, one of the key features of Aboriginal life writing is that it often takes into account the political task of uncovering the "colonial legacy" of assimilation in Australia; life writing is almost always engaged in a process of kinship restoration in the wake of this legacy.

---

[10] *Maban* is a term widespread in the northwest of Western Australia for a man of power and knowledge, capable of effecting changes in the bodies and minds of others through magical practices; it is also the term for the magic itself. Mudrooroo adopted the term *maban reality* to describe his particular brand of magical realism. See his "Maban Reality and Shape-Shifting the Past: Strategies to Sing the Past Our Way," *Critical Arts: South-North Cultural and Media Studies* 10, no. 2 (1996): 1–20.

In asserting that writing about self is the result of the editorial imposition of whiteness, Mudrooroo implicitly asserts that the reconstruction of Aboriginal subjectivity has no value beyond its marketing to the white reader, for instance to Aboriginal readers and collaborators. Might it not be possible to say that every piece of life writing is "a story about community" woven through a story about "self" rather than maintaining the splendid isolation of community and self, autobiography and life writing as irrevocably discrete sites of literary production? The act of maintaining such a purity of categories of self and community, autonomy and heteronomy misses precisely what is unique about the poetics, praxis, and politics of Aboriginal life writing.[11]

Sally Morgan's *My Place*, then, is simultaneously about self and community. *My Place* is difficult to box into a genre, since it combines elements of a memoir, an autobiographical bildungsroman, and collaborative efforts with Morgan's mother Gladys Corunna, grandmother Daisy Corunna, and great-uncle Arthur Corunna. *My Place* subtly unravels such claims as Mudrooroo's that this memoir is primarily about self by producing textual reverberations that both complicate and restore self through the life stories of Morgan's family members. *My Place* is chronologically tied to Sally's discoveries of her own Aboriginality and the order in which she collected her relative's stories. The first part of the book recounts Morgan's life growing up and her eventual speculation about her family's Aboriginal origins, which have been held back from her by Gladys and Daisy. One way to read this first part is as an autobiography of Morgan's discovery of her own Aboriginality. In the second part of the book, through the narratives of Gladys, Daisy, and Arthur, Aboriginality is positioned less as an authentic subject position and more as a process of personal and political consciousness formation that can only be understood within the colonial history of the disruption and rearticulation of kinship. Therefore, to deride the text as a narrative reduced to a process of self-discovery opens it to the criticism that this reflexivity is merely the result of "the tastes and expectations of a white readership and publishing industry" (Whitlock, 252). By enmeshing her own bildungsroman with the recovery and presentation of Gladys, Daisy, and Arthur's stories, Morgan makes a story of self inseparable from that of a community. Returning to Aboriginal tradition becomes simultaneously a process of uncovering the colonizing process that has withheld it from the subjects of the Stolen Generations and their families.

---

[11] Elizabeth Povinelli explores the complexities of self and community formation as the tension between autology and heterology in her *The Empire of Love: Toward a Theory of Intimacy, Genealogy, and Carnality* (Durham, NC: Duke University Press, 2006).

However, the aforementioned narrative of individual subjective plenitude does not adequately account for the complex kinship and communal responsibility making up Aboriginal subjectivity. A better way to read *My Place* is to emphasize the way the text engages a dialogic process of both self and community formation by interweaving autobiography with the life story of relatives. *My Place* reveals both the fracturing of community and cultural consciousness that assimilation brought about and, through the process of drawing together the family's multiple generations, suggests a practice of healing. The motif of healing resonates on a personal level for both Sally and Daisy as the novel closes with their mutual understanding brought about by Daisy's eventual decision to tell her part of the story before her death. This resolution comes as the final relinquishment of Daisy's reluctance to speak of her past—itself a legacy of her experience of colonizing oppression, her loss of her first child, and the fear of the loss of her children and grandchildren if they or the authorities were to learn of their Aboriginality.

The literary projects of life writers often lead them from self to community or, alternately, from community back to self. Where *My Place* has led Morgan to extensively engage in projects of community building and kinship restoration (such as *Wanamurraganya* and her extensive campaigns to improve Indigenous literacy), Pilkington Garimara's trajectory has been the inverse. Beginning her career in 1990 as a novelist with her *Caprice: A Stockman's Daughter*, Pilkington Garimara soon turned to life story. Her 1996 *Follow the Rabbit-Proof Fence* told the story of her mother and two aunts' escape from the infamous Moore River Native Settlement and long walk back to their families at the Jigalong Depot. Beginning her foray into life writing with this account of her extended family's struggles with colonialism, Pilkington Garimara then turned to positioning her own story in relation to this broader history. This trajectory—from family history to autobiography—is also echoed in the structure of each of her life accounts. Both *Follow the Rabbit-Proof Fence* and *Under the Wintamarra Tree* move from recounting the traditional lives and practices of her extended family to an increasing focus on the principle characters. In *Under the Wintamarra Tree*, the tension between restoring tradition and critiquing colonialism is brought out early on as Pilkington Garimara recounts the disruption of traditional food gathering practices in the northwest, first leading to her family's need to move to Jigalong. Recounting the traditional subsections of her people's marriage system, she is quick to note that the move to Jigalong brought them face to face with colonialism: "for the first time in their lives they were confronted with fences, a barrier that marked the boundary of a new owner and a method of control" (6). As the story progresses, like Jack McPhee, Doris successfully breaks through the barriers of white society, becoming a trained nurse before marrying into an increasingly abusive relationship with a Noongar man. The story, in this way, accounts for the insistent hegemonic force that divides Aboriginal people in their own relations, and Doris's successful survival allows her to carve out a space between self and community, "celebrating the resurrection of life itself" (199), such that the story functions in "the movement to heal our people" (208). As in McPhee's story, Pilkington Garimara's account of herself as Doris valorizes Aboriginal tradition, asserts the role of the self, and accounts for the legacy of colonialism as a barrier in either. This tension between the practice of poetically inscribing self through kinship and writing against the insistence of the colonizing legacy might serve as a thematic center to classroom discussions of Aboriginal life writing.

Collaboration, we have seen, is central to processes of Aboriginal life writing. It would do, then, to close with an emphasis on the role of texts themselves in the process of cultural restoration. To do so, I want to tell a partial story about a storyteller and elder. In Wagin, Western Australia, Noongar elder Angus Wallam spends much of his time advising the Southern Land Council. When I visited Wallam in 2009, he was assisting in the restoration of the Carrolup-Marribank Aboriginal Reserve on the site that was once an internment center for Indigenous children, Carrolup Native Settlement (Haebich, 165–87). Wallam was able to leave the settlement compound at times because of his family's close proximity. Wallam consequently lived "a semi-traditional" way of life (Wallam and Kelly, 29). He raised his family with this semitraditional knowledge and continues to impart it to his extended family. After arriving within the grounds of the reserve and singing a soft song to the spirits of those lost, he notes with wry and ironic humor that he was the "first boy in here" (Angus Wallam, personal interview, October 11, 2009). Wallam is, in other words, deeply involved in remembrance of the Stolen Generations. Indeed, Wallam recounted his oral history to historian Annette Roberts in the years prior to the 1995 National Inquiry into the Separation of Aboriginal and Torres Strait Islander Children from Their Families (Wallam). Yet he equally possesses much traditional knowledge of Noongar language and culture. Wallam teaches arrivals at the Carrolup-Marribank site not only about the legacy of child removal still denied (though thankfully decreasingly so) by non-Indigenous Australians but also about the salination attendant upon the waterways in the district and the spiritual beliefs surrounding the migratory patterns of the black swan as they lay their eggs (*nyoorok*) in these same waterways, to name only a few items of knowledge over which Wallam is a custodian. As such, *Corroboree*—a children's book he wrote in collaboration with younger Noongar writer Suzanne Kelly and illustrator Norma McDonald—is not a narrative of the Stolen Generations. The story's highlights include cutting Mallee bark and digging for *djoobak* (bush potato)—all practices that Wallam continues to pass on to Carrolup-Marribank visitors. *Corroboree* does not concern itself with the narratives of stolen children even as it is very much engaged in the restoration of tradition in the wake of this colonizing legacy. The writers of *Corroboree* imagine the time when the book's protagonist, Willin, lived autonomously with his family—perhaps a recollection of those times when Wallam was free from the Western Australian Department of Aborigines and took up his "semitraditional" life. While *Corroboree* does not signal itself as life writing, I raise this humble and illuminating book precisely because it is a regionally and culturally specific example of what it can mean to "write of life." This collaborative children's book involves Noongar people of several generations, and it allows young Noongar readers to learn the words of their language. *Corroboree* can be read as a fictionalized piece of life writing precisely because of its *poetics* of imagining—in Scott's terms—a regenerative Noongar *praxis* of life and language. Texts performing similarly restorative functions have followed in the region. For instance, Noel Kyar Morrison's *Carrolup Inspired* (2008). Like Wallam, Morrison has a large extended family whose members work in such areas as Aboriginal arts, land management, and prison reform. In more recent times, the politics of activism, while not disappearing, has been complemented by an engaged, ameliorative set of praxes. The poetics of life writing evinced in *Carrolup Inspired* and *Corroborree* are inextricably imbricated in the heteronomy of these praxes. Similarly, Kim Scott has engaged with his extended Wilomin family on a project of linguistic and cultural restoration, producing a series of bilingual books telling traditional *Noongar* stories. The construction of this project is emblematic of the reclamation and restoration brought about through the practice of life writing broadly conceived. Scott drew from the archive of American linguist Gerhardt Laves to uncover Noongar word sets. Collaborating with the descendants of Laves's "informants," the project combined the written record with the living recollection of language and stories embodied by Wilomin Noongar elders such as Lomas Roberts. The result is a collection of wonderful stories that also function as active instruments of cultural restoration, bringing community members together in productive collaboration and disseminating Noongar language throughout the community. Where the poetics of life writing has focused its political efficacy on revelation and memorialization, in this period following the 2008 apology to the Stolen Generations, it may be that this poetics will be increasingly concerned with the restoration of language, kinship, and community in regions like the southwest.

As I mentioned in my opening, Indigenous life writing is not the translation of an uninterrupted form of traditional knowledge. Indeed, to try to identify such an unchanging form of cultural knowledge would be to make a crucial mistake about the existence of continuity and change

across Aboriginal *poēsis* and *praxis*.[12] This mistaken positing of a full uninterrupted plenitude of traditional identity also reflects real political consequences for Aboriginal people; the discourse of native title, for instance,
often depicts Aboriginal culture as static—either whole and unchanged or
"washed away in a tide of history."[13] Aboriginal society is not the static
and fixed tradition that discourses of salvage anthropology from Spencer
and Gillen onward have attempted to render them (Baldwin Spencer, and
Gillen). Aboriginal societies are fluid and syncretic, changing with circumstances while maintaining the central tenets of their tradition. Indigenous
notions of life draw from both Indigenous traditions and the colonial and
postcolonial experience to which Indigenous life has become, for better
or worse, irrevocably bound. As Jackie Huggins argues significantly from
within the bounds of her mother's life story, Aboriginal people are not
fixed in the traditions that they continue and embody: "styles of dress,
speech, abode, where we shop or what car we drive do not lessen our
relation to Aboriginal culture and identity" (Huggins and Huggins,
"Excerpts," 73). Aboriginal life stories do not respond in isolation to
either only Australia's "hidden history and colonial legacy" or only to
some fixed imaginary of a precolonial tradition. Rather, Aboriginal life
stories simultaneously respond to colonial legacies and reconstruct meaningful models of kinship, community, land, and shared experience in relation to both precolonial and colonial experiences. The poetic practice of
community formation responds to a legacy of kinship fragmentation and
underscores the processual linkage of self and community. Against earlier
attempts to hierarchize genres of Aboriginal writing, critics and teachers
should emphasize the way Aboriginal writers produce works that cannot
be demarcated from the world, the community, or imaginings of their
regenerated future.

---

[12] Anthropologist W. E. H. Stanner famously argued that whereas the colonizing process of assimilation sought to transform Aboriginal people into cultural
Europeans, it was rather Aboriginal people who were often cunningly capable
of deciding the terms on which they accepted changes in their cultural forms.
Stanner wrote in 1958 that Aboriginal people do not "impress me as already or
as likely to be 'incorporated,' or 'absorbed,' or 'assimilated' into the surrounding
system of Europeanism. The very contrary is true. Various European things . . .
are data, facts of life, which the Aborigines take into account in working out their
altered system. . . . Unless we see both their contemporaneity and their specialisa-
tion, we set up a false model" (147, 164).

[13] The phrase "washed away in a tide of history," is Justice Olney's, and I use
it with significant irony (Members of the Yorta Yorta Aboriginal Community v.
Victoria [2001]). Povinelli considers the complexities of native title, cultural disruption, and cultural syncresis in her "The Poetics of Ghosts: Social Reproduction
in the Archive of the Nation" (2004).

# Works Cited

Agamben, Giorgio. *Homo Sacer: Sovereign Power and Bare Life.* Translated by Daniel Heller-Roazen. Stanford, CA: Stanford University Press, 1998.

Allen, Chadwick. *Blood Narrative: Indigenous Identity in American Indian and Maori Literary and Activist Texts.* Durham, NC: Duke University Press, 2002.

Bakhtin, Mikhail. "Forms of Time and of the Chronotope in the Novel." In *The Dialogic Imagination: Four Essays,* 84–258. Austin: University of Texas Press, 1981.

Baldwin Spencer, Walter, and Frank Gillen. *The Native Tribes of Central Australia.* 1898. Reprint, London: Macmillan, 1938.

Benterrak, Kim, Stephen Muecke, and Paddy Roe. *Reading the Country: Introduction to Nomadology.* Fremantle, WA: Fremantle Arts Centre Press, 1984.

Brewster, Anne. *Reading Aboriginal Women's Autobiography.* Sydney: Sydney University Press, 1996.

Brigg, Morgan. "Biopolitics Meets Terrapolitics: Political Ontologies and Governance in Settler-Colonial Australia." *Australian Journal of Political Science* 42, no. 3 (2007): 403–17.

Bunda, Tracey. "The Sovereign Aboriginal Woman." In *Sovereign Subjects: Indigenous Sovereignty Matters,* edited by Aileen Moreton-Robinson, 75–85. Crows Nest, NSW: Allen and Unwin, 2007.

Coffey, Essie. *My Survival as an Aboriginal.* Sydney: Ballad Films, 1978.

Davis, Jack. "John Pat." In *John Pat and Other Poems,* 2–3. Melbourne: Dent, 1988.

Griffiths, Michael R. "Biopolitical Correspondences: Settler Nationalism, Thanatopolitics, and the Perils of Hybridity." *Australian Literary Studies* 26, no. 2 (2011): 20–42.

———. "Settler Colonial Biopolitics and Postcolonial Iterability in Kim Scott's *Benang.*" In *Postcolonial Issues in Australian Literature,* edited by Nathanael O'Reilly, 157–84. Amherst, NY: Cambria, 2010.

Haebich, Anna. *For Their Own Good.* Nedlands: University of Western Australia Press, 1988.

Huggins, Rita, and Jackie Huggins. *Auntie Rita.* Canberra, ACT: Aboriginal Studies Press, 1994.

———. "Excerpts from *Auntie Rita.*" In *Indigenous Australian Voices: A Reader,* edited by Jennifer Scabbioni, Kay Schafer, and Sidonie Smith, 52–73. Brunswick, NJ: Rutgers University Press, 1998.

Krupat, Arnold. *For Those Who Come After: A Study of Native American Autobiography.* Berkeley: University of California Press, 1985.

Langford Ginibi, Ruby. *Don't Take Your Love to Town.* Sydney: Penguin, 1987.

Lockwood, Douglas. *I, the Aboriginal.* Adelaide: Rigby, 1962.

Members of the Yorta Yorta Aboriginal Community v. Victoria (2001) 110 FCR 244; 180 ALR 655, Full Federal Court, February 8, 2001.

Mignolo, Walter. "Delinking: The Rhetoric of Modernity, the Logic of Coloniality, and the Grammar of Decoloniality." *Cultural Studies* 21, nos. 2–3 (2007): 449–514.

Mirritji, Jack. *My People's Life: An Aboriginal's Own Story.* Milingimbi, NT: Milingimbi Literature Centre, 1976.

"Mixed Blood: Featuring Kim Scott, Thomas King, and David Malouf." Narrated by Daniel Browning. *Awaye!* ABC Radio National. March 1, 2008.

Moreton-Robinson, Aileen. *Talking Up to the White Woman: Indigenous Women and Feminism.* St Lucia: University of Queensland Press, 2000.

———. "Whiteness, Epistemology, and Indigenous Representation." In *Whitening Race*, edited by Aileen Moreton-Robinson, 75–88. Canberra, ACT: Aboriginal Studies Press, 2004.

Morgan, Sally. *My Place.* Fremantle, WA: Fremantle Arts Centre Press, 1987.

———. *Wanamurraganya: The Story of Jack McPhee.* Fremantle, WA: Fremantle Arts Centre Press, 1989.

Morrison, Noel Kyar. *Carrolup Inspired.* Fremantle, WA: Matilda Press, 2008.

Moses, A. Dirk. "Time, Indigeneity, and Peoplehood: The Postcolony in Australia." *Postcolonial Studies* 13, no. 1 (2010): 9–24.

Mudrooroo. *The Indigenous Literature of Australia: Milli Milli Wangka.* Melbourne, VIC: Hyland House, 1997.

———. "Maban Reality and Shape-Shifting the Past: Strategies to Sing the Past Our Way." *Critical Arts: South-North Cultural and Media Studies* 10, no. 2 (1996): 1–20.

Pilkington Garimara, Doris. *Caprice: A Stockman's Daughter.* St. Lucia: University of Queensland Press, 1990.

———. *Follow the Rabbit-Proof Fence.* St. Lucia: University of Queensland Press, 1996.

———. *Under the Wintamarra Tree.* St. Lucia: University of Queensland Press, 2003.

Povinelli, Elizabeth. "The Poetics of Ghosts: Social Reproduction in the Archive of the Nation." In *The Cunning of Recognition: Indigenous Alterities and the Making of Australian Multiculturalism*, 187–234. Durham, NC: Duke University Press, 2004.

———. *The Empire of Love: Toward a Theory of Intimacy, Genealogy, and Carnality.* Durham, NC: Duke University Press, 2006.

Roe, Paddy. *Gularabulu: Stories from the West Kimberley.* Edited by Stephen Muecke. Fremantle, WA: Fremantle Arts Centre Press, 1983.

Roughsey, Dick. *Moon and Rainbow: The Autobiography of an Aboriginal.* Sydney: A. H. & A. W. Reed, 1971.

Scott, Kim, and Hazel Brown. *Kayang and Me.* Fremantle, WA: Fremantle Arts Centre Press, 2005.

Scott, Kim, Lomas Roberts, and the Wirlomin Noongar Language and Stories Project. *Noongar Mambara Bakitj.* Crawley: University of Western Australia Press, 2011.

Stanner, W. E. H. "Continuity and Change Among the Australian Aborigines." In *The Dreaming and Other Essays*, 146–71. Melbourne: Black Inc. Agenda, 2009.

Unaipon, David. *Legendary Tales of the Australian Aborigines.* Edited by Stephen Muecke and Adam Shoemaker. Melbourne: University of Melbourne Press, 2001.

Wallam, Angus. Interview by Annette Roberts. Battye Library of West Australian History. Oral History Collection. OH 2552/20.

———. Personal interview. 11 October 2009.

Wallam, Angus, with Suzanne Kelly. *Corroboree.* Crawley: University of Western Australia Press, 2004.

Whitlock, Gillian. "From Biography to Autobiography." In *The Cambridge Companion to Australian Literature*, edited by Elizabeth Webby, 232–57. Cambridge: Cambridge University Press, 2000.

# 2: Australian Aboriginal Life Writers and Their Editors: Cross-Cultural Collaboration, Authorial Intention, and the Impact of Editorial Choices

*Jennifer Jones*

WHEN MARY ANN HUGHES complained in 1998 that critics were preoccupied with the process of editorial collaboration that shaped Australian Aboriginal texts, she argued that this focus led to the neglect of the literary merit of the work. While the collaboration of mainstream writers with editors primarily went unremarked, "in the case of an Aboriginal writer, the role of the editor in constructing the work is the issue which most readily springs to the fore" (56). Hughes remarked upon the then decade-long critical determination to materialize the traditionally invisible craft of editing. This critical preoccupation ran parallel with the second wave of Aboriginal life writing (Brewster, 44), which witnessed the transformation of Aboriginal publishing from marginal to mainstream, reaching beyond the local to global audiences (Haag, 12). The exponential increase in the publication of Aboriginal life writing was accompanied by the politicization of publication processes, including coproduction, that have conventionally been kept from public view.[1]

Sally Morgan's best-selling life narrative *My Place* (1987), a watershed in Australian Aboriginal publishing, also prompted critical interest in the politics of collaboration.[2] Australian critics responded with skepticism to the mass-market appeal of this multivoiced life story, which capitalized on burgeoning interest in Aboriginal affairs fostered by the celebration of the bicentenary of white settlement in Australia. Aboriginal scholars found a "soft analysis" (Huggins and Tarrago, 143) of the colonial past that allowed for a "catharsis" of white settler guilt (Langton, 31). Others speculated that the debutante author's manuscript "must have been

---

[1] An average of 6.8 books published per year during the 1990s, 15.2 books published per year from 2000 to 2004 (Haag, 8).

[2] In 1995, publisher Ray Coffey believed *My Place* had achieved the highest book sales in Australian publishing history (Little, 53).

heavily edited" to achieve such a polished and market-attuned outcome (Muecke, 135).

Critical interest in the relationship between an Aboriginal author and white editor then focused upon a court case involving editor Susan Hampton and Aboriginal author Ruby Langford Ginibi. Hampton apparently played such a comprehensive role in the two-year preparation of Langford Ginibi's *Don't Take Your Love to Town* (1998) that she believed she was entitled to joint copyright (Little Nyoongah, 35). Although Langford Ginibi warned the white editor not to "gubbarise my text. Don't Anglicise it,"[3] her text was labeled by influential critics as having been "comprehensively edited" (Shoemaker, 91) in a style that conformed "to the dictates of middle class literature" (Nyoongah, 377). As the editor's textual choices were not made public, these claims remain unsubstantiated.

Other more transparent cross-cultural collaborations in the era had also attuned critical attention to an apparent disparity of power and control between Aboriginal authors and their white editors. *Ingelba and the Five Black Matriarchs* (1990), by Aboriginal author Patsy Cohen and white scholar Margaret Somerville, foregrounded collaborative construction processes and Somerville's feminist praxis.[4] The representation of Aboriginal English, which was recorded verbatim in the text, prompted a spirited critical response. Black writer and activist Roberta Sykes found the disparity between the textual voices degrading, as "an excellent and superior form [is] reserved for the writer—to the detriment of the interviewees" (44).[5] Poet Lee Cataldi criticized Somerville's presumption to speak on behalf of Aboriginal women, asserting that "Patsy Cohen is not the speaking subject of this book. She does not control it" (52). Issues of power and control were pertinent, as many Aboriginal people then embarking upon authorship were in their senior years, choosing life writing as a culturally appropriate and accessible genre that could accommodate varying degrees of literacy. Aboriginal authors like Cohen, who was born in 1937 and reared in rural New South Wales, had often received segregated and inferior schooling that did not aim to educate Aboriginal

---

[3] *Gubba* is the term used to describe white people by Aboriginal people in southeastern Australia (Watson, interview with Ruby, 158).

[4] See also Patsy Cohen and Margaret Somerville, "Reflections of Ingelba," *Westerly* 36 (June 1991): 45–49.

[5] With a white mother and knowing little of her paternity, Roberta Sykes refers to herself as a "Black Australian." The publication of the first volume of her autobiographical trilogy *Snake Cradle* (1997), prompted debate in the Indigenous community over Sykes perceived adoption of an Indigenous identity. See Sonja Kurtzer, "Is She or Isn't She: Roberta Sykes and 'Authentic' Aboriginality." *Overland* 171 (Winter 2003): 50–56.

students beyond a third-grade standard.[6] Aboriginal matriarchs such as Alice Nannup, *When the Pelican Laughed* (1992), Evelyn Crawford, *Over My Tracks* (1993), and Rita Huggins, *Auntie Rita* (1996), preferred to dictate an oral narrative that could be transcribed by their Aboriginal or non-Aboriginal collaborators and then presented as a written text. The prevalence of such methodologies, combined with the politicization of these behind-the-scenes processes, influenced the development of protocols for collaborative publishing.[7]

It was also in the mid- to late 1990s that critical comparison of sections of an original manuscript with the published text first substantiated the impact of editorial intervention upon Aboriginal manuscripts. Two leading scholars in the field, Stephen Muecke and Adam Shoemaker, undertook a "literary repatriation" of Aboriginal activist, scientist, and preacher David Unaipon's *Legendary Tales of the Australian Aborigines* (2001). Unaipon wrote his text in the 1920s, but because of an unfortunate coalescence of circumstance, the stories were appropriated by and attributed to W. Ramsay Smith.[8] Muecke and Shoemaker identified the steps taken to dislodge Unaipon and restored the text to its original form. They also discussed the nature of custodianship in Aboriginal knowledge systems, which made "working in conjunction with others . . . not at all unusual for Unaipon" (Unaipon, *Legendary*, xx). Foundational Aboriginal writers often worked in cooperation with a non-Aboriginal person drawn from their circle of friends and acquaintances. Significant textual compromise was often the price Aboriginal authors paid for the assistance of these collaborators. In the remainder of this chapter, I will examine the cross-cultural collaborations between editors and foundational Aboriginal

---

[6] In the state of New South Wales, from 1938 to 1952, a special syllabus delivered vocational training fitting Aboriginal children for domestic service and farm labor rather than educating them. See Amanda Barry, "Broken Promises: Aboriginal Education in South Eastern Australia 1837–1937" (PhD Thesis, University of Melbourne, 2008). The last segregated Aboriginal school in New South Wales was not closed until 1960. See Jim J. Fletcher, *Clean, Clad and Courteous: A History of Aboriginal Education in New South Wales*. Carlton, VIC: J. Fletcher, 1989. Aboriginal affairs, including education, were administered differently in each state of Australia; some systems were more discriminatory than others.

[7] See, e.g., Margaret McDonnell and Gillian Whitlock, "Editing Ruthie: The Work in Theory and in Practise," *Journal of Australian Studies* 64 (2000): 135–41.

[8] Published as *Myths and Legends of the Australian Aboriginals* by W. Ramsay Smith, FRS, anthropologist and chief medical officer of South Australia in 1930, the author David Unaipon was not acknowledged in the text. See David Unaipon, *Legendary Tales of the Australian Aborigines*, ed. Stephen Muecke and Adam Shoemaker (Carlton South, VIC: Miegunyah Press, 2001), for a full discussion of the circumstances surrounding the appropriation of Unaipon's text.

writers in the social context of the protection, assimilation, and dawning self-determination eras. A close examination of the original oral manuscript of Ella Simon's *Through My Eyes* (1978) identifies her early attempts to indigenize the life-writing genre, and how Eurocentric editing hampered these innovations.[9]

Although Unaipon was robbed of the distinction of becoming the first Australian Aboriginal author in 1929, his production of a marketable manuscript was in itself a remarkable feat given the social environment, as racism made the concept of Aboriginal authorship anathema (Unaipon, *Legendary*, xxxiv). All mainland Australian states had protection policies that limited the civil rights of those people defined as Aboriginal (Taffe, 11). In most states, these policies relegated Aboriginal people to segregated stations and reserves,[10] "smooth[ing] the dying pillow" on the mistaken assumption that Aboriginal people were "dying out."[11] During this period, Theresa Clements published a seven-page pamphlet, *From Old Maloga: The Memoirs of an Aboriginal Woman*, telling her personal and family story, contesting the negative assessment of Aboriginal capacity, and claiming rights to land at Cummeragunja Aboriginal Station in southern New South Wales.[12]

It was not until 1951, after the exposure of racially motivated atrocities of the Second World War that overtly eugenicist policies were adapted, with State and Federal governments shifting to policies of cultural assimilation (Rowse, introduction, 178).[13] Soon after, in 1954, the Aborigines'

---

[9] I digitized and retranscribed the oral recordings in 2009, with the permission of her collaborator Anne Ruprecht and Ella Simon's cousin and the custodian of her work, Faith Saunders. The analysis is based upon my retranscription.

[10] In New South Wales, live-in managers supervised Aboriginal stations, while reserves were supervised by local police. See Tim Rowse, introduction to *Contesting Assimilation*, edited by Tim Rowse (Perth: API, 2005), 1–26.

[11] For example, in New South Wales the protection period spanned 1909–40. See James H. Bell, "Assimilation in New South Wales," in *Assimilation Now*, edited by Marie Reay (Sydney: Angus and Robertson, 1964), 59–71.

[12] Although this pamphlet is undated, the narrative suggests it was published after the 1939 Cummeragunja walk off; most probably during the Second World War, when Theresa Clements's daughter, Margaret Tucker, worked in a rope and then a munitions factory in Melbourne. Publisher John Edward Fraser of Fraser and Morphet, Prahran, died on December 28, 1945. It is unknown whether the business continued after his death. See Therese (Yarmuk) Clements, *From Old Maloga: The Memoirs of an Aboriginal Woman* (Prahran, VIC: Fraser and Morphet, 1939–45).

[13] Rather than maintaining growing numbers of Aboriginal people on segregated reserves, they were to be merged with the white population where they "must live and work and think as white Australians do so that they can take their place in social, economic and political equality with the rest of the Australian community" (Commonwealth).

Friend's Association published David Unaipon's six-page pamphlet, *My Life Story* (1954).[14] In 1962 a white journalist, Douglas Lockwood, published *I, the Aboriginal* based on transcribed interviews with Roper River man Waipuldanya. Although he presented it as a first-person narrative, Lockwood assumed authorship and Waipuldanya was unacknowledged (Rowse, introduction, n.p.). It was another seven years until the first mainstream book-length Aboriginal life story, *Lionel Rose, Australian* (1969), was published by world-champion Aboriginal boxer Lionel Rose. During this period (from 1958 to 1973), Aboriginal rights organizations such as the Federal Council for the Advancement of Aborigines and Torres Strait Islanders (FCAATSI) fought for social and legislative reform for Indigenous Australians and agitated to dismantle the policy of assimilation (Taffe, 114).[15] Aboriginal life stories published in the 1970s included several by activists with reputations established during this campaign. Oodgeroo Noonuccal, then known as Kath Walker, published *Stradbroke Dreamtime* in 1972. Charles Perkins published *A Bastard like Me* (1975), Margaret Tucker, *If Everyone Cared* (1977), Monica Clare, *Karobran* (1978), and Ella Simon, *Through My Eyes* (1978). All five authors acknowledged the role of non-Indigenous supporters and collaborators in fostering or facilitating their autobiographical project. The needs of the projected readership and the editor's own ambitions for the text, however, often competed with the aims of the author. Thus, despite their positions of esteem, most of these writers accommodated significant editorial emendation to their texts prior to publication.

Oodgeroo Noonuccal established a national reputation as a poet with her best-selling books *We Are Going* (1964), *The Dawn Is at Hand* (1966), and *My People: A Kath Walker Collection* (1970). Critics received her style as redolent of social protest rather than technically correct poetry, but Noonuccal was untroubled by the critique (Hodge, 65). Noonuccal was deeply involved in the national Aboriginal civil rights movement and relished any publicity if it assisted the aims of this cause. By the early 1970s, however, controversy and division within Aboriginal rights groups FCAATSI and the National Tribal Council had forced Noonuccal to rethink the link between her literary output and her politics (Jones, *Black*, 62–65). Noonuccal retreated from national public life, in which

---

[14] The pamphlet was reprinted from the Association's annual report. Unaipon worked as a subscription collector for the Aborigines' Friends' Association, travelling southeastern Australia lecturing and preaching for more than fifty years. See Philip Jones, "Unaipon, David (1872–1967)," in *Australian Dictionary of Biography* (Melbourne: Melbourne University Press, 1990), 303–5.

[15] Their landmark achievement was the 1967 alteration of the Australian constitution to remove negatively couched references to Aboriginal people and to allow the federal government to make special laws applying to Aboriginal people in concurrence with the states.

she had been active since 1958, and sought solace, support, and a quiet place to write at the home of her friend, Australian poet Judith Wright (Jones, "Why," 44–49). She drafted eight chapters of her first prose book, *Stradbroke Dreamtime*, which she envisaged as an innovative autobiography of childhood and a new expression of her epistemology and political praxis. Turning from poetry to prose and from adult to child audiences mirrored Noonuccal's shift from pan-Aboriginal politics to children's cultural education and environmental conservation. As she argued in 1979, "I'm sick and tired of talking to mentally constipated adults; they don't listen. It's the children who are going to change this world for the better, not the adults" (Lane, 33). The approach taken by Noonuccal's professional editor, however, substantially undermined Noonuccal's vision. In her manuscript, Noonuccal made the choice to break generic conventions by combining autobiography and fiction with traditional and contemporary legends. This approach challenged the individualistic and past-centered underpinnings of autobiography and asserted the relevance of Aboriginal tradition and spirituality for contemporary urbanized Aboriginal people. The editorial response was to reject the fictional stories and to reassert genre divisions between autobiography, traditional legends, and contemporary myth (Jones, *Black*, 31–34). Rather than representing a vital and contemporary Aboriginal culture, the text reasserted a primitivist interpretation that tethered Aboriginal culture to the romanticized past. Because she undertook this project at a low point in her physical and emotional health, Noonuccal did not counter the editorial changes. She was particularly upset when the publisher, Angus and Robertson, lost the name and address of the Aboriginal child chosen to illustrate the cover of the first edition, who went unacknowledged and unpaid (46). *Stradbroke Dreamtime* achieved healthy global sales, but Noonuccal remained unhappy with the presentation of book until the fourth edition was released in the year of her death (1993). Previous editions illustrated by non-Aboriginal artists had failed to reflect Noonuccal's worldview (46). Aboriginal artist Bronwyn Bancroft's bold and captivating Aboriginal designs finally communicated Noonuccal's vision.

Charles Perkins first came to fame as a soccer player and then to notoriety as the Aboriginal student leader of the Freedom Ride, which travelled around rural New South Wales in the summer of 1965 attempting to break the established color bar at local public facilities including swimming pools, picture theaters, town halls, and clubs (Curthoys). Perkins, who in 1965 also became the first Aboriginal Australian to graduate from an Australian university, had been "frequently encouraged" to write his life story by friend, mentor, and social reformer Reverend Ted Noffs of the Wayside Chapel in Sydney's red-light district of Kings Cross (Perkins, 5). Perkin's *A Bastard like Me* (1975) was transcribed from tapes recorded by Reverend Noffs. Although he enjoyed a high profile for his activism and leadership role in the federal Department of Aboriginal Affairs established by the Whitlam government, Perkins did not attract a mainstream publisher. The publication of his life story by Ure Smith, a small publishing house that previously specialized in the fine arts, reflected the difficulty Aboriginal writers faced in proving the financial viability of their projects. His book, described by critics as a "vigorous self-portrait," proved popular and sold eighteen thousand copies in the first twelve months (Corris, quoted in Read 332, 177). According to biographer Peter Read, Perkins's account of his life is characterized by an "awkward and jerky style" attributable to its transition from oral to written text (177). Scholars are yet to examine the oral manuscript, should it still exist, to substantiate the impact of this transition or how the distinct qualities of the Aboriginal oral tradition are reflected in the published text.

Like Charles Perkins, Margaret Tucker found willing collaborators and support from non-Indigenous friends who shared her worldview. Born in 1904, Margaret Tucker became a member of the Stolen Generations of Indigenous children when she was forcibly separated from her family in 1917.[16] She was trained for domestic service at Cootamundra Girls Home in the Riverina District of New South Wales, and upon release she served mistresses in suburban Sydney and on an isolated property near Walgett in northern New South Wales. Tucker received treatment that ranged from cruel to kindly, but it was never egalitarian, according to Jackie Huggins, "indicating a clearly oppressive relationship between Black and white, servant and boss/mistress" (*Sister*, 82). Although Tucker reunited with her family in 1925, she retained a suspicion of white people, particularly members of the upper classes who were most likely to engage an Aboriginal servant. Moving to Melbourne, Tucker became a founding member of the Australian Aborigines' League and participated in the Day of Mourning in Sydney in 1938, an event that is now recognized as a "turning point in capturing white public attention" for Aboriginal rights (Goodall, 230). Tucker's support of the Cummeragunja walk-off protesters in 1939 aligned her with Communist activists and gained her the title the Black Communist (Morgan and Bostock). Tucker's political affiliations later shifted from the Communist Party, and she joined Moral Re-Armament (MRA), a global religious organization, in 1956.[17] An

---

[16] Reflections on the experience of Indigenous child separation can be found in Doreen Mellor and Anna Haebich, eds., *Many Voices: Reflections on Experiences of Indigenous Child Separation* (Canberra, ACT: National Library of Australia, 2002).

[17] MRA was a multifaith organization, as adherents are directed by their conscience and the morality of their personal faith. MRA promoted the practice of absolute moral standards, active forgiveness, and reparation. Affiliates believed that world peace could be achieved through the influence of individual lives. MRA ideology suggested that profound personal change required harnessing a

upper-class white woman and MRA member who publicly apologized for the poor historical treatment of Australian Aboriginal people at a social gathering prompted Tucker's allegiance with MRA. Tucker attributed her release from bitterness to the influence of MRA teachings.

While Tucker's adoption of MRA teachings had a positive effect on her personal life, it later stymied the recollection of her political past. MRA presented itself as a world-transforming ideology: a "greater ideology" than Communism (Howard, 23). Tucker's Communist past thus became a contentious issue when she came to draft her life story. When Margaret Tucker decided to write her autobiography, she realized she would need support: a quiet place to write away from family and community obligations, emotional sustenance to recall painful life events, and help with initial editing. Tucker relied heavily upon her non-Indigenous MRA friends, who assisted at every turn. One of the outcomes of this facilitation, however, was the minimization of her formative political experiences as a Communist. Historically important material regarding Communist support of the fledgling Aboriginal rights movement that was available in Tucker's manuscript was removed or diluted prior to publication (Jones, *Black*, 137–42). Tucker's lasting alignment with MRA thus explains some of the editorial choices that shaped her life story.

The editorial treatment of Monica Clare's manuscript also reveals how Aboriginal voices that are clad in the trappings of a distinct ideological frame can influence the approach taken by the editor. This is particularly the case when the worldview prioritized by the manuscript has lost social credibility, holding a potentially negative impact on its capacity to attract a readership. Clare was also a member of the Stolen Generation, but she was never reunited with her family. In her adult years, she formed connections with the Aboriginal community at Wollongong on the south coast of New South Wales, becoming a committed socialist and activist for Aboriginal and women's rights. Clare's poor experience of formal education made her unsure of her authorial capacity, but she was determined to expose the ongoing practice of forced removal of Aboriginal children from their families. In the early 1970s, she approached two non-Indigenous friends from different social and political groups to read and help edit her manuscript (Jones, *Black*, 182–83). Clare's text was in the hands of these readers when she died suddenly in July 1973. White editors drawn from the Society of Women Writers and FCAATSI, Mona Brand and Jack Horner, eventually collaborated to finish manuscript preparation. This process took several years, during which time organized socialism in Australia had collapsed, the credibility of the ideology inextricably linked to its practice in the Soviet

---

"moral and spiritual force that is powerful enough to remake the world." MRA is now known as Initiatives of Change (Lean, 263).

Union.[18] Clare's manuscript, which made the unlikely combination of socialist realism with sentimental testimony exposing child removal, was edited to minimize both elements. Instead, the editors bolstered themes that could be linked to the Aboriginal rights movement, hoping to attract a readership that would be prepared to overlook the books remnant commitment to socialism. The Alternative Publishing Co-operative, established in 1976, finally published *Karobran* five years after the author's death.[19] This small-scale publishing house specialized in politically committed texts on a not-for-profit basis. *Karobran* fell into obscurity almost immediately. Critics began to engage with *Karobran* as an important but highly flawed text in the 1990s. Joy Hooton speculated about the "signs of editorial interference" (330–32), and Mudrooroo Narogin (Colin Johnson) observed that the text had obviously been "heavily compromised" (175). Both critics surmised the imposition of a socialist frame by the left-leaning editors, when they had actually attempted to minimize this preoccupation in the text. This misreading highlights the necessity of returning to the original manuscript to gauge how authorial intention was balanced with editorial license.

Aboriginal matriarch Ella Simon was a respected community leader at Taree on the midnorth coast of New South Wales. She was one of the first Aboriginal women at Purfleet Aboriginal Station to forge active links with the white community at nearby Taree, becoming a long-term member of several conservative Christian and women's community organizations, including the Country Women's Association and Quota Club.[20] Non-Indigenous women drawn from these organizations took practical steps to support Simon when she decided to record her life story, with one friend facilitating the recording, transcription, and editing of her narrative (Ruprecht). Simon recorded her life story between May and December 1973, sometimes in the company of a non-Indigenous friend (20 percent), most often while alone (60 percent), and also yarning with a relative (20 percent). Simon's awareness of the differing needs and interests of these audiences crucially influenced which topics she chose, the details she included, and the level of knowledge she presumed. She clearly envisaged a text that accommodated the distinct needs of these different audiences.

---

[18] See for example Stuart Macintyre, *The Reds: The Communist Party of Australia from Origins to Illegality* (Sydney: Allen & Unwin, 1998); Bernie Taft, *Crossing the Party Line* (Newham, VIC: Scribe, 1994).

[19] It had a print run of 250 hardbacks and 1000 paperbacks, and much of this inventory was remaindered when APCOL folded and on-sold its list.

[20] The Country Women's Association is a conservative rural women's group aligned with the Country Women of the World and equivalent to the Women's Institute movements in the United Kingdom and Canada. The closest US equivalents are the Home Bureaus founded in various states. Quota Club is an international women's service organization.

My analysis suggests that Simon's white editors did not share or understand this vision. The oral manuscript is far more wide ranging than the published text, which addresses the imagined white reader at the expense of an Aboriginal audience. Approximately 45 percent of the total number of topics addressed to the imagined reader was finally included in the published text. Thirty percent of topics narrated to a non-Indigenous friend were included, but only 15 percent of topics recorded in dialogue with an Aboriginal relative were included. The editors clearly shaped the text to meet the interests and needs of an anticipated non-Indigenous audience.

The decision to prioritize the interests of a non-Indigenous audience held consequences for the oral features of the text, especially the use of repetition. Repetition is a characteristic of storytelling in oral cultures, and Simon frequently repeated stories and motifs as she recorded her oral manuscript in the three different settings described above. Theorist Walter Ong suggests that narrative originality in oral cultures is prompted by the need to manage particular audiences: "every telling the story has to be introduced uniquely into a unique situation" (41). When Simon repeated the same story, each rendition differed in emphasis and detail in response to the particular audience and the teaching intent of the narration. The table below lists the fourteen topics repeated in Simon's oral manuscript; eight topics are repeated twice, five topics repeated three times, one topic repeated seven times, and one topic repeated on eight occasions.

| | Audience type | | |
|---|---|---|---|
| Topic repeated | Imagined reader | Family member | White friend |
| Legendary Winmurra Women | 1 | — | 1 |
| Regional language differences | 1 | — | 2 |
| Massacres | 1 | — | 2 |
| Grandmother's racial heritage | 2 | — | 1 |
| Miscegenation | 3 | 3 | 2 |
| Bush food | 5 | 1 | 1 |
| Bora grounds | 1 | 1 | — |
| Ella's marriage experience | 2 | — | — |
| Echidna legend | 1 | — | 1 |
| Scrub turkey legend | 1 | — | 1 |
| Spear fishing | 1 | 1 | — |
| Traditional tools | 2 | — | — |
| Grandfather building Purfleet | 2 | — | — |
| Coolumbra legend and the 1912 flood | 1 | 1 | 1 |

Repetition in the oral narrative reflects the importance of particular top-ics relative to Simon's narrative aims. For example, Simon's concentration upon miscegenation and the ongoing practice of traditional food gathering relates to her concern to substantiate the cultural belonging of people of mixed Aboriginal and non-Aboriginal descent.[21] In all of these cases, the multiple narrations are consolidated by the editors and represented only once in the published text, if they were included at all. The example pro-vided below demonstrates how the editorial prioritization of the needs of the imagined white reader stripped this foundational Aboriginal life story of a communal voice. The communal nature of Aboriginal life writing is now acknowledged as an important feature of the genre (Moreton-Robinson).

## The Relationship between Repetition, Content, and Audience: The "Spear-Fishing Narrative"

When Ella Simon recorded sections of her life story narrative in conversation with her cousin Maude, they adopted the conventions of Indigenous yarn-ing. Yarning is a communal activity where "each participant . . . assist[s] and confirm[s] the other's memories" (Barker, 9.7). The maintenance of family and community oral history relies upon the verification of personal accounts, as stories may have more than one custodian. Oral history is highly esteemed and valued as intrinsically trustworthy by Aboriginal people, particularly in comparison with official records that may have proven false or defamatory (Nugent). In this example, the oral versions establish the cultural importance and continued practice of spear fishing. They highlight the unfair and poten-tially corrupt practices of officials in positions of authority. The versions differ significantly, however, in their narrative style and teaching aims.

### "Spear-Fishing Narrative"; Addressed to Imagined Reader (Tape 2 Side A)

They lived there all their life on the seaside, all their lives, but I was a dry-lander and therefore I did not know half the names of the fish—they really laughed about that because they thought I was such an old dry-lander. The very first day he took me out to Forster to go to visit

---

[21] During the protection and assimilation eras, people of mixed descent who had lighter skin tones were not officially designated as Aboriginal. They were expected to relin-quish their Aboriginal culture to live and behave as white people. Official government policy supported the racist classification according to proportion of "Aboriginal blood": full blood, half caste, quarter caste. etc., with full bloods believed to be the only "real" Aboriginal people. For further discussion of Ella Simon's use of bush tucker narratives, see Jennifer Jones, "Perpetuating White Australia: Aboriginal Self-Representation, White Editing and Preferred Stereotypes," in *Creating White Australia*, ed. Jane Carey and Claire McLinsky (Sydney: Sydney University Press, 2009), 156–72.

his people; he took me out to an island by boat. He stood up in the boat; he had a spear which he speared the fish for our dinner. When we went to shore he give the others a lovely flathead, a good sized one. I really enjoyed this grilled fish. I was amazed how he could see the fish on the bottom, on the sand under the water. He educated me; he showed me how to find the fish and how to look for them when they lay on the bottom—what it looked like. Then after we were married, the spear was finished, spearing, because the Inspectors stopped the Aborigines from carrying their spears, which they would carry to spear fish. They reckoned that they were getting more fish or destroying fish, I don't know. It's just some of those things of civilisation; that we did not have any more use for our spears. The Aborigines did not have too many fishing lines and they relied on them. Out at Forster they often had spears. Those days there was not too much money to buy things like that, we had to save up for fishing trips. We would buy these lines to catch the fish, which he was always fond of and happy. The family was as fond of fish as he was; they cleaned up their fish bones as good as the father. But when I see the spear fishermen now I wonder. Here's the spear-fishermen today where ever you go on the shore. There is so many of them, and they can buy so many lines; they don't have to destroy the fish like they are. (Simon, "Through")

Born and raised in the coastal hinterland, Simon establishes the cultural differences between herself and her husband's people. This version attributes restrictions on spear fishing to the pressure of civilization and recounts how this disadvantaged Aboriginal people. Simon carefully establishes that Aboriginal people, who used natural resources responsibly, could not afford to legally fish because of the prohibitive cost of purchasing fishing tackle. She accuses the plethora of contemporary spear fishers of waste, given the ease with which they can purchase fishing lines, and especially compared to her family, who "cleaned up their fish bones as good as [their] father."

The second version of this story is a family discussion of spear fishing that takes place between Ella Simon and her cousin Maude. The discussion maintains oral knowledge of the practice of spear fishing within the family, the historical whereabouts and depletion of natural resources, and contests the discriminatory banning of spear fishing with traditional weapons. This ban also becomes a topic for humor, as a fair-skinned family member asserts his cultural rights by defying the ruling.

### "Spear-Fishing Narrative"; Discussion with Family Member (Tape 4 Side A)

> ELLA: Granny Simon, and she used to tell us about coming down and getting boats and fishing—catching the first flat head. And Old Dick Lester, they used to call him Blue Dick.
> MAUDE: Yeah, Blue Dick: Grandfather.

ELLA: Yeah, your grandfather, well, she used to talk about him a lot with her mother, you know. How they used to get in the boats, fishing around; all the fish that used to come out of the river, Wallamba River and there was tonnes of fish used to come out of the river then. But what is it like today? You can scarcely get a scale, a decent fish anyway.

MAUDE: And if they didn't catch, they'd spear them, you know.

ELLA: Yeah, do you remember that spearing episode; I remember Joe used to carry a spear.

MAUDE: Kel and Henry used to go spearing.

ELLA: You know they stopped them from carrying a spear.

MAUDE: They did say something about it.

ELLA: They stopped them carrying weapons. They used to go spearing and they stopped them, they wouldn't allow them. Somebody to do with the Council at Forster, he stopped them from carrying the spear. When you think of what they use when they go spearing fish today, and the poor old Abo had the old original spear with his prongs; and they reckon that he was taking all the fish out of the river—probably taking too many away from them! [The white officials].

MAUDE: One of my boys, young Rick, you know Rick. He has real Abo in him, although he is very fair, but he has that Abo in him. He used to go spearing, and I told him, I said, "You'll get into trouble, son. You're not supposed to spear the fish." And he said, "Look, all I've got to do is tell them I'm an Abo!" [*laughter*]

ELLA: [*laughing*] That wouldn't make any difference; they stop you just the same!

MAUDE: "Tell him I'm an Abo [because] that's the way they had to get their food." Ah, he was funny, he was. (Simon, "Through")

In this yarning narrative, Maude is amused by the absurd suggestion that telling an official "I'm an Abo" might prompt them to overlook a misdemeanor. While the family recognized Rick's cultural belonging, the "real Abo in him," the majority of white Australians still believed Aboriginality was reflected in skin color, not culture.

## "Spear-Fishing Narrative"; Version in Published Text

I'd been a "drylander" all my life and my husband had always lived by the sea. The first time I tasted lobster was when I went out with him to meet his father and family.[22] . . . My husband took me in a boat up the lake. I was amazed at how he could stand up in the

---

[22] At this point, the published text amalgamates a separate narrative about Ella Simon's dislike of lobster. I have excluded it for the sake of brevity.

little boat without rolling it over, see the fish and spear them with
only one throw. That was really something. He showed me how to
spot the fish but, soon after we were married, the authorities banned
the Aborigines from spear fishing. They reckoned they were taking
too many fish. Yet how about all the spearfishermen you see today!
Anyway, I never did get to try standing up in that little boat and
throwing a spear at fish. That was a great shame. (Simon, *Through*)

The published version of this spear-fishing story both abbreviates and
depoliticizes the narrative. The inclusion of the word "anyway," suggests
that Ella Simon is resigned to the unjust denial of cultural rights, while
the suggestion that she "never did get to try" spear fishing implies the
tradition has been relinquished. The editor preferred to produce a bland,
seamless first-person narrative that was acceptable to a non-Indigenous
audience rather than accommodating political critique or multiple voices.
The discussion format of the yarn, which concentrates on family history
and cultural maintenance, was incompatible with stereotypes regarding mixed racial heritage and the ongoing practice of culture. Similarly,
Simon's political commentary on the importance of hunting and gathering as a supplement to meager Aboriginal incomes suggested white
Australians were unfair to Aboriginal battlers. Simon attempts to incorporate Aboriginal people into a central tenet in Australian cultural self-
understanding, the ideology of a "fair-go" for battlers, and mounts an
appeal for an end to discrimination.[23]

The spear-fishing narratives demonstrate how Simon adapted or indigenized the life-writing genre by using the oral storytelling strategy of
repetition to deliver distinct messages to Aboriginal and non-Aboriginal
audiences. Unfortunately, her editors stripped the repetition and the con-
versational approaches from the narrative, aligning it with the Western
convention of a single autobiographical protagonist. Although the treatment of the spear-fishing narrative may appear to be minor, it holds rami-
fications for the integrity of the text when extended across all topics. The
treatment of the spear-fishing narrative is representative of the editorial
impact upon the text as a whole; it denies the indigenization of the narrative style, alters the tone, and reduces the range of content.

Many Aboriginal authors recount their experience of being edited,
seen as perfunctory negotiations by white professionals, as a series of
compromises (Heiss 66). Given her failing health, Simon accepted compromise as the price of publication. As her friend Anne Ruprecht recalls,
"She was just pleased to get the book finished . . . as long as the main
thread of the story was there, she was happy" (Jones, "Perpetuating,"
162). Authors, such as Ruby Langford Ginibi, who continued to write

---

[23] *Battlers* refers to hardworking and stoic Australians who struggle against
adverse social, economic, or environmental conditions.

and deal with the publishing industry soon became more proactive. Langford Ginibi's second book, *Real Deadly* (1992), was deliberately "written orally" to develop her distinctive narrative style and to avoid undue editorial interference (Heiss, 75). Langford Ginibi's depictions of urban Aboriginal life particularly appealed to Aboriginal audiences, as Nugi Garimara (Doris Pilkington) comments, because of the pertinence of her stories to "their lives, their history" (Watson, interview with Nugi, 33). Langford Ginibi's appeal is clearly founded upon the strength of her voice and community stories, yet the white editor of her next book, *My Bundjalung People* (1994), "couldn't see the relevance" of her historical research and made extensive cuts (Heiss, 75). By the time Langford Ginibi began working with her son Nobby and white academic Penny van Toorn on *Haunted by the Past* (1999), she had "learned how to deal with" publishing professionals and developed strategies to retain more control of her text (Watson, interview with Ruby, 158). Van Toorn functioned as a "surrogate stranger" or "sounding board" to anticipate the needs of a non-Indigenous audience while ensuring that the oral feel of the text remained paramount: "Ruby . . . wanted [the readership] to be able to hear her voice in their mind's ear so in no circumstances was I to sacrifice the sense of her voice speaking" (18). Langford Ginibi's *All My Mob* (2007), a compilation of new and republished stories, was edited by industry professional Janet Hutchinson. In 2007 Hutchinson's growing specialization in Aboriginal publishing included work by esteemed academic Martin Nakata and award-winning novelist Tara June Winch. *All My Mob* reiterates Langford Ginibi's "defiantly oral" style, now identified as the familiar "voice of an old friend and teacher," and continues to communicate her Aboriginal cultural perspective (Harley).

One of the recognized features of Aboriginal life writing published after 1988 is its communal focus. By including the views and voices of the family and community, Aboriginal authors maintain important oral traditions and communicate their distinct cultural perspective to Aboriginal and non-Aboriginal audiences. This has been a priority for Aboriginal writers since the first Aboriginal life story was published. Writing from marginalized positions in the protection, assimilation, and dawning self-determination eras often required that Aboriginal authors pragmatically accept changes to their text as a price of publication. Although critics have speculated that editorial interference reoriented foundational Aboriginal life writing to meet the projected needs of white, middle-class audiences, it was not until the mid-1990s that these claims have begun to be substantiated. Evidence of textual compromise, such as that presented in this chapter, supports arguments for cultural awareness in the Australian publishing industry. Meanwhile, the determination of Aboriginal writers, including Ruby Langford Ginibi, has attuned mainstream audiences to listen differently, cultivating respect for indigenized narrative forms.

# Works Cited

Barker, Lorina. "'Hangin' Out' and 'Yarnin': Reflecting on the Experience of Collecting Oral Histories." *History Australia* 5, no. 1 (2008): 9.1–9.9.

Barry, Amanda. "Broken Promises: Aboriginal Education in South Eastern Australia 1837–1937." PhD Thesis, University of Melbourne, 2008.

Bell, James H. "Assimilation in New South Wales." In *Assimilation Now*, edited by Marie Reay, 59–71. Sydney: Angus and Robertson, 1964.

Brewster, Anne. *Literary Formations: Post-Colonialism, Nationalism, Globalism*. Carlton South: Melbourne University Press, 1995.

Cataldi, Lee. "Ingelba and the Five Black Matriarchs." *Refactory Girl* 36 (1990): 52–53.

Clare, Monica. *Karobran: The Story of an Aboriginal Girl*. Sydney: Alternative Publishing Co-operative, 1978.

Clements, Theresa (Yarmuk). *From Old Maloga: The Memoirs of an Aboriginal Woman*. Prahran, VIC: Fraser and Morphet, 1939–45.

Cohen, Patsy, and Margaret Somerville. *Ingelba and the Five Black Matriarchs*. North Sydney: Allen and Unwin, 1990.

———. "Reflections on Ingelba." *Westerly* 36 (June 1991): 45–49.

Commonwealth Government, Department of Territories. "Assimilation of Our Aborigines." Canberra, ACT: Government Printer, 1958.

Crawford, Evelyn, with Chris Walsh. *Over My Tracks*. Ringwood, VIC: Penguin, 1993.

Curthoys, Ann. *Freedom Ride*. Sydney: Allen and Unwin, 2002.

Fletcher, Jim J. *Clean, Clad and Courteous: A History of Aboriginal Education in New South Wales*. Carlton, VIC: J. Fletcher, 1989.

Goodall, Heather. *Invasion to Embassy*. Sydney Allen and Unwin, 1996.

Haag, Oliver. "From the Margins to the Mainstream: Towards a History of Published Indigenous Australian Autobiographies and Biographies." In *Indigenous Biography and Autobiography*, edited by Peter Read, Frances Peters-Little, and Anna Haebich. Canberra, ACT: Australian National University E Press, 2007.

Harley, Alexis. "Memoir: Story Gathering—All My Mob by Ruby Langford Ginibi." *Media/culture.org.au*. http://reviews.media-culture.org.au/modules.php?name=News&file=article&sid=2108.

Heiss, Anita. *Dhuuluu-Yala = to Talk Straight: Publishing Indigenous Literature*. Canberra, ACT: Aboriginal Studies Press, 2003.

Hodge, Bob. "Poetry and Politics in Oodgeroo: Transcending the Difference." In *Oodgeroo: A Tribute*, edited by Adam Shoemaker. 57–76. St Lucia: University of Queensland Press, 1994.

Hooton, Joy. *Stories of Herself When Young: Autobiographies of Childhood by Australian Women*. Oxford: Oxford University Press, 1990.

Howard, Peter. *The World Rebuilt*. London: Blandford Press, 1951.

Huggins, Jackie. *Sister Girl: The Writings of Aboriginal Activist and Historian Jackie Huggins*. St Lucia: University of Queensland Press, 1998.

Huggins, Jackie, and Isabel Tarrago. "Questions of Collaboration." *Hecate* 16, nos. 1–2 (1990): 140–47.

Huggins, Rita, and Jackie Huggins. *Auntie Rita*. Canberra, ACT: Aboriginal Studies Press, 1996.

Hughes, Mary Ann. "An Issue of Authenticity: Editing Texts by Aboriginal Writers." *Southerly* 58 (Winter 1998): 48–58.

Jones, Jennifer. *Black Writers White Editors: Episodes of Collaboration and Compromise in Australian Publishing History*. Melbourne: Australian Scholarly, 2009.

———. "Perpetuating White Australia: Aboriginal Self-Representation, White Editing and Preferred Stereotypes." In *Creating White Australia*, edited by Jane Carey and Claire McLinsky, 156–72. Sydney: Sydney University Press, 2009.

———. "Why Weren't We Listening: Oodgeroo and Judith Wright." *Overland* 171 (Winter 2003): 44–49.

Jones, Philip. "Unaipon, David (1872–1967)." In *Australian Dictionary of Biography*, 303–5. Melbourne: Melbourne University Press, 1990.

Kurtzer, Sonja. "Is She or Isn't She: Roberta Sykes and 'Authentic' Aboriginality." *Overland* 171 (Winter 2003): 50–56.

Lane, Terry. *As the Twig Is Bent*. Melbourne: Dove Communications, 1979.

Langford Ginibi, Ruby. *Don't Take Your Love to Town*. Ringwood, VIC: Penguin, 1988.

———. *Haunted by the Past*. St. Leonards, NSW: Allen and Unwin, 1999.

———. *Real Deadly*. St. Leonards, NSW: Allen and Unwin, 1992.

Langton, Marcia. *Well, I Heard It on the Radio and I Saw It on the Television: An Essay for the Australian Film Commission on the Politics and Aesthetics of Filmmaking by and about Aboriginal People and Things North*. Sydney: Australian Film Commission, 1993.

Lean, Garth. *Frank Buchman: A Life*. London: Constable, 1985.

Little, Janine. "Placing Authority in Aboriginal Women's Prose." In *Voices of A Margin: Speaking for Yourself*, edited by Leonie Rowan and Jan McNamee, 45–58. St. Lucia: University of Queensland Press, 1995.

Little Nyoongah, Janine. "That's Doctor Ginibi to You: Hard Lessons in the History and Publication of Ruby Langford Ginibi." *Southerly* 58, no. 2 (1998): 31–47.

Macintyre, Stuart. *The Reds: The Communist Party of Australia from Origins to Illegality*. Sydney: Allen & Unwin, 1998.

McDonnell, Margaret, and Gillian Whitlock. "Editing Ruthie: The Work in Theory and in Practise." *Journal of Australian Studies* 64 (2000): 135–41.

Mellor, Doreen, and Anna Haebich, eds. *Many Voices: Reflections on Experiences of Indigenous Child Separation*. Canberra, ACT: National Library of Australia, 2002.

Moreton-Robinson, Aileen. *Talkin' Up to the White Woman: Aboriginal Women and Feminism*. St Lucia: University of Queensland Press, 2000.

Morgan, Alec, and Gerald Bostock. "Lousy Little Sixpence." Australia: Sixpence, 1983.

Morgan, Sally. *My Place*. Fremantle, WA: Fremantle Arts Centre Press, 1987.

Muecke, Stephen. *Textual Spaces: Aboriginality and Cultural Studies*. Kensington: University of New South Wales Press, 1992.

Nannup, Alice, Lauren Marsh, and Stephen Kinnane. *When the Pelican Laughed*. Fremantle, WA: Fremantle Arts Centre Press, 1992.

Narogin, Mudrooroo. *Writing from the Fringe: A Study of Modern Aboriginal Literature*. South Yarra, VIC: Hyland House, 1990.

Nugent, Maria. "Aboriginal Family History: Some Reflections." *Australian Cultural History* 23 (2003): 143–54.

Nyoongah, Mudrooroo. "'Couldn't Ya Cry If Ya Couldn't Laugh': The Literature of Aboriginality and Its Reviewers." *SPAN* 34/35 (1992–93): 376–83.

Ong, Walter J. *Orality and Literacy: The Technologizing of the Word*. London: Routledge, 1982.

Perkins, Charles. *A Bastard Like Me*. Sydney: Ure Smith, 1975.

Read, Peter. *Charles Perkins: A Biography*. Ringwood, VIC: Viking, 1990.

Rose, Lionel, with Rod Humphries. *Lionel Rose, Australian*. Sydney: Angus and Robertson, 1969.

Rowse, Tim. "Indigenous Autobiography in Australia and the United States." *Australian Humanities Review* 33 (August–October 2004). Accessed November 29, 2012. http://www.australianhumanitiesreview.org/archive/Issue-August-2004/rowse.html.

———. Introduction to *Contesting Assimilation*, edited by Tim Rowse, 1–26. Perth: API, 2005.

Ruprecht, Anne. Interview with Jennifer Jones. Sydney, 2004.

Shoemaker, Adam. *Mudrooroo*. Pymble, NSW: Angus and Robertson, 1993.

Simon, Ella. *Through My Eyes*. Adelaide: Rigby, 1978.

———. "Through My Eyes: Oral Narrative." Albury, NSW: Private collection of the author, n.d.

Sykes, Roberta. "Staying Put." *Australian Left Review* 119 (July 1990): 44.

Taffe, Sue. *Black and White Together*. FCAATSI: The Federal Council for the Advancement of Aborigines and Torres Strait Islanders 1958–1973. St. Lucia: University of Queensland Press, 2005.

Taft, Bernie. *Crossing the Party Line*. Newham, VIC: Scribe, 1994.

Tucker, Margaret. *If Everyone Cared*. Sydney: Ure Smith, 1977.

Unaipon, David. *Legendary Tales of the Australian Aborigines*. Edited by Stephen Muecke and Adam Shoemaker. Carlton South, VIC: Miegunyah Press, 2001.

———. *My Life Story*. Adelaide: Aborigines Friends Association, 1954.

Van Toorn, Penny. "A Book by Any Other Name: Towards a Social History of the Book in Aboriginal Australia." *Australian Literary Studies* 24, no. 2 (2009): 5–20.

Walker, Kath. *The Dawn Is at Hand*. Brisbane: Jacaranda, 1966.

———. *My People: A Kath Walker Collection*. Brisbane: Jacaranda, 1970.

———. *We Are Going: Poems*. Brisbane: Jacaranda Press, 1964.

Watson, Christine. Interview with Nugi Garimara/Doris Pilkington. *Hecate* 28, no. 1 (2002): 23–28.

———. Interview with Ruby Langford Ginibi and Penny van Toorn. *Hecate* 25, no. 2 (1999): 156–63.

# 3: Contemporary Life Writing: Inscribing Double Voice in Intergenerational Collaborative Life-Writing Projects

*Martina Horakova*

THE GENRE OF Australian Indigenous life writing has, particularly in the 1990s, proliferated into a large critical field that, mirroring the quantity, popularity, and diversity of published life stories, examines various aspects of these narratives.[1] One of these aspects is the nature of collaboration among participants, both Indigenous and non-Indigenous, in the process of eliciting, recording, writing, editing, and publishing such accounts. A number of scholarly studies have examined the complexities of this process and noted the long and notorious history of editorial intervention in the production of mostly orally transmitted life stories, an intervention that frequently led to some degree of misrepresenting Indigenous voices and cultural values (Jacklin, "Critical," 56). From ear-

---

[1] I use the term *life writing* to refer to a large group of personal narratives that may involve not only coherent and chronological but also fragmented and achronological strategies for telling one's own or another's life story. Life writing embraces auto/biographical accounts, collaborative oral history projects, and communal and collective life narratives that are told in various modes (including, e.g., memoir, confessional and trauma narratives, testimonies, tribal histories, histories of particular places, etc.). This term also serves to capture aptly the frequent confluence of writing life and writing history in Indigenous life writing, inscribing both individual and collective identity at the same time. As such, I understand the term to be more inclusive and less rigid than the established genre of auto/biography in the Euro-American literary tradition, a genre that has traditionally centered on the developmental, progressive aspect of one's subjectivity. Sidonie Smith and Julia Watson, among other proponents of auto/biography theory, assert that the genre of auto/biography, celebrating the "autonomous individual and the universalizing life story," emerged in the Enlightenment and has become canonical in the West (3). Arnold Krupat, a critic of North American indigenous life writing, perceives indigenous life writing, on the contrary, as presenting a different nature of the "self," a kind of alternative to the centrality of the individual subject in Western autobiography (*Ethnocriticism*, 201).

lier "as-told-to" autobiographies to variously negotiated and complex collaborative oral history projects integrating multiple voices, the issues of power relations, authority, authenticity, representation, accommodation, and resistance come to the surface in any attempt to examine the mechanics of producing Indigenous life writing.[2] One may wonder about the motives for paying such close attention to the ways in which Indigenous life stories are produced. Not surprisingly, this has to do with the genre itself: it has been widely acknowledged that Indigenous life writing has become an important vehicle for retrieving previously repressed histories of colonial violence, forced assimilation, and state intervention, and, therefore, it has been identified as a site of resistance (Brewster, *Reading*, 2–3; Nettlebeck, 43; Grossman, 174). As a result, the genre involves some important ethical issues, and the methods of its production significantly determine the ways the narratives are read, reviewed, and consumed.[3]

Australian Aboriginal authors, aware of the amount of the earlier oral accounts variously misrepresented by white authorities, anthropologists, and mainstream editors, have begun seizing control of their own writing (Van Toorn 3). One of the subgenres in Indigenous life writing has been characterized by collaboration among the members of an extended family, in which a younger member typically records, transcribes, writes, and edits orally transmitted life stories of his or her community elders, relatives, or even entire families and clans. These intergenerational collaborations often combine oral family history with written auto/biography. In her acclaimed, albeit critically controversial, autobiography, *My Place* (1987), Sally Morgan combines first-person accounts of her family members with her own story.[4] She develops this strategy further in *Wanamurraganya: The Story of Jack McPhee* (1989), which retells her grandfather's life. The 1990s saw a proliferation of intergenerational life writing, particularly by Aboriginal women: Ruby Langford Ginibi extends the story of her return to her homeland to

---

[2] The term *as-told-to* autobiography has been used predominantly in the context of North American indigenous life writing. Arnold Krupat provides an overview of the use of the term in *Dictionary of Native American Literature*, ed. Andrew Wiget (New York, Garland, 1994), 169–70.

[3] For an illuminating contribution to the notion of ethics in reading cross-cultural life writing, see Michael Jacklin, "Consultation and Critique: Implementing Cultural Protocols in the Reading of Collaborative Indigenous Life Writing," in *Indigenous Biography and Autobiography*, ed. Peter Read, Frances Peters-Little, and Anna Haebich (Canberra, ACT: Australian National University E Press, 2008), 135–45.

[4] For a detailed overview of critical responses by both Indigenous and non-Indigenous public intellectuals and the core of the debate provoked by Morgan's *My Place*, see Michele Grossman's "Out of the Salon and into the Streets: Contextualizing Australian Indigenous Women's Writing," *Women's Writing* 5, no. 2 (1998): 169–92.

include those of her family members in *My Bundjalung People* (1994) and relates her son's life in *Haunted by the Past* (1999). In *Follow the Rabbit-Proof Fence* (1996), Doris Pilkington Garimara interweaves voices of her mother and two aunts as she depicts their homecoming journey after having been forcibly removed to Moore River Native Settlement in Western Australia. Jackie Huggins records a biography of her mother Rita in *Auntie Rita* (1994), while Rosemary van den Berg records a biography of her father in *No Options, No Choice* (1994).

The popularity of intergenerational life writing extends into the twenty-first century: in *Shadow Lines* (2003), Stephen Kinnane revisits the life history and marriage of his Indigenous grandmother and non-Indigenous grandfather. In *Kayang and Me* (2005), Kim Scott, a Noongar writer, collaborates with his elder Hazel Brown to formulate his ancestors' collective biography, while registering his own subjectivity in the text.[5] In these projects, it might be argued that the Indigenous informants who have been previously "written out" of the collaborative life writing are now finding their way back. In addition, some of the recent narratives not only foreground the elders' stories but they also examine their influence on the younger members' own paths as the younger generation negotiate their identities, their sense of belonging to the country, and their relationships to both Indigenous and non-Indigenous people.

Two of these narratives, in particular, stand out formally and poetically from the others and indicate the variety of directions intergenerational collaborations have taken. Rita and Jackie Huggins' *Auntie Rita* and Kim Scott and Hazel Brown's *Kayang and Me* exemplify an innovative narratological approach to the production of collaborative projects in the sense that they expose the nature of collaboration in an explicitly dialogic, self-reflective, and introspective mode of writing that deliberately draws attention to its own textual construction and framing devices. They are both double-voiced narratives presenting two equally authoritative narrative voices (though on different grounds), formally marked off by different fonts, thus signaling a clear shift, both visual and textual, in subjectivity. While the other collaborative life-writing projects mentioned earlier may demonstrate similar strategies of integrating multiple voices, dialogicity, and relationality, this formal separation of the two voices throughout the selected accounts is unique. In *Auntie Rita* and *Kayang and Me*, neither

---

[5] The references to intergenerational life writing provided here are by no means exhaustive; they merely serve to illustrate a certain tendency. A complex bibliography of Indigenous auto/biographies is provided by Oliver Haag in "From the Margins to the Mainstream: Towards a History of Published Indigenous Australian Autobiographies and Biographies," in *Indigenous Biography and Autobiography*, ed. Peter Read, Frances Peters-Little, and Anna Haebich (Canberra, ACT: Australian National University E Press, 2008), 5–28.

speaker's expression is suppressed; this *double voice* communicates two—sometimes conflicting, sometimes complementary—perspectives. While the central narratives in both texts, authored by Rita Huggins and Hazel Brown respectively, can be read as more traditional in their imperative to reiterate the story of what it meant to be Aboriginal in Australia throughout the twentieth century, it is equally important to examine the voices of the two younger writers, namely Jackie Huggins and Kim Scott. They are both urban, university-educated, established writers who take an active role in promoting Aboriginal culture and repeatedly draw public attention to issues of social injustice and inequality within the Aboriginal population. In these terms, both Huggins and Scott might be viewed as representatives of the contemporary Aboriginal cultural and intellectual elite.

What is illuminating in these two collaborative projects is the way in which Jackie Huggins's and Scott's narrative sections disclose their own subjectivities, making their presence in the text much more visible than is common in similar accounts. This is a feature that is shared, for instance, in Stephen Kinnane's *Shadow Lines*. Kinnane, similar to Kim Scott, sets out on a journey to initiate and maintain a dialogue with his ancestors across time and space, combining imaginative journal entries, archival materials, and his own observations as a contemporary urban writer who is, among other things, confronted with the demands and rewards of his extended Indigenous family. Jackie Huggins, Kim Scott, and Stephen Kinnane all deliberately problematize their apparently transparent roles in the collaborative process: they are far from holding the position of a mere scribe; on the contrary, they take an active role in framing the texts. As writers and editors who have considerable control over the final version, they comment, explain, reflect on, and sometimes even intervene in the narratives of their respective relatives. As will be shown later, Jackie Huggins does this, for example, by supplementing historical and archival information to contextualize her mother's life story. In *Kayang and Me*, which may be seen as a poetic counterpart to *Auntie Rita* (published approximately ten years earlier), Kim Scott steps into Hazel Brown's narrative in introspective passages that constantly ask questions, express doubts, interpret, and reinterpret what he has heard from his Noongar relatives. He often returns to conversations between him and Hazel Brown that took place in between the recordings and uses them to articulate more general meditations. Sometimes this becomes a source of creative tension between the two voices, such as when Aunt Hazel tries to explain the complicated genealogy to her younger relative and Scott restages the conversation with Aunty Hazel about one of their ancestors:

> I asked Aunty Hazel about Harriette and Fanny: which one was Granny Winnery? "Well," she said. . . . "I don't know, not for sure. We can't. I only know what people said, . . . And what Daddy said,

that your father was our people. Cousin, he said. I believed him, and I still believe 'em now. They knew what they were talking about. They kept track of people." I didn't like it. Suddenly, ours seemed a tenuous connection, and there were no papers to help me out. "That's white man's stuff," Aunty Hazel said, as if my reliance on paper was a disrespectful challenge. Her emphasis was on the authority of the old people's word and their sense of importance of place. I respected that authority. . . . But I also like genealogical diagrams and sheets of paper. (Scott and Brown, 78–79)

This emphasis on the uneasy interaction between the authority of the spoken word and archival material evokes similar strategies in other intergenerational life-writing narratives—*Auntie Rita, Follow the Rabbit-Proof Fence*, and *Shadow Lines* among them.[6] The reader senses a split between being invited to retrace the process of sifting through archival materials, on the one hand, and being invited to follow a family member in her subjective recollection, on the other. As a result, the incompleteness, the impossibility of encompassing the entire history in the text—experienced by the younger researcher/writer (because of the missing perspectives in historical documents) as well as by the older family member (because memory is, of course, never complete)—occupies an important position in the text. Consequently, the narrative is powerful in its dialectical relationship between what is revealed, found out, and resolved and what is hidden, lost, and unresolved.

While I have mentioned previously that the formation of what I called a double voice in *Auntie Rita* and *Kayang and Me* is unique from the narratological point of view, it is also crucial to emphasize that dialogicity and multiple voices as such are implied, in various forms, in the majority of intergenerational life-writing projects. One of the earlier intergenerational narratives that have problematized the conventions of the as-told-to accounts is Sally Morgan's *My Place* (1987), a story of the quest for identity and ancestral belonging. I am going to bypass the complex debate about whether *My Place* does or does not

---

[6] Jackie Huggins occasionally integrates transcripts of some of these archival materials in *Auntie Rita* (49–50). Doris Pilkington Garimara effectively employs the strategy of juxtaposing period archival documents, such as police correspondence, newspaper clippings, and official records, with her mother's and aunts' oral accounts of what happened to them in *Follow the Rabbit-Proof Fence*. The notion of archive as an institutional apparatus developed by the colonial establishment into a vicious system of surveillance is noted by, e.g., Anne Brewster in "Aboriginal Life Writing and Globalisation: Doris Pilkington's *Follow the Rabbit-Proof Fence*," *Australian Humanities Review* 25 (March–May 2002), accessed January 10, 2011, http://www.australianhumanitiesreview.org/archive/Issue-March-2002/brewster.html.

embrace the individualism and isolation that, in the European post-Enlightenment tradition, permeates conventional autobiographical narratives.[7] Instead, I will reaffirm Morgan's strategy of stepping out of her own autobiographical story and into the lives of the family members. Here Morgan temporarily adopts the role of a biographer, even an anthropologist (since what she is after is recovering a family genealogy), who elicits, records, and transcribes the life stories of her great-uncle Arthur Corunna, her grandmother Daisy Corunna, and her mother, Gladys Milroy. This tactic is complemented by a shift in the narrative voice, as all three stories employ the first-person point of view. In a way, Morgan defers her narrative authority and yields the narrative space to her Aboriginal family to speak for themselves. This independence of the three testimonies of the principal narrator (supported by their formal separation through their own title and a clear closure) has been, even though tentatively, related to Mikhail Bakhtin's notion of heteroglossia (Jaireth, quoted in Docker, 7). Morgan's role as an autobiographer and biographer at the same time may preview some of the more complex strategies employed in later collaborative life-writing projects, most notably in *Auntie Rita* and *Kayang and Me*.

In order to locate more precisely some aspects of its double-voiced structure and its narrative complexity, I now turn to a closer examination of *Auntie Rita*. In this piece of life writing, two Aboriginal women, a mother and a daughter, relate the life story of Rita Huggins, who was born in the early 1920s, spent her early childhood in the region of the Bidjara-Pitjara people (an area now known as Carnavorn Gorge, in Queensland), and then was forcibly removed, along with her community, to the Cherbourg Aboriginal Reserve. Rita's life story continues with her work as a domestic, her brief marriage, motherhood, widowhood, single-parenthood, and her role as one of the leaders in the Aboriginal political movement in the 1960s. Rita Huggins told her life story to her daughter, Jackie Huggins, who taped, transcribed, and, as has been suggested, actively commented on it. In addition, the written story was published in collaboration with a non-Indigenous editor, Alison Ravenscroft.[8]

---

[7] In his 1998 article about *My Place*, John Docker, before presenting his own intriguing reinterpretation of *My Place* as an intertextual diasporic novel, provides a useful overview of the major influential (and mostly critical) readings of Morgan's text (among them Eric Michaels's, Stephen Muecke's, Bain Attwood's, Jackie Huggins's and Subhash Jaireth's engagements), which, simply put, position the narrative in terms of foregrounding a unified, homogenous, individualistic self at the expense of communal and collective storytelling that they associate with more "authentic" Aboriginality.

[8] However, the position of Ravenscroft in the genesis of the book is somehow ambivalently assessed. In *Auntie Rita*, Ravenscroft is unacknowledged on the cover as either a coauthor or an editor and is only marginally (though positively)

It is particularly illuminating to compare the subjectivities that Jackie and Rita Huggins inscribe in the narrative, as these reveal a productive tension stemming from close collaboration and an intimate relationship. In her article on *Auntie Rita*, Rocío G. Davis argues that it discloses "dialogic selves," which she defines as "dual voices with separate perspectives, within the context of Bakhtinian notions of double-voiced, continuing deconstruction of narrative structure and tradition executed on the level of narration" (279–80). Rita's narrative authority is complemented by Jackie's equally authoritative voice, which sometimes contributes to and sometimes challenges Rita's perspectives and opinions. This relationship, presented in a comparable way in *Kayang and Me*, can be described in terms of intersubjectivity, characterized by scholar Michael Jackson as "a site of conflicting wills and intentions," and it is placed at the center of the narrative structure (quoted in Davis, 278). I suggest that such treatment of the two subjectivities, including the decision to maintain the two voices literally present on the page throughout the narrative, has been, so far, quite exceptional in Australian Indigenous intergenerational life writing.

In the foreword to *Auntie Rita*, entitled symptomatically "Writing the Book," Rita Huggins almost immediately takes pains to emphasize her agency and narrative authority: "This book tells the story of my life. These are my own recollections. I speak only for myself and not how others would expect me to speak" (1). Most likely aware of the extent to which Indigenous peoples have been misrepresented in various kinds of Western cultural media, she claims her own voice as subject, not an object of another's gaze, as has so often been the case. So, even before her narrative begins, Rita Huggins, in a fairly simple and straightforward manner, asserts control over her memories and textual performance. That this may not be so transparent is shown subsequently: in the same foreword, with her voice formally marked off in italics, Jackie Huggins, the daughter-biographer, problematizes the process of writing the book:

> *After getting many of Rita's memories on tape, I began, through naivity,* [sic] *to translate my mother's voice, trying to do it justice while knowing that this book would have a predominantly white audience.*

---

mentioned in Jackie's foreword to the book (4), which would point to her role as a mere facilitator in the process of writing the book. Nevertheless, in Christine Watson's interview with Jackie Huggins, which details the three-way collaboration, Ravenscroft's quite important contribution to resolving the impasse regarding the book's structural directions is generally highlighted and praised by Jackie Huggins (Watson, 149–51). The idea of *Auntie Rita* as a three-way collaboration is also supported by Penny van Toorn (17). My own analysis, however, treats *Auntie Rita* as a two-way collaboration, taking into account the authority of Jackie Huggins's voice and her previous experience with non-Indigenous editing.

> *This was my first cardinal sin. . . . Although Rita speaks a standard*
> *English, her voice often got lost amid my own as I attempted to "pro-*
> *tect" her from non-Aboriginal critics.* (3; italics in the original)

This quote invites a closer examination of Jackie Huggins's complex position within the collaborative process. At first, having assumed the role of the "translator" of her mother's voice, Jackie implies that she will be speaking *for* her mother and controlling the narrative in a way remindful of non-Indigenous editors who have, by various means, modified and shaped Indigenous accounts for intended readerships. Indeed, she makes it clear that she counts on a "predominantly white audience," while Rita, in contrast, expects her readers to be primarily Aboriginal (1). This discrepancy between Rita's and Jackie's anticipations seems to prompt Jackie to "protect" her mother from non-Aboriginal critics while transcribing her mother's way of speaking. However, Jackie hurries to admit that ultimately she resisted this impulse to intervene by translating. Therefore, she finds herself in a difficult situation, faced with the dilemma of keeping her mother's voice intact and truthful yet, at the same time, being self-conscious enough to inscribe her own self within the final form. In the end, Jackie does exercise a certain power over the voice of her "subject," as she "organizes, prompts, supports, contradicts, corrects, explains, and generally constructs that narrative," but she certainly avoids modifying or appropriating her mother's voice (Davis, 281). In addition, scholar Michele Grossman suggests that such narrative organization is "counter-discursive" because it "resists the history of 'translation' and the concomitant narrative unification of Aboriginal experience, history, practice and belief by non-Aboriginal academics and 'experts'" (184). In other words, while Rita is the central subject of the narrative, Jackie Huggins, similarly to Scott, Kinnane, and Pilkington Garimara, becomes its dominant framing voice.

The complexity of the narrative framing in *Auntie Rita* is revealed further on by a peculiar contrast in Jackie's own voice. On the one hand, Jackie Huggins's remarks disclose the voice of a university-educated historian and a political activist for Aboriginal causes. This voice provides, in a rather detached way, explanatory notes and additional comments for Rita's recollections of her life, placing them in a wider sociohistorical context. For example, Rita's account of her community's removal to the reserve is supplemented by Jackie's detailed overview of the historical background of the system of native settlements and surveillance of Aboriginal people in Australia in the first half of the twentieth century (14, 33). In such passages, Jackie's tone is rather angry and confrontational: she adopts a clear political stand that condemns racism in Australia and actively participates in creating a counterknowledge of Aboriginal history. The tendency to combine auto/biographical accounts and family memoirs with historiography is a common technique in Indigenous life writing (Schaffer and Smith, 100–101). In *Follow the Rabbit-Proof Fence*, for instance, Doris Pilkington Garimara uses particular strategies to create a sense of a larger historical frame: before she unfolds her mother's and aunts' joint odyssey, she recreates the Western Australian landscape with a mythofictional account of pre-contact and early contact times that depicts the area as an idyllic, imagined, and decolonized space.

Jackie Huggins's voice in the passages where she directly addresses her mother becomes, on the other hand, much less formal, deprived of its academic, didactic tone. In contrast to Jackie's professional voice, it is personal, soothing, and supportive, occasionally stepping out of Standard English to embrace Aboriginal English phrases. It is precisely in these passages that the self-reflective and introspective nature is exposed. The intimacy between the two women transpires, for example, when Rita recollects painful memories, such as when, as a young single mother working as a domestic, she had to give up her first child, Marion (42), or when, after giving birth to her second daughter, Gloria June, her father rejected her as a "disgrace to the family" (47). In these moments, Jackie responds in a quiet, confessional, and almost forgiving tone, initiating a private dialogue with her mother. Significantly, she reveals here her own personal narrative, weaving the two life stories together by emphasizing the similarities in their lives as Aboriginal women and mothers:

> *I can just imagine what it must have been like in your time to be a single mother, not once but twice. . . . For me, being a single mother has meant independence, freedom, choice, acclaim, unreserved happiness, status and power over my own life, among other things. All of which you were never afforded. . . . All I want to say to you is that it's okay. All your children and grandchildren love you, understand you and forgive you because being a single, Black and penniless pregnant woman in your time was your greatest test and punishment.* (47–48; italics in the original)

A similar imaginative leap of empathy is sensed in *Shadow Lines* as well: Kinnane carefully revisits all the places and events that played a major role in his grandparents' lives, as he tries to get a clearer, more complete picture of what it must have been like to "have an uncertain lifeline" (51).

Agency and authority in *Auntie Rita* are presented as a contested ground on yet another level: at times Rita, as the subject and narrator of the story, clearly decides not to publicize certain details that still carry painful significance and shame for her. Obviously, the silences and gaps can be interpreted, psychoanalytically, as a way of dealing with repressed trauma. The reading of Indigenous life stories in the light of trauma studies often situates them as testimonies that bear witness to colonial brutality.[9] However, contextualizing Indigenous life writing within the history of collaboration between Indigenous informants and white editors demonstrates that self-censorship and the deliberate hiding of strategic information from outsiders (especially information concerning religious knowledge, the geographical locations of sacred sites or groups of people, or the identification of white fathers, for example) have been powerful means of resistance (Muecke, 128; Jacklin, "Collaboration," 35). Aboriginal people, having suffered from long-term exposure to pressure to speak from white authorities and anthropologists, have developed what Stephen Muecke calls a "discursive strategy [in] the form of *non-disclosure*" (128; italics in the original). In Indigenous life writing, such as *Auntie Rita*, the significant difference between collaboration with non-Indigenous editors and collaboration with the Indigenous community and family members is that Indigenous editors and biographers can generally recognize and retain the silences of their elders in a sensitive manner. This is not to suggest that none of the non-Indigenous editors choose to respect the self-censorship of their Indigenous informants, nor does this imply that all Indigenous writers recording the life stories of their relatives or elders do respect their silences.[10] Rather, the intergenerational collaborative projects reveal complex negotiations and shifting power relations between the participants.

The issue of preserving the subject's nondisclosures is intricate in *Auntie Rita*. Importantly, Jackie sometimes chooses *not* to respect her mother's silences in her desire to provide, in her eyes, the appropriate historical context for Rita's painful memories. For example, Rita's silences

---

[9] The notions of collective trauma, memory, remembering, forgetting, and healing have become crucial in analyses of minority literatures, combining literary theories with knowledge stemming out of disciplines such as clinical psychoanalysis. Kay Schaffer and Sidonie Smith, *Human Rights and Narrated Lives: The Ethics of Recognition* (New York: Palgrave Macmillan, 2004), explain the recent surge of interest in life writing of marginalized groups as a need to bear witness to the violent and painful histories that have shaped many modern nations. Major studies of trauma theory in relation to minority literatures, including indigenous life writing, are Cathy Caruth, *Trauma: Explorations in Memory* (Baltimore: John Hopkins University Press, 1995); Cathy Caruth, *Unclaimed Experience: Trauma, Narrative, and History* (Baltimore: Johns Hopkins University Press, 1996); and Shoshana Felman and Dori Laub, *Testimony: Crises of Witnessing in Literature, Psychoanalysis, and History* (New York: Routledge, 1992).

[10] One of the examples of such ambiguity in terms of respecting one's silences and self-censorship is provided in Sally Morgan's *My Place*, where Morgan, in the process of writing her family's life stories, describes her difficulties in persuading her grandmother Daisy to tell her life story to be recorded and written down. In the end Sally does get Daisy's story on tape; however, she has to come to terms with the fact that certain things from Daisy's life, such as the identities of Daisy's father and grandfather, will never be shared with her.

(that the readers learn about from Jackie's interventions) refer to the cruel regime of the native settlement: regular beatings and lockups as a form of punishment for "misbehavior" may have resulted in an internalized self-hatred and self-blame (34, 36). At other times, however, Jackie decides to comply with her mother's self-censorship, such as when it comes to exposing more information about the father(s) of Rita's two eldest daughters. In spite of the obviously close relationship between the two women, it is also possible to interpret Rita's silences as a resistance strategy aimed not only at readers but also at Jackie herself, simply showing that certain aspects of Rita's memorized life cannot be accessed, even if the biographer/editor is a close person. On the other hand, as resistant and selective as Rita may be about sharing some of these particular details with the reader, her authority is sometimes explicitly reduced by Jackie's intervention. Rita herself comments on this: "There are some parts of my life that I probably didn't want to have in the book because to me they are shame jobs. But they are part of the story and Jackie tells me, in her loving way, that I don't need to feel ashamed" (2). In the end, it is clearly indicated that Jackie's insistence on incorporating some details from Rita's life that Rita herself would have excluded is not driven by a desire to violate or appropriate Rita's voice but rather by a desire to confront non-Indigenous readers with the shameful history of the treatment of Aboriginal people in the missions. Thus, by offering her own perspective and by choosing to no longer be silent, Jackie is consciously alluding to and resisting the silence enforced upon generations of Aboriginal people by white Australia.

Another sphere in which *Auntie Rita* introduces innovative aspects is the representation of female indigeneity and the mother-daughter relationship. Similar to the complexity of the construction of textual frames, the site of womanhood and motherhood is also ambivalent and manifold. Motherhood acquires a new meaning here, as more traditional notions of Aboriginal motherhood are combined with modern, predominantly urban experiences. The result is a hybridized image of a traditionally strong mother figure at the center of the family clan, on the one hand, and an image of an urban, single mother who sees her role in the public sphere, especially in political activism, on the other. Thus, this image blurs the boundaries between the categories of mother/private and non-mother/public by combining the two in both Rita's and Jackie's lives. In a way, Rita complicates the conventional Western model of a mother and housewife: altogether, she mothers five children; however, the first two daughters, Mutoo and Gloria, are illegitimate, and Rita does not mention their father(s). She actually says very little about her pregnancies, both outside and inside her marriage to Jack Huggins. Rita says that, because she was young and working as a domestic under the Aborigines Protection Act, which gave her no choices in regard to arranging her own life, she left her first daughter to be raised by her parents, who took her in as their own daughter, in accordance with Aboriginal values of extended families and the care of children (42). After five years, having obtained exemption papers from the Director of Native Affairs that allowed her to leave her work and travel wherever she wanted, Rita was pregnant again with Gloria and running away because "in those days it was a scandal to be an unmarried mother, especially now that I was considered a respectable and 'free' Aboriginal woman" (44–45). The disgrace that society in those times attached to single motherhood and Rita's desire to become a "respectable woman" in white middle-class terms resonate with the prevailing dominant culture's values and assimilationist policies applied to "half-caste" Aboriginal women. After marrying Jack Huggins, Rita paradoxically becomes this "ideal" mother and housewife, only to be left a single mother again after her husband's sudden death. Juxtaposed to the image of a single mother trying to overcome poverty in an alienating city is the notion of a wider Aboriginal community and the extended family of which Rita is part: significantly, after the tragic death of her daughter Gloria, Rita takes in her four young grandchildren. Additionally, with her own children still living with her, she becomes a mother again in her early fifties. It is also mentioned several times in the narrative that Rita has taken in some of her female relatives and friends, although she herself does not have a proper place to stay. This image of Rita, embodied in the word *auntie* in the book's title, depicts her as a matriarch taking care of the people around her and strengthens the notion of the traditional Aboriginal kinship system that Rita, in spite of her mostly urban life experience, represents.

The depiction of the mother-daughter relationship complements the construction of the double voice running through the pages of *Auntie Rita*. As was already suggested, the life story of Rita Huggins, although being the primary concern of this collaborative life writing, is sometimes subtly, sometimes more explicitly, complemented by her daughter's personal account. Through Jackie's comments, memories, and allusions, readers learn about her life as well. In the second half of the book, when Rita's children, including Jackie, enter the narrative, it is actually the memories of her own childhood that Jackie uses to create a fuller picture of her mother's life. For example, she comments on her early experience of Rita's involvement in political activism and offers a different perspective on what it was like to be taken as a small child, by her mother to political meetings in the evenings or to be left behind, along with her siblings, because of Rita's lifestyle amid the urban whirl of meetings, dances, and parties, or to face extreme poverty and racism (69–71). In spite of this divergence, Jackie mostly recounts her memories of a happy childhood, surrounded by her sisters and brother, in a family with a strong mother figure, and exposed to the values of extended family ties, sharing, and belonging to a large urban Aboriginal community in Brisbane (70–77). The depiction of the mother-daughter relationship in *Auntie Rita* is enriched by the intimate and introspective passages that illuminate the strengths as well as the weaknesses, the dialogues as well as the silences, of these two women. In this way, Jackie, as a daughter-auto/biographer, reconstructs her mother's life and succeeds in providing a positive role model for future representations of female indigeneity. Finally, by presenting two subjective perspectives on the political and social meanings of Aboriginal femininity a generation apart and thus providing a commentary on the developments in the position of Indigenous women in Australia during the twentieth century, both Rita and Jackie are able to seize control over the marketed representations of Indigenous womanhood. Again, in spite of the relative popularity and a wide range of Indigenous women's life writing in Australia, the way in which the mother-daughter relationship is played out in this particular narrative is exceptional.

To conclude, in their focus on a double-voiced nature and an explicit dialogic form, both *Auntie Rita* and *Kayang and Me* represent dissident narratives that challenge assumptions made in the debates surrounding both Indigenous life writing and auto/biography studies. *Auntie Rita*, for example, has been hailed as a unique collaborative project that stands out among other Aboriginal women's life writings published in the 1990s (Grossman, 174; Nettlebeck, 51). Michele Grossman, for instance, positions *Auntie Rita* as one of the few collaborative projects that has the potential to disrupt the tendency to homogenize Aboriginal women's life writing as a genre primarily associated with the historicizing impulse, realist documentary style, political tone, collective identity, and oppositional strategy (176, 183). Indeed, it seems that *Auntie Rita* shows a self-consciousness about the genre that earlier life writing does not possess. Those life stories have generally relied more on the historical turn, creating an imperative for their subjects to speak out and write about the hidden histories of racial oppression and cultural genocide as realistically as possible. In contrast, *Auntie Rita* and *Kayang and Me*, while addressing these issues and still having a strong political agenda, propose a new dynamic of which self-reflective and self-conscious examination of the poetics of the genre form an inseparable part.[11]

---

[11] While *Kayang and Me*, because of its relatively recent publication, has so far attracted fewer scholarly engagements and reviews than *Auntie Rita*, those available to me focus on slightly different aspects than those that interest me in this article. For instance, Fiona Probyn-Rapsey, "Complicity, Critique and Methodology," *Ariel: A Review of International English Literature* 38, nos. 2–3 (2007), offers an enriching reading of Scott and Brown's narrative in terms of the structural ambivalence of historical resistance and complicity, emphasizing negotiation, contestation, and disunity as important elements of Scott's writing.

Another sphere in which double-voiced intergenerational Indigenous life writing may be considered dissident is auto/biography studies and, in particular, feminist and postcolonial interventions into the theory of auto/biography. Feminist critiques have repeatedly drawn attention to the notions of relationality and collective identity as constituent elements in women's auto/biographies and life writing.[12] Recently, some critics have extended this premise to postcolonial life writing written by both women and men.[13] As far as Indigenous life writing is concerned, some scholars have also supported the argument about its predominantly relational and collective subjectivities.[14] But, as Grossman has shown, *Auntie Rita* complicates some of these claims about Aboriginal women's life writing as privileging collective identities at the expense of autonomous individuality (184). In other words, while Rita's and Jackie's subjectivities are firmly anchored in their "mutual Aboriginality," they are also "fighting with [their] tongues" (Huggins and Huggins, 2), each speaking for herself. A similar tendency can be observed in *Kayang and Me*, where the two voices, although in a constant dialogue, are clearly visually separated.

The dissident character of intergenerational Indigenous life writing that inscribes the double voice can be detected in two more aspects. First, the double-voiced structure, presenting two different modes of writing, will inevitably attract a mixed audience. Some readers might prefer the storytelling of Rita Huggins and Hazel Brown; others will be drawn to the metanarrative passages by Jackie Huggins and Kim Scott. Second, the unique form of braiding older relatives' life stories with critical reflections on contemporary indigeneity is a valued contribution for promoting

---

[12] See, e.g., Sidonie Smith and Julia Watson, *Reading Autobiography: A Guide for Interpreting Life Narratives* (Minneapolis: University of Minnesota Press, 2001).

[13] See, e.g., Bart Moore-Gilbert, *Postcolonial Life-Writing: Culture, Politics and Self-Representation* (London: Routledge, 2009).

[14] It is illuminating to draw on comparative scholarship of North American indigenous life writing here. The idea of the collective subject is present, e.g., in Arnold Krupat, *The Voice in the Margin: Native American Literature and the Canon* (Berkeley: University of California Press, 1989), in which Krupat explores the development of the "dialogic models of the self" in Native American life writing produced either individually or collaboratively with a nonindigenous editor. He argues that in Native American autobiography the self is not, typically, "constituted by the achievement of a distinctive, special voice that separates it from others, but, rather, by the achievement of a particular placement in relation to the many voices without which it could not exist" (133). This argument is reiterated by Kathleen M. Sands, who makes the following comment about Native American women's collaborative life writing: "Dialogue emphasizes kinship and relationality in terms of placement within the community social structure. This, of course, is directly antithetical to the privileging of individuality, of uniqueness, at the core of Euro-American autobiography" (144).

specific interactions between Indigenous elders and younger writers. Texts such as *Auntie Rita*, *Kayang and Me*, and *Shadow Lines* are instructive precisely because they emphasize both benefits *and* difficulties of intergenerational collaborative projects. They do not aspire to produce a resolved, seamless life-writing account. Rather, they point to the instability of various dialogues and negotiations. In the light of John Fielder's observation that "colonial power relations are characterized by the tendency to not listen, to not enter into dialogue, to not reciprocate, and to not enter into respectful relationships with Aboriginal peoples as equals," it seems that these collaborative narratives, in their desire for explicit dialogic structures, clearly attempt to dissociate from and "write back" to previous colonial monologic representations of Aboriginal lives (10). After all, this process of writing back, as it is implied in the texts analyzed here, is a process that may occur not only between Indigenous storytellers and their mainstream, non-Indigenous readerships, but also among contemporary Aboriginal descendants themselves, whose crosscultural experience, it seems, has become an increasingly valuable medium for situating their identities.

# Works Cited

Brewster, Anne. "Aboriginal Life Writing and Globalisation: Doris Pilkington's *Follow the Rabbit-Proof Fence*." *Australian Humanities Review* 25 (March–May 2002). Accessed January 10, 2011. http://www.australianhumanitiesreview.org/archive/Issue-March-2002/brewster.html.

———. *Reading Aboriginal Women's Autobiography*. Sydney: Sydney University Press, 1996.

Caruth, Cathy. *Trauma: Explorations in Memory*. Baltimore: John Hopkins University Press, 1995.

———. *Unclaimed Experience: Trauma, Narrative, and History*. Baltimore: Johns Hopkins University Press, 1996.

Davis, Rocío G. "Dialogic Selves: Discursive Strategies in Transcultural Collaborative Autobiographies by Rita and Jackie Huggins and Mark and Gail Mathabane." *Biography: An Interdisciplinary Quarterly* 28, no. 22 (2005): 276–94.

Docker, John. "Recasting Sally Morgan's *My Place*: The Fictionality of Identity and the Phenomenology of the Converso." *Humanities Research* 1 (1998): 3–22.

Felman, Shoshana, and Dori Laub. *Testimony: Crises of Witnessing in Literature, Psychoanalysis, and History*. New York: Routledge, 1992.

Fielder, John. "Country and Connections: An Overview of the Writing of Kim Scott." *Altitude* 6 (2005): 1–12.

Grossman, Michele. "Out of the Salon and into the Streets: Contextualizing Australian Indigenous Women's Writing." *Women's Writing* 5, no. 2 (1998): 169–92.

Haag, Oliver. "From the Margins to the Mainstream: Towards a History of Published Indigenous Australian Autobiographies and Biographies." In *Indigenous Biography and Autobiography*, edited by Peter Read, Frances Peters-Little, and Anna Haebich, 5–28. Canberra, ACT: Australian National University E Press, 2008.

Huggins, Rita, and Jackie Huggins. *Auntie Rita.* 1994. Reprint, Canberra, ACT: Aboriginal Studies Press, 2005.

Jacklin, Michael. "Collaboration and Resistance in Indigenous Life Writing." *Australian-Canadian Studies* 20, no. 1 (2002): 27–45.

———. "Consultation and Critique: Implementing Cultural Protocols in the Reading of Collaborative Indigenous Life Writing." In *Indigenous Biography and Autobiography*, edited by Peter Read, Frances Peters-Little, and Anna Haebich, 135–45. Canberra, ACT: Australian National University E Press, 2008.

———. "Critical Injuries: Collaborative Indigenous Life Writing and the Ethics of Criticism." *Life Writing* 1, no. 2 (2004): 55–83.

Kinnane, Stephen. *Shadow Lines.* Fremantle, WA: Fremantle Arts Centre Press, 2003.

Krupat, Arnold. "Collaborative Indian Autobiographies." In *Dictionary of Native American Literature*, edited by Andrew Wiget, 169–70. New York: Garland, 1994.

———. *Ethnocriticism: Ethnography, History, Literature.* Berkeley: University of California Press, 1992.

———. *The Voice in the Margin: Native American Literature and the Canon.* Berkeley: University of California Press, 1989.

Moore-Gilbert, Bart. *Postcolonial Life-Writing: Culture, Politics and Self-Representation.* London: Routledge, 2009.

Morgan, Sally. *My Place.* Fremantle, WA: Fremantle Arts Centre Press, 1987.

Muecke, Stephen. *Textual Spaces: Aboriginality and Cultural Studies.* Sydney: New South Wales University Press, 1992.

Nettlebeck, Amanda. "Presenting Aboriginal Women's Life Narratives." *New Literature Review* 34 (1997): 43–56.

Pilkington Garimara, Doris. *Follow the Rabbit-Proof Fence.* St. Lucia: University of Queensland Press, 1996.

Probyn-Rapsey, Fiona. "Complicity, Critique and Methodology." *Ariel: A Review of International English Literature* 38, nos. 2–3 (2007).

Sands, Kathleen Mullen. "Cooperation and Resistance: Native American Collaborative Personal Narrative." In *Native American Representations: First Encounters, Distorted Images, and Literary Appropriations*, ed. Gretchen M. Bataille, 134–49. Lincoln: University of Nebraska Press, 2001.

Schaffer, Kay, and Sidonie Smith. *Human Rights and Narrated Lives: The Ethics of Recognition.* New York: Palgrave Macmillan, 2004.

Scott, Kim, and Hazel Brown. *Kayang and Me.* Fremantle, WA: Fremantle Arts Centre Press, 2005.

Smith, Sidonie, and Julia Watson. *Reading Autobiography: A Guide for Interpreting Life Narratives*. Minneapolis: University of Minnesota Press, 2001.

Van Toorn, Penny. "Indigenous Australian Life Writing: Tactics and Transformations." In *Telling Stories: Indigenous History and Memory in Australia and New Zealand*, ed. Bain Attwood and Fiona Magowan, 1–20. Crows Nest, NSW: Allen & Unwin, 2001.

Watson, Christine. "To Sit Down and Write That Book" (Interview with Jackie Huggins). *Hecate* 26, no. 2 (2000): 146–54.

# 4: European Translations of Australian Aboriginal Texts

*Danica Čerče and Oliver Haag*

SINCE THE LATE 1970s, books authored or coauthored by Australian Aboriginals have been translated into well over seventeen different languages, with continental Europe being the most prolific and largest market for this literature in translation (Haag, "Indigenous Australian," 2). Translations of Aboriginal literature into European languages are a comparatively recent phenomenon—the first translated book authored by an Aboriginal to be sold in Europe was the Polish edition of Kath Walker's *Stradbroke Dreamtime* in 1977. As statistical evaluations of bibliographies have shown, translation of Aboriginal literature has increased since the 1988 Australian bicentennial, with roughly ninety translations published so far.

Though the number of translated works written by Australian Aboriginals reflects the increasing interest in their culture, the way these books are translated and marketed often distorts the author's original intentions and distorts how Australian Aboriginals are perceived by many European communities. For example, many books authored by Europeans about Aboriginal cultures are often still deceivingly advertised as "Aboriginal" literature.[1] There is also the tendency in Europe to perceive the translations in terms of their cultural value, rather than their literary significance (Haag, "Indigenous Literature," 52). Finally, the European reception of Aboriginal literature often reflects the European audiences' idealized, exotic views of Aboriginal Australians, which is connected with the marketing of this literature in Europe, consequently reinforcing outdated stereotypes.

---

[1] See Haag, "Indigenous Australian Literature in German: Some Considerations on Reception, Publication and Translation." Special Issue, *Journal of the Association for the Study of Australian Literature.* (2009): 1–17; and Di Blasio, "A Path of Words: The Reception of Autobiographical Australian Aboriginal Writing in Italy," in *Indigenous Biography and Autobiography,* ed. Peter Read, Frances Peters-Little, and Anna Haebich (Canberra, ACT: Australian National University E Press, 2009), 29–39.

Currently, the most popular languages that Australian Aboriginal literature is translated into are Slovene, Italian, Dutch, and German. This essay will focus on Sally Morgan's *My Place* and Doris Pilkington Garimara's *Follow the Rabbit-Proof Fence* (in subsequent editions entitled *Rabbit-Proof Fence*) in these four languages, to reveal how these translations have in many ways misrepresented the original text for the purposes of adapting each translated text to the target audience's culture. Our definition of *adaptation* parallels scholars Aldo Di Luzio, Susanne Guenthner, and Franca Orletti's: "the translation of culture which aims at making the experience of other peoples understandable" to target readers (Mazi-Leskovar, 59). Particularly in cases when readers are exposed to a remote culture, closeness to the source text does not guarantee that a translation will be well received by the target audience. Most critics agree that translators have to aim for a balance between comprehensibility and foreignness (Anderman and Rogers). When evaluating translation, it is thus of particular importance to establish whether it is a faithful reproduction of the source text and at the same time communicatively acceptable for the contemporary target readers. According to Lawrence Venuti, one of the most prominent figures in modern translation theory, the communication of the foreign experience through "domestic" means cannot but be "partial and second-order," but many translators succeed in transposing the narrative into another cultural environment without sacrificing the original text (*Translation*, 468–69). Venuti's claim undoubtedly applies to the Slovene translation of Sally Morgan's *My Place*, which is why we begin this discussion with the smallest of the four markets.

An immediately noticeable difference between the Slovene translation of Morgan's autobiography and the original publication by Fremantle Arts Centre Press in 1987 is its tripartite division. Like Morgan's *My Place for Young Readers* (1990), an abridged version of the original text, and unlike the source text, the Slovene translation published in 2007 by Založba Miš consists of three separate books, subtitled *Sallyina zgodba* (Sally's story), *Zgodba Arturja Corunne* (Arthur Corunna's story), and *Mati in hči* (Mother and daughter). The translation of the title itself, from *My Place* into *V objem korenin*, also deserves some attention. Whereas in several other European publications the title is a word-for-word translation, Tamara Bosnič took the liberty of translating it with a poetic noun phrase meaning "in the embrace of the roots." Judging by the title, it would be reasonable to assume that the entire text is translated with sophistication and poetic finesse. However, this is hardly the case, with Bosnič regularly manipulating the stylistic patterns and register of the source text. Rather than finding a style that would achieve the same effect as the original, Bosnič did not hesitate to occasionally simplify sentences by omitting various words (very often adjectives) or by reformulating long sentences into shorter and easier ones for her target audience of young readers. The following paragraph, for example, is simplified to the extent that it reads as a kind of resume:

> Razvajanje pa je šlo predvsem v smeri neomejenega števila lizik in sadja; za novo obleko, igrače ali knjige ga je še vedno primanjkovalo. Leto prej nas je peljala na Kraljevsko predstavo, z več zasluženega denarja pa je to leto načrtovala ogled *na nivoju*. (107)

which might be back-translated into English like this:

> This indulgence took the form of unlimited lollies and fruit mainly; for new clothes, toys or books it [money] was still insufficient. A year before, she took us to the Royal Show; with bigger earnings, this year she was planning to see the performance *in style*.

In the original, however, the paragraph reads:

> This indulgence took the form of unlimited lollies and fruit, rather than new clothes, toys or books. She'd managed to take us all to the Royal Show the year before, and this year, she told us that, because of her new job, we would really do it *in style*. (68)

Given the three books' manufacture, special for their eye-catching covers and appealing typeface that allowed for no more than twenty-nine lines per page, the publisher too seems to have been aiming at a young audience. Intriguingly, some Slovene bookstores display the book in the youth and children's section.

Bosnič operated with an awareness of what was acceptable or alien to the target culture, but her presuppositions regarding Slovene readers' knowledge of the source text's culture were not always correct. Only rarely did she find a literal translation insufficient for a certain culturally remote phenomenon, situation, or word and supplemented it with an additional explanation or description. For example, she thoroughly explained the word *Vegemite* as a "traditional dark brown Australian food paste made from yeast extract and vegetable, which is usually consumed as a spread for toast . . . or as a substitute for salt," but this is the only footnote in the first book. Occasionally, the translator used synonyms relevant to Slovene culture to explain a native Australian word (*vojni ujetniki* for *POW transport*, *loterija* for *raffles*), which contributes to the assimilation of the text into Slovene culture, whereas at other times she retained some words and expressions that have almost no communicative function for a Slovene readership, such as *Guy Fawkes Night, Anzac Day, Frere Jacques, softball, Fantail toffee*, and some others, thus, reinforcing the foreignizing effect. Nor was it appropriate to simply omit those culturally marked words that seem to have been too problematic (e.g., *Avon ladies*).

Not only is the cultural repository contained in the original book somewhat problematic in a text addressing a Slovene readership; the source language, with its occasional departures from Standard English, also presents difficulties. Noted sociolinguist David Limon is right to claim that the communicative acceptability of any translated text depends on both how the translator deals with the cultural and conceptual foreignness of the source text and how he or she deals with the differences between the two languages (641). Of prime importance for the translator here is to differentiate incidental differences between the two linguistic systems (e.g., word order) from the writer's conscious departures from conventional stylistic and lexico-grammatical norms implemented by colloquialisms, unusual order of sentence elements, double negatives, sound reductions, and so on (641). Given the differences between the linguistic systems of Slovene and English, establishing a similar mixture of formal and informal language to that in the original text is surely not an easy task. But this should not be an excuse for almost neglecting this kind of stylistic marker, as is the case with Bosnič's translation. With a few exceptions, all of them lexical, Bosnič failed to reconstruct the colloquial speech of the original. In the chapter "Drinking Men," for example, she tried to preserve the flavor of slang by occasionally using words other than those from the formal vocabulary, like *mularija* and *ženšče*, pejorative terms meaning *kids* and *woman* respectively, informal expressions *fentati* and *žreti* for the verbs *to kill* and *eat* in the original text, a pejorative adjective *zarukani* for *stupid*, and so on. Several other examples show that the translator paid scant regard to Aboriginal English diction by using grammatically correct Slovene literary language:

> "Če ti bodo še kaj težili zaradi starega denarja, jim reci, da nič ne veš o tem." . . . "Babica," sem se nasmehnila, "nikogar iz vlade ne bo, ki bi kaj takega počel." (153)
> "Ničesar ne veš punca." . . . "Me spet poskušaš prelisičiti, ne? Aah, ne morem ti zaupati. Nisem neumna, veš. Ničesar ne bom rekla. Ničesar, slišiš!" (169)

Translated back into English these passages might read like this:

> "If they pester you about the old money, tell them that you don't know anything about it." . . . "Grandmother," I laughed, "there won't be anybody from the government to do something like this."
> "You don't know anything girl." . . . "Are you trying to deceive me again? Aah, I can't trust you. I'm not stupid, you know. I won't say anything. Anything, do you hear?"

The original text, however, reads as follows:

"If they pester you about the old money, you just say you don't know nothin.'" . . . "Nan," I half laughed, "no one from the government is gunna come round and do that." (96)

"You don't know nothin, girl." . . . "You're tryin' to trick me again. Aaah, you can't be trusted. I'm not stupid, you know. I'm not saying nothing. Nothing, do you hear." (105)

This passage shows that, although Bosnič closely followed the author's words and thoughts and even retained the exact punctuation, she failed to reconstruct the departure from grammatical norms with a similar effect as the double negative in the source text, and she also used formal vocabulary. For example, instead of translating the verb *to trick* with the expressive Slovene idiom *potegniti za nos*, Bosnič used a very formal equivalent, *prelisičiti*.

The translations of the Aboriginal English words, such as *blackfella*, *boong*, and *tucker* are also quite interesting. Bosnič translated both *blackfella* and *boong* as *črnuh*, which is a very offensive Slovene word for a person belonging to a dark-skinned race, whereas *tucker* is rendered into a neutral Slovene word, *hrana*, meaning "food." When handling swearing, the translator preserved the slang flavor and the expressiveness of idioms. Rather than using their English counterparts, she chose phrases and words that are more typical of Slovene, which adds to the domestication of the translation.

Andreja Blažič-Klemenc, in her Slovene translation of Doris Pilkington Garimara's *Rabbit-Proof Fence*, entitled *Zajčja ograja*, also translated the word *blackfella* as *črnuh*. Her choice, implying cultural insensitivity, is a good example that domestication is, in Lawrence Venuti's definition, "an ethnocentric reduction of the foreign text to the target cultural world" and thus not always beneficial for democratic geopolitical relations (*Translator's*, 20). It also justifies Venuti's claim that "insofar as foreignizing translation is a form of resistance to ethnocentrism and racism, cultural narcissism and imperialism," it is highly desirable today (20).

There are only a few discrepancies in the meaning of certain words between the translation and the original text, but this is not detrimental to the story itself. Putting aside the translator's inability to deal with colloquialisms and some other minor flaws, she deciphered, understood, and reconstructed the original text's model of the world and offered a complete equivalent of the intertextual narrative perspective. However, these were not at the expense of the communicative function of the translation. One the one hand, Blažič-Klemenc presupposes information known to the Slovene readership; while on the other hand, she brings Aboriginal culture closer. Yet, her translation reveals some inconsistencies. These are particularly evident in geographical names containing words like *sound, river, lake, desert*, and *route*. In most cases, she provided a literal translation of these words, whereas in some others she retained them in English. In replacing the unknown and strange with elements familiar to the target readership, the translator also made some mistakes. For example, when Blažič-Klemenc translated the expression *native settlement* in "The Moore River Native Settlement," she omitted the adjective *native* and merely rendered it as *naselje* (a group of houses and buildings where people live). To provide a clearer translation she should have used *naselbina*, which means "settlement of indigenous people" or ethnic minority. As evident from this definition, this noun is self-sufficient without the accompanying adjective. Clearly, the Slovene translator failed to establish an important aspect of Australian reality, whereas—as discussed later—the Italian version retains "Moore River Native Settlement" in English.

As for Aboriginal words, they are kept in their original form and explained in the glossary at the end of the book. The Slovene version of the glossary is longer than that in the original (the words added are *coolamon*, *gidgee*, *mallee*, *marri*, *mulga*, *neked*, *wandoo*, and the Latin expression *Chamaelaucium uncinatum*). In addition, the translated text contains some words (*mulga*, *woomera*, *woodarchy*, *dawuja*, etc.) that are domesticated only insofar as to follow the rules of Slovene declination.

Like Tamara Bosnič, who was not mindful enough of the colloquial language in *My Place*, Andreja Blažič-Klemenc failed to reconstruct Pilkington Garimara's colloquial diction. Rather, she produced grammatically correct sentences and mainly used words from the formal vocabulary. For example, "We gotta get away from this bad place" (86) is rendered in her translation as "Proč moramo s tega zloveščega kraja" (138), which when translated back into English reads, "We have to go away from this sinister place." This latter sentence is not only grammatically correct, but is also very formal: the adjective *bad* is translated with the word *zlovešč* (sinister, ominous), which is rarely used in the Slovene language. Clearly, the oral characteristics of Aboriginal literature have in this instance not been translated into Slovene. Several other examples give evidence that the translator gave preference to formal words (*grobijan* for *cheeky fullah*, *prebežnice* for *young gel runaway*) and gave undue respect to the conventional order of sentence elements, declination, gender, verb forms, and other stylistic markers of standard Slovene.

The failure to satisfactorily reconstruct colloquialisms in Aboriginal texts is a characteristic that other Slovene translations share. Similarly, the unauthorized "editorial intrusions" to Aboriginal texts (e.g., shorter, simplified sentences), discussed by leading Aboriginal literature scholars including Adam Shoemaker, are not exclusive to Bosnič's translation of *My Place* but can also be found in other Slovene translations of Aboriginal literature, particularly in the 2003 collections of poetry, *Vesolje okrog kuščarja* (translated and collected by Bert Pribac and David Brooks), and *Konec sanjske dobe* (translated by Bert Pribac).

In contrast to Slovene translated texts, Italian translations of the two texts provide a real encounter between target readers and the authors. One likely reason for this difference could be that the Italian translations of Australian Aboriginal work have a longer tradition than they do in Slovenia (the first Italian version of a book by Aboriginal author was published in 1995—Colleen Shirley Perry and Roberta Sykes's *Mum Shirl*; Slovenes got the first translation as late as 2003). Marina Rullo's 2004 Italian translation of *Rabbit-Proof Fence*, entitled *Barriera per conigli* (a literal translation of the English title), is an example of the work of a translator who not only transposed the narrative into another cultural environment without sacrificing the original text but also enriched the original with several commentaries in the footnotes. In addition to some bibliographical information, Italian readers get information about terms such as *Dreamtime, corroborree, tea-tree, Christmas tree,* and *rainbow snake*. Unlike the Slovene version, the Italian version not only retains Aboriginal words, which are then explained in the glossary, but also geographical names containing the words *sound, river, lake, desert, beach, route,* and similar (il Moore River Native Settlement, la Eighty Mile Beach, il Savory Creek, etc.). The latter are assimilated only insofar as they are preceded by an Italian article. There are, however, some inexplicable deviations from this tendency, such as translating *The Great Australian Bight* (*il Grande Golfo australiano*), *Ethel Creek Station* (*l'allevamento di Ethel Creek*), and *the Swan River Colony* (*la colonia di Swan River*). Like the Slovene translator of this book, Rullo translated the titles of two books mentioned in the source text, *Diary of Ten Years* (*Diario di dieci anni*) and *The Fatal Shore* (*La riva fatale*), while retaining the titles of the *Illustrated Melbourne Post* and *Challenger*.

As for the reproduction of the source text's combination of formal and informal language, Rullo managed to establish a similar mixture by choosing colloquial expressions where possible and establishing conscious departures from standard Italian through contractions: for example, *un po'* instead of *un poco* (a little), irregular word order, and the omission of words. Some examples from the original text read as follows:

> "They got a Mardu policeman, a proper cheeky fullah. He flog 'em young gel runaway gels like you three." (91)

> "Oh shut up and stop whining." (93)

> "We're not sleeping in the bunna again, eh Dgudu?" (93)

> "We got a long way to go yet." (94)

These were rendered in Italian translation like this:

> "Hanno un poliziotto mardu, un prepotente. Piglia a bastonatele ragazzine che scappano come voi tre." (128)

"Oh, chiudi il becco e piantala di frigare." (131)

"Non dormiamo mica un'altra volta in una tana, eh, dgudu?" (132)

"Abbiamo ancora un sacco di strada da fare." (135)

The translation shows that Rullo translated every constituent part of the text in a literal manner, thus creating an accurate translation. They also demonstrate her sensibility for the spirit of both languages and their colloquialisms. Although in some cases the flavor of diction is almost lost when rendered back into English, the back translation might be the following:

"They have a cop, a cheeky fellow. He flogs young girls that do a moonlight flit."

"Oh, shut your mouth and stop whining."

"We're not sleeping in the hole again, right, eh, dgudu?"

"We still have long way to go."

In these examples, the translator used informal words like *un prepotente* (a rude and disrespectful person) for *cheeky fullah*, the phrases *pigliare a bastonate* for *to flog* (literally meaning "beat with a stick") and *chiudi il becco* for *shut up* (literally meaning "shut your beak"), the expressions *mica* and *un sacco di* to emphasize negation and long distance respectively (both structures are used only in colloquial diction).

Rullo was less successful in dealing with the word *blackfella*: she rendered it into Italian as *un muso nero*, using the ethically problematic word for a black person. (The English equivalent for the word *muso* is "gob," an informal expression for someone's mouth, used in the phrase "shut your gob." In Italian, this word is also used in the informal collocation *muso brutto*, meaning "a very annoying person.") Maurizio Bartocci, on the other hand, the Italian translator of *My Place*, paid attention to the complexity of cross-cultural communication: he retained this Aboriginal English word, as well as the words *boong* and *abo*, and provided the explanations in footnotes.

If the only criterion in assessing the quality of a translation were the footnotes, *La mia Australia* (My Australia), as Morgan's autobiography is entitled in Bartocci's Italian translation, would have few rivals. Numerous annotations clearly indicate that Bartocci did not regard the act of translating as mere "linguistic transference of signifiers" but as a cross-cultural communication (Suoqiao, 374). The annotations can be divided into two groups: those that contribute to the in-depth understanding of the narrative, regardless of the cultural background of readers, and those that address cultural contexts of the source text that have no equivalent in the target readers' culture. For example, the translator provides thorough background information about the historical figure Guy Fawkes and the terms *Repatriation scholarship, AMP building, Anzac Day*, and several others. Conversely, the notes accompanying the novel's discussion of different medical products consumed by the family succinctly explain culturally marked terms like *Laxettes* (a medicine for constipation) and *Enos* (an antacid); the opening pages of the book provide information on *Fantails* (a candy), *Vegemite* (a sandwich spread), and *jarrah* (coffee). Without listing further examples, and putting aside a few words specific to Australian culture that the translator did not make comprehensible to Italian readers (e.g., the word *raffles*), we can see that in Bartocci's version, translation and transmission of culture go hand in hand.

Bartocci's ability to attentively follow Morgan's words and thoughts without distancing the text from the target readers resulted in the book's unprecedented success in Italy. First published in 1997, *La mia Australia* has been republished twice and has sold more than 35,000 copies. It is not hard to notice that Bartocci was mindful of both cultural differences and the source text's language. As in the source text, the characters in the translation communicate in the language characterized by "essential grammar, poor syntax and elementary vocabulary" (*La mia*, 501). In the original text the passage reads:

> "We were both poor bastards stuck on a POW transport bound for the camps, Italian job she was, when *Boom!* a bloody Pommy sub got us right up the Mediterranean! Jesus bloody Christ, I'll never forget that one. Anyhow, we stayed afloat and beached on the Greek coast. I couldn't move, I was wounded in the chest. I thought I'd cashed in me chips. Then ya know what happened?"
> "No, what?" I whispered. (31)

In the Italian version, this passage is rendered as follows:

> "Eravamo entrambi dei poveri bastardi bloccati su un mezzo di trasporto POW diretto ai campi, una roba italiana, quando *Boom!*, un cazzo di sottomarino inglese ci becca proprio in mezzo al Mediterraneo! Cazzo. Non me lo scorderó mai. Comunque, andammo alla deriva e ci arenammo sulla costa greca. Non riuscivo a muovermi, ero ferito al torace. Pensavo di tirar le cuoia. E invece sai che é successo?"
> "No, cosa?" sussurrai. (41)

which might be back-translated into English like this:

> "We were both poor bastards stuck on a POW transport bound for the camps, Italian stuff, when *Boom!* Fucking English sub hits us right in the middle of Mediterranean. Dick. I'll never forget.

Anyhow, we stayed afloat and beached on the Greek coast. I couldn't move, I was wounded in the chest. I thought I'd cashed in me chips. But, you know what happened?"
"What?" I whispered.

The above is just one among many examples that show the translator's sense of the nuances of both languages. With his careful choice of informal words and expressions, like *bastardo* (bastard), *roba italiana* (what is made in Italy, Italian stuff), *cazzo* (penis), the verb *beccarci* (to hit somebody), *tirare le cuoia* (to cash in one's chips), and so on, and by deliberately distorting syntactic rules by omitting words or final letters—*No, cosa?* (No, what?) instead of the correct *No, che cosa?* *tirar* instead of a correct *tirare* with a final vowel *e*—the translator produced a counterpart with a slang flavor similar to that of the source text. It is safe to say that Bartocci's translation functions as a literary text in its own right and not merely as a reproduction of another text.

The German and Dutch translations of the two books pose different problems than the Slovene and Italian versions. Because of the closeness of German and Dutch and the similarities in the translations, they will be discussed together. The German title of *My Place*, *Ich hörte den Vogel rufen* (I heard the bird calling), takes up the title of the last chapter, "The Bird Call." In German, this title evinces more literary finesse than a literal translation, already indicating the sophisticated technique employed in the translation of the text. The German rendition is characterized by a careful balance between literal and free translation. The structure of sentences, for example, has been adapted to a highly readable German style that occasionally departs from the original meaning:

> "All those years, mum," I said, "how could you have lied to us all those years?" "It was only a little white lie," she replied sadly. (135)

The German translation reads:

> "All diese Jahre, Mum," sagte ich, "wie konntest du uns all diese Jahre anlügen?" "Ich war mit meiner Weisheit am Ende," antwortete sie traurig. (158)

Translated back into English this passage means,

> "All those years, Mum," I said, "how could you have lied to us all those years?" "I was at my wit's end," she replied sadly.

Whereas the first sentence has been accurately translated, the translation of *white lie* as *mit meiner Weisheit am Ende sein* (being at my wit's end) produces a completely different reason for the lying. This reason is implicit in the historical context of the story: the protagonists were forced to adopt a different racial identity—Indian instead of Aboriginal—in order to protect their family from harm, especially the removal of its children. The reason for lying is thus given as a comparatively minor lie, hence a "white lie." In the original, the expression "white lie" can be read as a minor lie as well as one caused by white society, thus rendering the oppressive white society responsible for the lie. The translation, in contrast, is free of historical context. The correct translation would have been *Notlüge* (white lie). Yet *Notlüge* sounds more trivial than the more formal expression "to be at one's wit's end."

The Dutch translation is a similarly careful balance between literal and free translation. The Dutch version was first published in 1991 under the title *Terug naar Corunna* (*Back to Corunna*) and republished in 1994 under the title *Mijn plek* (*My Place*). Here, too, the beauty of the language has been given primacy—the Dutch version has even fewer colloquialisms than the German one. The passage quoted above, for example, has been translated as follows:

> "Al die jaren, mam," zei ik, "hoe heb je al die jaren tegen ons kunnen liegen?"
> "Het was alleen maar leugentje om bestwil," antwoordde ze sip. (139)

In back translation this reads,

> "All those years, Mum," I said, "how could you have lied to us all those years?"
> "It was just a white lie," she replied embarrassedly.

The Dutch translation reproduces nearly the same meaning as the English text—only the word *sip* (embarrassedly) differs in meaning from *sadly*.

Another peculiarity of the German translation is the frequent use of English terms left untranslated, such as *blackfella*, *Mum*, and *Aussie*. These terms are easily understandable by German speakers. Only few terms specific to Australia have been omitted, most conspicuously *Vegemite sandwich*, which has been translated as *Pausenbrot* (snack bread), with its Australian characteristics completely concealed. Other terms have not been translated but adapted to a German pronunciation. *Corroborees*, for one, has been given as *Korroboris*, briefly explained in a subordinate clause as a dance. The Dutch version, in contrast, employs Dutch terms for Australian words, such as *Australisch* (i.e., Australian instead of Aussie), *zwart mens* (black human) for *Blackfella*, and *boterhammen met marmite* (bread with marmite) for *Vegemite sandwich*, which refers to the better-known British version of the product. Thus, the German translation tends to foreignize particularly Australian expressions, whereas the Dutch rendition tends to domesticate such cultural specificities. Importantly, in stark contrast to the Slovene and Italian versions, the German and Dutch editions do not translate the terms *Blackfella* and *zwart mens* with words carrying a pejorative racial meaning.

Another form of foreignization and domestication lies in the translation of dialogues that are replete with colloquialisms. In both Dutch and German, dialogues have been rendered into a spoken but correct language in that the word order reflects native language. Some words have been contracted, as is customary in oral conversation—like *nich* instead of *nicht* or *'ne* instead of *eine*—and colloquial terms have been translated into similar colloquialisms—like *nee* for *naah*. The Dutch dialogues are distinguished by the use of fewer colloquialisms and contractions (for example, *'t* for *dat*). The infrequency of such contractions reflects the more obvious strategy of domestication in the Dutch rendition of the text. In both instances, the colloquialisms do not result in an incorrect language. Rather they reflect the use of an informal language, thus mirroring the oral origin of the source text:

> "You know, Sal . . . all my life, I been treated rotten, real rotten. Nobody's cared if I've looked pretty. I been treated like a beast. Just like a beast of the field. And now, here I am . . . old. Just a dirty old blackfella." (352)

This version has been translated into German as follows:

> "Weißt du, Sal, . . . mein ganzes Leben lang bin ich mies behandelt worden, richtig mies. Niemand hat sich je drum gekümmert, ob ich hübsch aussehe oder häßlich, ob es mir gut geht oder schlecht. Bin behandelt worden wie ein Tier. Wie ein Tier auf dem Feld. Und jetzt . . . bin ich alt. Nur ein dreckiger alter Blackfella." (402)

A literal translation of the German text reads thus:

> "You know, Sal . . . all my life, I have been treated rotten, really rotten. Nobody has cared if I look pretty or ugly, if I am doing fine or badly. I have been treated like a beast. Just like a beast of the field. And now . . . I am old. Just a dirty old blackfella."

Strategies of foreignization and domestication can be observed in this short passage. First, the text has been domesticated by being translated into a grammatically correct German (*I have been treated* instead of *I been treated*) and colloquialisms have been rendered into widely used modes of contraction (*drum* instead of *darum*; *bin* instead of *ich bin*). At the same time, elements of foreignization have been included (e.g., *blackfella*). Most strikingly, the translator amended an entire sentence which does not exist in the original (*nobody has cared if I look pretty or ugly, if I am fine or bad*).

The Dutch translation of this passage reads as follows:

> "Weet je, Sally ... mijn hele leven ben ik slecht behandelt, heel slecht. 't Kon niemans schelen of ik er mooi uitzag. Ik been als een beest behandelt. Gewoon als een stuk vee. En hier ben ik nu ... oud. Gewoon een oud zwart mens van niks." (366)

Literally translated, this paragraph means,

> "You know, Sally ... my whole life I've been treated badly, very badly. Nobody's been interested if I've looked pretty. I was treated like a beast. Just like a piece of beast. And now, here I am ... just an old black human of nothing."

This translation is close to the original and departs only in relation to grammar in that it uses correct Dutch syntax, eschews colloquialisms like *Sally* for *Sal*, and uses the negative expression *zwart mens van niks* (black human of nothing) instead of *dirty blackfella*. The Dutch text presents Morgan's story in a less vulgar language, but these adaptations are minor.

The Dutch and German translations of *Rabbit-Proof Fence* have experienced similar success as *My Place*, with the German edition reprinted three times in the first year of publication. The Dutch version retains the same title as the original, and the German translation carries the English title, *Long Walk Home*, which already indicates the foreignization employed in the translations. Almost all Australian words and geographical names, like *banksia tree*, *heathlands*, and *camp*, have been maintained in the original. In a similar fashion, Aboriginal names like *marbu* and *Mardu* have been left untranslated. As with the translation of *My Place*, the style in both translations is fluid. At the same time, the translations remain close to the original text. This strategy is certainly easier to pursue in Germanic than Slavic and Romanic languages because of the closeness of German and Dutch to English. But the strategy of remaining close to the original also leads to a few difficulties in translating the historical contexts of the story. For example, the original book begins thus:

> The trek back home to Jigalong in the north-west of Western Australia from the Moore River Native Settlement just north of Perth was not only a historical event, it was also one of the most incredible feats imaginable, undertaken by three Aboriginal girls in the 1930s. (xi)

The German version reads,

> Die Wanderung dreier Aborigine-Mädchen von der Eingeborenensiedlung Moore River nördlich von Perth zurück in ihren Heimatort Jigalong im Nordwesten Australiens war nicht nur ein historisches

Ereignis, sondern gleichzeitig eine unvorstellbare Leistung. Sie fand in den dreißiger Jahren des 20. Jahrhunderts statt. (9)

Literally translated this means,

The hike of three Aborigine girls from the native settlement Moore River north of Perth back to their hometown Jigalong in the northwest of Australia was not only a historical event, but, at the same time, an unimaginable effort. It took place in the '30s of the twentieth century.

The German translation is stylistically smooth and quite literal. Only northwestern Australia has been substituted for *Western Australia*. A distortion, however, results from the literal translation of *Moore River Native Settlement* as *Eingeborenensiedlung More River*. This literal translation is grammatically correct, yet the word *Siedlung* (settlement) carries the connotation of a living place where people gather by free choice. The English term *settlement*, to be sure, has not the connotation of force but needs to be understood as part of the name of a historical institution that used *settlement* in a deliberately euphemistic fashion, thereby negating the forcible character of child removal associated with this institution. The literal translation thus suggests that Aboriginal people indeed simply settled in Moore River without any curtailment of freedom. Thus, in this instance the strategy of a literarily proper translation fails to translate the historical dimension of the story. The Dutch version of the same passage gives *Moore River Settlement* as *opvoedingskamp* (education camp), which rather accentuates the history of this institution (9). Occasionally, however, the Dutch version, too, does not do full justice to the original historical meaning:

When the invaders encountered the Nyungar people of the Great Southern region, they were pleased to find friendly, hospitable people. At first, the Aboriginal men welcomed the sealers and whalers. (4)

The translation reads:

Toen de blanke zeelieden voor de eerste keer in contact kwamen met de Nyungar-bevolking van de Great Southern Region, werden ze aangenaam verrast door hun vriendelijkheid and gastvrijheid. De aboriginals verwelkomden de walvisvaarders hartelijk. (18)

Literally translated into English, this paragraph means:

When the white sailors first came into contact with the Nyungar people of the Great Southern Region, they were pleasantly surprised by their friendliness and hospitality. The Aboriginals warmly welcomed the whalers.

The Dutch version employs a method of foreignization, using the English term *Great Southern Region* and remains close to the meaning of the original while evincing a fluid style. But there are three exceptions to this rather literal method of translation. One is the translation of the term *invaders* as *white sailors*. Thus, to Dutch readers, the historical significance of the term *invasion* has not been brought to the page. The second exception is the omission of the translation of the term *sealers*. The third departure from the original text is the rendition of *they were pleased to find friendly, hospitable people* as they *were pleasantly surprised by their friendliness and hospitality.* "Being pleased" and "being surprised" convey different meanings, for the latter suggests an anticipation of the Aboriginal people being potentially unfriendly and inhospitable.

The Dutch and German translations of *Rabbit-Proof Fence* and *My Place* are characterized by a fluid style despite having remained close to the structure of the original. This form of translation can be considered representative of the majority of Dutch and German translations of Australian Aboriginal literature, as is the case with, for example, Archie Weller's *De donkere kant van de maan* (1988), translated by Babet Mossel; David Unaipon's *Mooncumbulli* (2005), translated by Gabriele Yin; and Melissa Lucashenko's *Außen eckig, innen rund* (2000), translated by Johanna Ellsworth. In contrast to the Slovene and Italian translations, the German and Dutch editions do not employ any negatively charged racial terms and are distinguished by foreignization rather than domestication. The difficulty with the Dutch and German translations lies with the concealing of significant historical information either because the translator was not fully acquainted with interracial Australian history or because the beauty of language was considered of more importance than the translation of the historical contexts of the stories.

As this discussion has shown, European translations of Aboriginal literature cannot be described as homogeneous. Rather, there are significant differences in the respective languages of translation, suggesting a diverse pattern of European reception of Aboriginal literature. Methods of foreignization and domestication have been employed to different extents in various languages of translation. Whereas some translations are successfully translated into the target audience's culture, others do not provide a real encounter between the target readership and the author. In particular, this is the case with Slovene translation of *My Place*: the translator went too far with her interventions into the text, while the publisher was manipulative regarding the design of the book. Yet, it is not the interventions by translators that appear problematic, not least because some of them seem to be necessary in order for the target text to be comprehensible for a culturally estranged readership. Rather, the problem lies with the extents to which these interventions have been made and whether they produce a different meaning from the original text, as has been shown with the literal translation resulting in the loss of historical information. Given that much of Aboriginal literature is permeated with the past, an adequate translation of historical context underlying the respective stories is imperative. The translators' insensitivity to historical details has thus resulted in one of the gravest problems in the European translations of Australian Aboriginal texts. The conception of the Slovene version of *My Place* as a book tailored to children is equally problematic. Finally, the use of racially prejudiced terminology in the Slovene and Italian versions portrays Aboriginal authors as using racist terminology. The use of such terminology tends to reinforce rather than counteract racism, rendering the meaning of the translations highly different from the original texts.

Translating Australian Aboriginal texts is a complex task involving difficult negotiations across cultural, linguistic, and historical contexts. On the positive side, translators have largely avoided the trap of exoticism. But, on the negative side, they have failed to convey important cultural and historical information contained in the texts.

# Works Cited

Anderman, Gunilla, and Margaret Rogers. *Translation Today: Trends and Perspectives.* Clevedon, UK: Multilingual Matters Limited, 2003.

Di Blasio, Francesca. "A Path of Words: The Reception of Autobiographical Australian Aboriginal Writing in Italy." In *Indigenous Biography and Autobiography*, edited by Peter Read, Frances Peters-Little, and Anna Haebich, 29–39. Canberra, ACT: Australian National University E Press, 2009.

Di Luzio, Aldo, Susanne Guenthner, and Franca Orletti. *Culture in Communication: Analyses of Intercultural Situations.* Amsterdam, Netherlands: John Benjamin, 2001.

Haag, Oliver. "Indigenous Australian Literature in German: Some Considerations on Reception, Publication and Translation." Special Issue, *Journal of the Association for the Study of Australian Literature.* (2009): 1–17.

———. "Indigenous Literature in European Contexts: Aspects of the Marketing of the Indigenous Literatures of Australia and Aotearoa/New Zealand in German- and Dutch-Speaking Countries." *Journal of the European Association of Studies on Australia* 2, no. 1 (2011): 47–69.

Limon, David. "Slovene Novel in English: Bridging the Cultural Gap." In *Slovenski roman,* 637–43. Ljubljana: Center za slovenščino kot drugi / tuji jezik pri oddelku za slovenistiko Filozofske fakultete Univerze v Ljubljani, 2003.

Lucashenko, Melissa. *Außen eckig, innen rund* [*Steam Pigs*]. Translated by Johanna Ellsworth. Frankfurt am Main, Germany: Alibaba, 2000.

Mazi-Leskovar, Darja. "Leatherstocking Tales: 20th Century Slovenian Translations." *Acta Neophilologica* 42, nos. 1–2 (2009): 57–68.

Morgan, Sally. *Ich hörte den Vogel rufen* [*My Place*]. Translated by Gabriele Yin. Berlin, Germany: Orlanda Frauenverlag, 1991.

———. *La mia Australia* [*My Place*]. Translated by Maurizio Bartocci. Ancona-Milano, Italy: Theoria, 2000.

———. *Mijn plek: Autobiografie over drie generaties Aboriginals* [*My Place*]. Translated by Eva Wolff. Amsterdam, Netherlands: In de Knipscheer, 1994.

———. *My Place*. Fremantle, WA: Fremantle Arts Centre Press, 1987.

———. *My Place for Young Readers*. Fremantle, WA: Fremantle Arts Centre Press, 1990.

———. *Terug naar Carunna: De koppige reis van een Aboriginal vrouw op zoek naar haar verlden* [*My Place*]. Translated by Eva Wolff. Amsterdam, Netherlands: An Dekker, 1991.

———. *V objem korenin* [*My Place*]. Translated by Tamara Bosnič. Dob pri Domžalah, Slovenia: Miš, 2007.

Pilkington Garimara, Doris. *Barriera per conigli* [*Rabbit-Proof Fence*]. Translated by. Marina Rullo. Varese, Italy: Giano Editore S.r.l., 2004.

———. *Long Walk Home: Die wahre Geschichte einer Flucht quer durch die Wüste Australiens* [*Rabbit-Proof Fence*]. Translated by Edith Beleites. Reinbek, Germany: Rowohlt, 2003.

———. *Rabbit-Proof Fence*. New York: Miramax Books, 2002.

———. *Rabbit-Proof Fence: De vlucht naar huis* [*Rabbit-Proof Fence*]. Translated by Koen Scharrenberg. Rijswijk, Netherlands: Elmar, 2003.

———. *Zajčja ograja* [*Rabbit-Proof Fence*]. Translated by Andreja Blažič-Klemenc. Nova Gorica, Slovenia: Eno, 2008.

Pribac, Bert. *Konec sanjske dobe: Antološki prerez sodobne avstralske aboriginske poezije.* Ljubljana, Slovenia: Društvo, 2003.

Pribac, Bert, and David Brooks. *Vesolje okrog kuščarja.* Ljubljana, Slovenia: Mladinska knjiga, 2003.

Shoemaker, Adam. "The Poetry of Politics: Australian Aboriginal Verse." In *Black Words White Page: Aboriginal Literature, 1929–1988.* Canberra, ACT: Australian National University E Press, 2008. Accessed October 14, 2008. http://epress.anu.edu.au/bwwp/mobile_devices/ch08.html.

Suoqiao, Qian. "Confucius as an English Gentleman: Gu Hongming's Translation of Confucian Classics." In *Discontinuities and Displacements: Studies in Comparative Literature*, 373–82. Rio de Janeiro, Brazil: Aeroplano, 2009.

Unaipon, David, and Karl Merkatz. *Mooncumbulli: Mythen und Legenden der Australischen Aborigines* [*Legendary Tales of the Australian Aborigines*]. Translated by Gabriele Yin. CD. Wien, Austria: Bilby-Hörbücher, 2005.

Venuti, Lawrence, ed. *The Translation Studies Reader.* London: Routledge, 2000.

———. *The Translator's Invisibility: A History of Translation.* London: Routledge, 1995.

Walker, Kath. *Widziadła* [*Stradbroke Dreamtime*]. Translated by Anna Przedpelska-Trzeciakowska. Warszaw, Poland: Nasza Księgarnia, 1977.

Weller, Archie. *De donkere kant van de maan: Roman uit Australië* [*Day of the Dog*]. Translated by Babet Mossel. Houten, Netherlands: Het Wereldvenster, 1988.

# 5: Tracing a Trajectory from Songpoetry to Contemporary Aboriginal Poetry

*Stuart Cooke*

Aboriginal poetry enjoyed a tremendously rapid evolution during the latter half of the twentieth century. In 1964, Oodgeroo Noonuccal published *We Are Going*, the first book of poetry by an Aboriginal author. Since the 1970s, poetry has been at the forefront of Aboriginal political expression. Poets like Noonuccal, Kevin Gilbert, and Lionel Fogarty have used the medium to forge new possibilities for the expression of contemporary Aboriginal thought. At the beginning of the twenty-first century, established poets like Fogarty and emerging talents like Samuel Wagan Watson and Ali Cobby Eckermann are some of the most widely read and exciting poets in Australia. However, while these poets are gaining increased attention, their position within Western critical discourse remains somewhat awkward. Literary critics have seldom rigorously engaged with *oral* Aboriginal poetry, thereby failing to acknowledge the extensive Indigenous cultural heritage of contemporary Aboriginal writers. Instead, musicologists and anthropologists have been left to research oral Aboriginal poetics, but within an empirical framework that generally denudes the songpoems of their poetic qualities.[1] Consequently, there is an enormous lacuna in Australian literary studies about the relationship of contemporary Aboriginal poetry to traditional forms of songpoetry. This relates to a larger, more willful ignorance of the relationship between the *voice* of the poet and the *text* that is printed on the page. I will argue in this essay that to separate these two modalities is to deny the importance of much of the Aboriginal poetic tradition.

In order to trace a trajectory between the avant-garde of contemporary Aboriginal poetry and the poetics of Aboriginal songpoetry, I am concentrating on three examples of Aboriginal poetics. Before I continue, I should point out that these examples are not meant to represent the

---

[1] Important exceptions include T. G. H. Strehlow's *Songs of Central Australia* (Sydney: Angus & Robertson, 1971); and the recent book by John Bradley, with Yanyuwa families, *Singing Saltwater Country: Journey to the Songlines of Carpentaria* (Sydney: Allen & Unwin, 2010).

entire tradition of Aboriginal poetry. They exist at particularly crucial points along a continuum of Aboriginal literature, but other writers— be they the aforementioned Gilberts and Wagan Watsons, or others like Alexis Wright and Kim Scott—also occupy important positions within the same milieu. For the first of the examples, I draw the reader's attention to a brief discussion of some of the characteristics of Aboriginal song-poetry, particularly from central Australia and the western Kimberley.[2] At the other end of the trajectory, we will come to the work of Lionel Fogarty (1958–), a Murri poet whose work not only extends the boundaries of Australian poetry but also of the English language. In between these apparently unrelated literatures, I place *Gularabulu* (1983), a collection of stories narrated by Paddy Roe (1912–2001) and transcribed by theorist and critic Stephen Muecke. We can read *Gularabulu* as a nexus of oral and written literatures: a place where Aboriginal oral poetics merge with modernist typography to become a literature that resists classification by Western criticism. Its position in Aboriginal literature is crucial because it allows us to better understand the relationships between the poetics of contemporary poets like Fogarty and traditional forms of oral songpoetry. *Gularabulu* is also a pioneering example of how Aboriginal literature can act as a political mediation between Indigenous and settler philosophies. Roe's stories do not grant full disclosure of his culture to a non-Indigenous audience. Rather, he skillfully designs each narrative so that the uninitiated reader is only given glimpses of a larger, more complex worldview.

A general understanding of some of the most striking characteristics of songpoetry allows us to note their subsequent re-emergence in the work of poets like Roe and Fogarty. The evocative imagery of many central Australian and western Kimberley songpoems vividly depicts open-ended situations rather than a sequence of actions with a clear conclusion. T. G. H. Strehlow emphasizes that the poetry tends to contain verbs of ongoing states, which he demonstrates by frequently using the progressive present in his translations (420). For John Bradley, the fact that such songpoetry can never be described in the past tense tells us that the poems are in constant movement through country, "flowing like a living conduit of meaning, ever present" (106). Consider the following curse song, from a women's ceremony carried out by a wronged wife who wishes to punish her rival. As the women sing the curse song, two women make two long digging sticks before cutting off their locks and pubic hair, which they work into plaits. The plaits are tied to two neckbands, and these are attached to the two digging sticks, which now represent the mythical plait

---

[2] Structurally, songpoems from the Western Kimberley and central Australia share many similarities. Their features are relevant to us here because author Paddy Roe was the owner of a number of important Western Kimberley song cycles.

women (*tjǐmbarkŋa*). A women's dance is executed around these "image-sticks"; the outlines of a snake are drawn to the intonation of the verse:

The tjǐmbarkŋa plaits are lying there:
She is continually wasting away without hope.

With bleaching teeth she is lying there,
With [shriveling] brain she is lying there.

Her eyeballs are projecting from their sockets;
Her head has grown too large for her.

The plait woman keeps on crying and crying;
In her loneliness she keeps on crying and crying.

The tjǐmbarkŋa plaits are breaking her life;
The avenging woman is breaking her life.

(Strehlow, 394)

This is potent poetry, intended to sing into another person the state being evoked in the song. The digging sticks are like constant shadows beneath the activity, yet the poetic is porous enough to allow for the present moment to move and change, and it is not concerned with delimiting the moment with reference to a linear time scale. For all we know, the moment might endlessly perpetuate, or it might fragment and decompose into other moments; neither of these possibilities is of concern, however. What is of concern is *movement*. This is a crucial aspect of songpoetry: for all of its porosity, it nevertheless has a *direction*. The songpoem, in turn, is powerful and *pointed*: its power does not radiate indiscriminately but has a very particular velocity. In other words, the poetic does not incorporate everything to become a meaningless totality but rather flows in a particular direction, maintaining enough flexibility to respond to changes in the environment without losing too much speed.

The poem above is an example of how, in much Aboriginal song-poetics, there is a tendency towards the reduction of the parts of speech to mainly verbal or substantival elements: the poetic vocabulary consists largely of nouns and verbs. This is indicative of songpoetry not only from central Australia but from the Kimberley and Arnhem Land, too.[3] The absence of adjectives is indicative of the fact that "the language of song is deprived of much of its denotative power so that its evocative potential can be enhanced in rhythmic and sound patterns" (Rosenfeld, 180). Yet adjectival paucity also indicates a poetic that is resistant to delimiting its

---

[3] See, e.g., Margaret Clunies Ross, "The Structure of Arnhem Land Song-Poetry," *Oceania* 49, no. 2 (1978): 128–56; Ray Keogh, "*Nurlu* Songs from the West Kimberley: an Introduction," *Australian Aboriginal Studies* 1 (1989): 2–11.

environment by confining it within the language of a descriptive survey. The poetry does not seek to encompass the country but needs to form a relationship *with* it. Objects remain free to enter into partnership with, or break away from, language; without adjectival anchors, a phrase cannot become "inaccurate" because the object to which it refers has changed in some way. Rather than stopping to layer a place with descriptive detail, the songpoem keeps flowing. Instead, objects or places can be emphasized by repetition, or by *returning* to them periodically, as we can see here in Margaret Clunies Ross's translation of the poem, "Wama-Dupun (Sugar Bag and Hollow Log)" (these repetitive, emphatic structures will reemerge in Paddy Roe's oral narratives):

> Tree-trunk, wood of the Tree,
> Spirit Women belonging to Sugar Bag hang up their honey-baskets. . .
> the bees are hurrying back, hurrying back. . .
> Wood of the Tree,
> Tree-trunk, wood of the Tree,
> Sugar Bag, exuding viscous drops, hot dark Sugar Bag,
> dry Tree with Sugar Bag inside, dry wood,
> fat, fermented Sugar Bag at the Tree's mouth,
> beeswax and cells filled with honey.
>
> (148–49)

For the songpoem is not only a spoken text but also a musical assemblage of various human and nonhuman actors. Invariably it comes to the poet in a dream from spirit beings, which live in country. It is up to the poet to then edit and refine the spirits' gift. The subsequent performance of the poem disperses it across a network of actors and back to country. Around Broome, for example, the performance of a *nurlu* series often involves the progression, song by song, along a particular track. If there is a chorus, or a group of "back-up" singers, it will follow the main singer and repeat his verses, rising in song after his voice has faded, and fading as his voice rises again. This song-dialogue is known as *tracking* (Benterrak, Muecke, and Roe 55). In this way, the focus on an individual's voice (something so prominent in Romantic poetics) is dispersed across the ensemble. In other words, the emphasis on any particular subjectivity recedes amid multiple subjectivities. Of more importance is the exchange *between* bodies, on the tracking, rather than on a particular body. A good performance of a songpoem depends on the creation of a good assemblage (spirit[s]-poet-singers-country), rather than on what any one person says or does.

A primary task for a critical discussion of Aboriginal songpoetry, therefore, is to understand that the poems are, as Jerome Rothenberg writes, "almost always part of a larger situation" (96). Once we discard the European notion of "poem" as a purely text-based object that one studies in literature departments at universities, we can begin to appreciate the truly multimedia complex of the songpoem. Writing of his experience of "translating" such songpoetry, Rothenberg remarks that "there was no more reason to present the words alone as independent structures than the ritual-events, say, or the pictographs arising from the same source. Where possible, in fact, one might present or translate all elements connected with the total 'poem'" (96).

Here, we need to develop some different critical criteria that allow for proper discussion of writing that has such a close relationship to oral poetry. As distinctively oral traditions, Bob Hodge and Vijay Mishra argue, Aboriginal literary cultures possess "a set of qualities that have been disvalued in the post-Gutenberg regime of literary discourse" (75). These include "an absence of closure, generic fluidity, the dimension of performance, and a specific attitude to the potency of the spoken word" (75). Without due consideration of these factors, it is impossible to come to a proper understanding of the thick textures of Aboriginal poetics. Indeed, since the category of orality can so easily be used reductively, it is important to emphasize what Hodge and Mishra call "the full scope and complexity" of an "oral" culture: "An oral culture is a complex semiotic system which is by no means exclusively oral. Various forms of art and performance play crucial roles in the totality of cultural production and reproduction. In such a system the oral mode will consist of a set of genres which will not all correspond exactly to any equivalent in English" (76).

As we will see, oral cultures have not been made "obsolete" by other media, but rather they continue to acquire new pathways and partnerships in an ever-expanding network of global modes of communication. It is extremely misleading, therefore, to trace the development of culture from "simple" oral forms to advanced literary forms when the emerging "global village" is threatening the very status of grammatical axioms (76).

\*　　\*　　\*

*Gularabulu* refers to a vast, luminal region of land and sea. Gularabulu is "the coast where the sun goes down," a large area of coastal country in the western Kimberley, stretching from La Grange in the south, right through Broome, and north to Dampier Land (Roe and Muecke, i). It encompasses tribal groupings of the Garadjeri, Nyigina, Yaour, Nyul-Nyul, and Djaber-Djaber tribes, and urban and nonurban lands. People from these various communities come together regularly.[4] In the same spirit of community, then, "Roe stresses that these stories belong not just

---

[4] Recently, however, tensions have inflamed between some of these groups over a proposal to construct a gas plant at Walmadan (James Price Point). Some

to him, but to all these people" (i). Gularabulu includes Broome, too, which is the home of plenty of whitefellas; consequently, to tell stories that are "for everybody" involves a difficult negotiation of cultures and contexts. Rather than shy from it, Roe embraces the challenge. He talks to whitefellas so that "they might be able to see us better than before" (i). What non-Indigenous people get to *see* during Roe's narration is a central concern of his poetics.

Roe's narratives have a distinctly contemporary feel and echo many of the qualities outlined above by Hodge and Mishra. Their fractured objectivity and the absence of any controlling, authorial point of view gesture at a plenitude of evolving explanations for how they have come to be. Each piece is certainly a story, but Muecke chooses to display each one on the page as a poem, reminding us of the close relationship between the text and the spoken word. The narratives, just like their genres, can be traced across a diverse range of communities, not only those on the southern coast of the Kimberley but also those with which Muecke is involved.[5] In other words, *Gularabulu* articulates a multicultural process of negotiation. The most important songpoetry has the power to maintain country and to relate living things—human and nonhuman—to each other (Bradley, 106). Such song cycles integrate, as well as evoke, various parts of an environment. Similarly, Roe's stories do not dwell in a single location or genre but need to keep moving *between* places in an effort to connect them. The driving motivation behind the stories "lies in the way that they interact with and make coherent the present-day social context" (Roe and Muecke, viii). Like the songpoems, the stories in *Gularabulu* "actively construct forms of social existence, ensuring *cohesion* and *flexibility* in responding to the major problems facing Aboriginal people" (Hodge and Mishra, 73, emphasis mine).

On Gularabulu country, no place is still or unchanging. The ground is alive with meat ants; the horizon is thrashing acacias or ragged swells. Roe's stories, like the places in which they are told, are both stationary and moving: "stationary" because they are clearly *located* in a particular space, "moving" because their energy and anaphora grant them lives of their own, thoroughly captivating Muecke, who takes them from local yarns into the global realm of literature, from oral narrative into written poetry. To illustrate this, a brief elucidation of a passage from "Mirdinan" will be useful; the following scene tells of a *maban* (medicine man) who

---

Djaber-Djaber people are disputing the native title of Joseph Roe, Paddy's son. See http://www.abc.net.au/news/stories/2010/06/21/2932052.htm.

[5] In their format and their attention to poetics, Muecke's transcriptions develop the relationship between oral history and poetry as pioneered by North American scholar Dennis Tedlock.

sees his wife with another man, then goes back to his camp to wait for her and confront her:

> . . . "Hello" he seen this man and woman in the mangroves, sitting
>     down --
> oh he come right alongside --
> he seen everything what they doin' (Laughs) you know --
> they sitting down --
>
> so, he seen everything --
> so he wen' back --
> he wen' back home firs' --
> he still waitin' for his missus -
> his missus come up oooh --
> prob'ly half an hour's time --
> the woman must have give him time you know -
> "oh mus' be nearly time for my oldfella to comeback" -
> but he was about half an hour late might be, his man was there
>     already with the fish he was -
> the oldfella was cooking --
> fish, aaah they had a talk there --
> that was about, dinner time --

(Roe and Muecke, 4)

Here, the narrative arc is not a smooth, uninterrupted line, but it is punctuated with a variety of complex rhythms accentuated by repetitions. Certain phrasal elements carry over a number of lines, such as "he seen . . . he seen" and "sitting down . . . sitting down," before the pause after line 4. Then, the steady accumulation of anaphoric rhythm in the next five lines ("so, he seen . . . so he wen' . . . he wen' . . .," etc.) increases the momentum. Roe's short, sharp phrases, however, mean that he acquires a surplus of breath as well as momentum, and the energy begins to spill; when it *does* spill we reach the climax of the arc: the old-fella was not "half an hour late" as his wife supposed but was already waiting for her in the camp!

After the long line depletes his breath, however, Roe retreats to the smaller phrases. Such deft use of rhythm is not only an aesthetic affect; it has a very explicit relationship with movement and with *time*. The problem of this extract relates to the different speed at which each character moves—the wife too slowly, the *maban* too quickly. As the rhythm increases, so does the maban's speed, which allows him to get back to camp before his wife. So there is an important connection between the world of the story and Roe's own physiology (his lungs). This connection is translated by Muecke into a material relationship between the typography on the page and the story-world, which remains mediated by the qualities of Roe's speaking voice. It is futile to say these stories are settled in locales when, like the Dreaming ancestors of which some are about, they keep these locales alive by *moving*, both in spoken performances (mediated by breath rhythms) and by distribution across spaces (mediated typographically by breath rhythms). Rhythm signals motion and the passing from one country into another.

Were Roe interested in decorative or ornamental flourishes, he would slow his scenes down with heavy, animated images; each elaborate image, weighed down with such detail, would become static. Like songpoetry, however, Roe's lines are sparsely detailed, perhaps to minimize the strain on his voice. When speed needs to be reduced in order to emphasize something, rather than layering imagistic detail upon the line, Roe will use what Muecke calls a "cross parallelism" (Muecke). Consider a portion of "Djaringgalong," when Djaringgalong, a giant bird, finally returns to his nest:

> *tjipeee* they hear-im -
> he's coming they can hear-im -
> somewhere here - (Laugh)
> they hear-im he's comin' back -
> so they get ready these two bloke -
> (Soft) these two bloke get ready -
>
> (Roe and Muecke, 79)

Using cross-parallel phrasing, Roe takes information from one line and repeats it in the following line, but this time as a mirror image. Cross parallelism occurs because, if we assign "he's coming" the letter A and "they can hear-im" the letter B, we can see that these two parts are switched in the next line. That is, the first line consists of **A[he's coming]** + **B[they can hear-im]**, which becomes **B[they hear-im]** + **A[he's coming back]** two lines later. The same pattern recurs in the final two lines, where **A[so they get ready]** + **B[these two bloke]** becomes **B[these two bloke]** + **A[get ready]**. By utilizing this sort of spliced anaphora, the story never stops moving, but Roe is still able to change his speed. The change of movement exerts a gathering power: overlapping the information in such a way slows the pace of the story considerably and creates a seductive rhythm in the speaking voice, drawing the listener/reader closer (Muecke). This circular, repetitive structure also echoes some of the defining characteristics of longer songpoems.

Roe's Aboriginal English, as Muecke notes in his introduction, is a crucial mode of communication between Aboriginal people of various language groups. It is also a way in which Indigenous and non-Indigenous Australians can communicate. For Muecke, Roe's use of such language in these stories could represent "the language of 'bridging' between the vastly different European and Aboriginal cultures"

(Roe and Muecke, iv). Consequently, one could say that Roe's language is an articulation of a distinct mode of contemporary Aboriginal poetics and politics: one that is *in between*. Here, it matters as much that Roe's stories articulate his country as it does that non-Indigenous readers *enjoy* his performance of them. Consequently, the narratives depend on Muecke's response; it is important for Roe that Muecke understands him and that he *performs* as a listener (v). One touching moment comes to mind from "Worawora Woman," where the story is paused to find out if Muecke is uncomfortable about Butcher Joe lighting up a cigarette. Roe continues only once Muecke has said, "Oh that's all right" (33).

This is not to say that *Gularabulu* is all about talking to a white audience, however. Often Roe threads his stories with words and phrases that are left unexplained and mysterious to those unfamiliar with his native Nyigina language or culture. In a veiled aside during "Djaringgalong," for example, Roe laughs and says to one of his countrymen, "*binabi-naba*," the meaning of which is never explained (80; italics in original). And a large chunk of one of Roe's *djabi djabi* songpoems is included in "Mirdinan" with only a very basic gloss (13). By repeating these fragments of stories or songs, different patterns of tradition are imprinted on contemporary texts. Roe's voice is, therefore, an example of what Hodge and Mishra call an "Aboriginal Polyphony" (Hodge and Mishra, 107). Rather than a text that represents a "pure" Aboriginality, Roe's is a "composite and federalist" literature that speaks a variety of languages and can live in different places (107). We will also read Lionel Fogarty's poetry in this light, but many other major works of Aboriginal literature function in this way, too, including Alexis Wright's *Carpentaria* (2006), which fuses Aboriginal modes of storytelling with magical realism, or Anita Heiss's *Mr. Right* series (2007–11), which are important for being the first examples of "Aboriginal chic-lit." In these texts, as in *Gularabulu*, polyphony articulates the great diversity within the regions of intersection between Aboriginal and settler societies.

What is the nature of the new cultural system of representation into which Roe sends his stories? While written discourses are often valued more highly than oral ones in this system, a genealogical link with oral modes is nevertheless a marker of exceptionally high status within Western literary culture (Hodge and Mishra, 75). Roe's stories exploit this link. Like his stories, the most famous members of the Western canon show the marks of their preliterary origins: retarded narratives, prolepsis, bricolage. Western drama and poetry are still realized in the oral mode, though they circulate in written forms. Even the novel relies heavily on dialogue (75–76). In turn, Muecke's typography does not eliminate or disregard the context of Roe's speech but makes use of it in another form. This is not an "escape" from the confines of the oral or an attempt to belittle its significance within larger cultural contexts, either. Like songpoetry, Roe's stories are always *more* than spoken language. Roe's is "a complex semiotic system"; in his stories, as in song, various forms of drawing and performance also play crucial roles. Roe growls, sings, rasps a boomerang, and draws pictures in the dirt, or members of his audience will interject and contribute to the story. It is more accurate to say that Roe's poetic consists "of a set of genres which will not all correspond exactly to any equivalent in English" (Hodge and Mishra, 76). Like Édouard Glissant's Creole storyteller, who "is surprising in his talent for relentlessly bringing together the most heterogeneous elements of reality," Roe's poetics is "an uninterrupted process of revelation: of putting into a *relation*" (200, emphasis mine).

Glissant's concept of relation has to do with understanding how the storyteller or poet might make sense of the world by moving among its various elements and allowing them to coalesce, or relate, of their own accord. The result could be a kind of bricolage. For the authors of *Reading the Country* (one of whom is Paddy Roe), bricolage is a practice and a way of living as much as it is a poetics. Bricolage involves roaming through the aftermath of colonization and picking up useful bits and pieces to keep things going or to make them function better. Since the European invasion, Aboriginal people have been forced into this poetics of relation: to become fluid and fringe dwelling, to neither totally assimilate foreign materials nor totally ignore them. The brico- lage poet moves nomadically, passing through cultures like a rhizome through soils. Thus, bricolage is flexible and adaptive, even subversive: it will never completely exchange one set of meanings for another, often leaving things half complete (Benterrak, Muecke, and Roe, 148–50). In this way, by leaving anomalous details in the mix (an untranslated word or phrase, perhaps) it is always disruptive of "the normal" linguis- tic rules. Roe's English is an example of a bricolage of Aboriginal and English languages: as we will also see with Fogarty, he juxtaposes forms so that new meanings and rhythms can emerge, which can elicit gentle pleasure "in seeing the edifice of language tremble a little as it becomes a kind of poetry" (151).

In various ways, Muecke is a partner to Roe's bricolage or part of a trajectory towards other audiences. He helps the stories survive but is not wholly assimilated into Nyigina language and culture. He is not exactly a mediator in the same sense that a translator is, either, because here Roe controls much of the mediation. When Roe is telling the story of Djaringgalong, for example, he requires assistance from his com- panion, Donald, with a "whatname"—*gurdjarda*—from the Nyigina. Incorporating the word into his story without ever translating it into English, Roe draws a line between Nyigina and white worlds before Muecke has a chance to mediate:

they get their two spears -
an' that whatname -
we call-im (Question to Donald in Nyingina) *garbarda* eh? (Donald:
    Mm) -
*gurdjarda* we call-im he got that

(Roe and Muecke, 79)

Nevertheless, Muecke's role as editor means that he must make some difficult decisions concerning just how opaque his transcriptions of the stories should be. His introduction, summaries, and footnotes, while extremely helpful, are far from comprehensive or extensive; Roe's story-poems constitute without doubt the biggest presence in the book. Yet Muecke's typographical decisions reflect his interest in modernist poetics, with lines of uneven length and a very sparse use of punctuation like commas or capital letters. In this case, then, "the Translator" is a blurred confluence of two people. The task of trying to "locate" the place where this poetics occurs becomes yet more problematic, therefore, for it moves freely between not only languages but *subjects*. In *Gularabulu* we will never arrive at a single location of language or a small clearing in which the Poet is producing his lyric. This text is always moving between two authors or shooting off in some other direction.

*　*　*

Born at Barambah Mission, now known as Cherbourg Aboriginal Reserve, Lionel Fogarty is of the Yoogum and Kudjela tribes.[6] He received very little education at Mergon High School and learned almost nothing about Western literature. His earliest relationship to poetry involved "going down to the township of Mergon and in the park areas there or in the outskirts of Mergon, or even in Cherbourg, just sitting down with young folks as well as old folks and just listening to their gossip, rumours, yarns, storytelling" (Fogarty and Mead).

Fogarty's introduction to poetry and the emphasis on orality and storytelling by "old folks" parallels the oral Aboriginal tradition of which Paddy Roe was a part. Indeed, despite the fact that Western literature provided him with the technology or the "medium" to write, Fogarty maintains that his greatest influences have come from oral Aboriginal sources:

In some of my writings, when I read them myself I get a thing that
ancestors give me this, and at the same time I get a thing that some

---

[6] Throughout the twentieth century, Aboriginal people from many disparate tribal groups were forcibly removed to Cherbourg, which became the largest settlement of its kind in Queensland.

whites have given me this. . . . I believe I read some stuff after I started learning to read, some white man's writings, I'm not saying they influenced me, influence is the wrong word for me to use, but I believe I got a medium of some sort from some of the white writers.

. . . I think that the most influence on my life, in literary terms, was from people who are the down and outs, the ones who didn't really care about employment, that were in the parks. These were the people, street talks, these kind of things, lane walks, that's what influenced my life in terms of writing.. . . . An old man by the name of Bob Landis was the greatest poet in Cherbourg, poetry used to just flow out of his mouth, out of his heart and out of his mind, was a great influence to me. (Fogarty and Mead)

Like a songpoem's place in a larger, communal performance, Fogarty's position as a member of a wider community is central to an understanding of his poetics. His I can be his own, or that of his local community, or even that of Aboriginal people across the whole continent:

we are a clan
we are clean
are we to inflame our truth:
My people over Australia . . .

    (Fogarty, "Dulpai," 96)

Indeed, in Fogarty's poetry we see taking place what John Kinsella calls "a communalising of the lyrical I" (Kinsella 156). Certainly, one need only look at *Yerrabilela Jimbelung* (2008) to find a concrete example. The book's subtitle, *poems about friends and family*, is the first clue to a piece of literature that deliberately evades the traditional association of the poetry book with a single author or origin. Here, three poets have contributed and are listed as follows on the front cover:

by Lionel Fogarty with
Yvette Walker and Kargun Fogarty.

Yvette Walker and Kargun Fogarty, Lionel's son, are both emerging poets. The book is still clearly anchored by the presence of Lionel, who writes the first and the longest introduction and whose poems are the last in the volume. Nevertheless, the reader is struck by the lack of authorial demarcation on the contents page, and we find that Fogarty's poems actually occupy about a third of the volume—no more than either segment of the new poets. So Fogarty's is an extremely generous and democratic gesture, to allow two other voices to occupy a position as privileged as his own, but there is also a very important, and no less striking, tactical maneuver going on here. "We wish to withdraw all poems from the

buildings and put them in open spaces," writes Fogarty, a significant statement that suggests two things (quoted in Fogarty, Walker, and Fogarty
6). Firstly, it would seem that Fogarty wants to initiate a kind of "ransack-
ing" of those institutions and places of power that have to date insisted
on particular readings of poems or of particular, canonical selections of
poems. Secondly, it seems Fogarty wants to return poems to the contexts in which they were generated—namely, in country, where, as with
songpoetry, *communities* gather and bring them into being. "We belong
to different styles," writes Kargun, "yet like the corroboree—one story—
many voices—same song" (quoted in Fogarty, Walker, and Fogarty, 8).

The allusion to a corroboree signals a key facet of much contemporary Aboriginal poetry—not only by Fogarty but also in books like *little bit long time* (2009), by Ali Cobby Eckermann and Samuel Wagan
Watson's *Smoke Encrypted Whispers* (2004). The inheritance of Aboriginal
oral, collaborative, and performative traditions has a "spectral presence"
in what Philip Mead calls Fogarty's "guerrilla surrealism" (Mead, 428).
"The reason why I'm a poet is so I can perform," Fogarty says. "Whatever
I write, I have to perform it, and so that others can also perform my
writings!" (Fogarty, 4). His rhythms are densely performative and often
anaphoric, ignited by internal and enjambed rhymes that crystallize in a
flurry of Aboriginal English and Australian idiom. Recalling the progressive present tense of songpoetry, the poems describe dynamic, ongoing
environments:

> Heart of European capsule my luxuriant
>     love's poems
> Heart of Australia capsule all animus
>     native's binding vessel universal
> Heart of earth clank beat landscaped
> bloods slashed by depopulated
> Heart perfect dream time rhyme
> Moral lead self ambition and loyalty
>     runs breasts of many disguises
> Hearts never beaten interest inextricably
>     rest tensions by reached high-minded
>                    (Fogarty, 17)

In poems like "Heart of a european . . ." it is the sonic similarities
of words, their capacities for rhyme and half rhyme, that drives the progression as much as any desire to accurately elucidate semantic content.
Here, we are reading the result of a complex and difficult translation
process, from a moving, sound-based poetic tradition to one based primarily in the visualization of images. What makes Fogarty's poetry so
distinctive, however, is the fact that he has refused to surrender to the

prevailing standards of Western poetics. In the words of Colin Johnson, "He writes in a manner which is the response of an Aboriginal song-man against the genocide inflicted on his language and the tyranny imposed on him by a foreign language" (quoted in Mead, 426). As a poet wielding the language of the invader, then, Fogarty's achievement is to destroy the impositions of that language and to create a written poetic that is often confusing but always intensely lyrical—a combination of elements that might befit the freely moving, ambiguous, and many-sided song languages of his ancestors.

If Fogarty's poems were nothing more than descriptions of a single, discrete self, they would leave themselves too vulnerable to confinement, ceasing to be available for reinterpretation and performative elaboration. To this end, his page becomes "a field of myth-thought, of song-dream continuity, a place that refuses closure" (Kinsella, 158). In order to keep refusing closure, the poems need to keep *moving*. Whereas in *Yerrabilela Jimbelung* the inclusion of other poets' work produces a sense of community through which the idea of the poem or the poetic passes in order to produce startling differences, in *Minyung Woolah Binnung* (2004) the realm of the "poetic" involves a bricolage of text and visual artworks (see fig. 1). In contrast to the relationships among the poets in *Yerrabilela Jimbelung*, then, of primary importance to *Minyung Woolah Binnung* are the relationships between word and image:

> Fogarty poses a fundamentally organic relationship between self, culture, politics and art practice. This is echoed throughout the book by stimulating drawings that synthesise a type of post-representational avant-gardism with distinctive symbolic content. . . . Anthropomorphic figures multiply across pages into any number of organic utterances, their lines, circles and patterns worked and reworked as territories of sensual connection. (Minter, 53)

This process of organic multiplication and reproduction between visual and textual artwork is analogous to the process of relation at work in the poems themselves. Consider the final segment of "Heart of a european . . .":

> Australia land of the and and?
>    free and figures federally
>    natives buy versed new things
> Until flower wait for bees diverse
> Until flounder waits for good dirt
> So heart of girls from Europeans
> Those masculine reminiscences debts
> all heart landed even sky hearts here
> Australia skate smoothed.

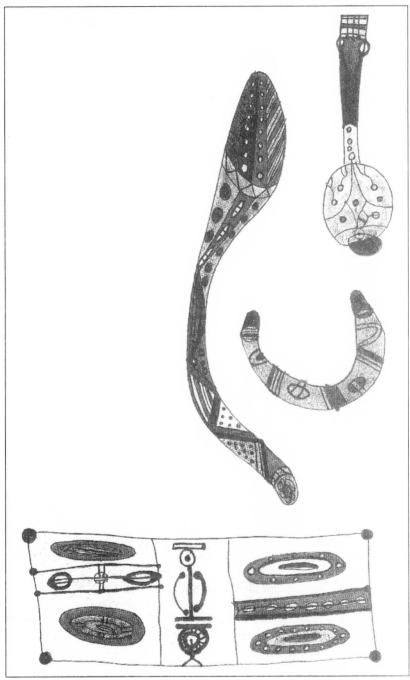

*Fig. 1. "territories of sensual connection" in Fogarty's* Minyung Woolah
Binnung *(25). Reproduction permission granted by Fogarty.*

In this extract, as in many of Fogarty's poems, an act of *smearing* is taking place: the integrity of signifying words is deliberately questioned. There are portions of grammatically correct English here, but no sooner do they appear than they have dissolved into a kind of word-music. Consequently, those intelligible phrases have the effect of punctuating the swirl of rhythm and rhyme with moments of clarity, which the reader "clings" to, as if stopping at the occasional water hole to rest before moving on through the scrub. The phrases jostle and commingle into a smaller, poetic bricolage, similar to the more macroscopic bricolage of poem and artwork in the book at large. *Movement*, rather than transparent, intelligible language, produces the poetry; there is nowhere for the eye to rest:

Australia land of the. . .

free. . .

natives buy. . .

. . . flower wait for bees. . .

. . . girls from Europeans. . .

Those masculine reminiscences. . .

The rise of Aboriginal poetry publishing over the past fifty years is not only indicative of Aboriginal poets embracing Western literary forms. What the development also traces is the continued evolution of an oral poetics with a history far longer than that of the printing press. Aboriginal poetry continues to be characterized by a strongly performative dimension, where the spoken word acquires an undeniable potency and a marked proximity to the written text. Aboriginal oral culture has always been a complex semiotic system; in this chapter, we have seen the performative, multimedia semiotics of songpoetry become a bricolage of various media *and* languages in Roe's *Gularabulu* and subsequently in Fogarty's poetry. This bricolage points to a communal poetic culture, in which the importance of the single Poet who individually composes his or her poems is negligible next to an assemblage of actors, each of whom has an important role to play in the production of the poetic "text." Finally, at the level of the poetics themselves, common to each kind of poetry is an emphasis on the progressive nature of the present moment, with an end to reveal dynamic, moving environments. As fluidly as it negotiates a variety of Indigenous and non-Indigenous genres and art forms, Aboriginal poetry articulates and maintains myriad connections between human and nonhuman worlds. At the intersection of written and oral poetics,

*Gularabulu* reveals the connections between contemporary, avant-garde Aboriginal poetry and its musical, oral heritage.

## Works Cited

Benterrak, Kim, Stephen Muecke, and Paddy Roe. *Reading the Country: Introduction to Nomadology*. Fremantle, WA: Fremantle Arts Centre Press, 1984.

Bradley, John, with Yanyuwa families. *Singing Saltwater Country: Journey to the Songlines of Carpentaria*. Sydney: Allen & Unwin, 2010.

Clunies Ross, Margaret. "The Structure of Arnhem Land Song-Poetry." *Oceania* 49, no. 2 (1978): 128–56.

Fogarty, Lionel. "Dulpai—Ila Ngari Kim Mo-Man." In *Macquarie PEN Anthology of Aboriginal Literature*, eds. Anita Heiss and Peter Minter, 93–99. Sydney: Allen & Unwin, 2008.

———. *Minyung Woolah Binnung (What Saying Says): Poems and Drawings*. Southport: Keeaira Press, 2004.

Fogarty, Lionel, and Philip Mead. "Lionel Fogarty in Conversation with Philip Mead." *Jacket* (October 1997). Accessed July 15, 2012. http://jacketmagazine.com/01/fogartyiv.html.

Fogarty, Lionel, Yvette Walker, and Kargun Fogarty. *Yerrabilela Jimbelung: Poems about Friends and Family*. Southport, QLD: Keeaira Press, 2008.

Glissant, Édouard. *Poetics of Relation*. Translated by Betsy Wing. 1997. Reprint, Ann Arbor: University of Michigan Press, 2006.

Hodge, Bob, and Vijay Mishra. *Dark Side of the Dream: Australian Literature and the Postcolonial Mind*. Sydney: Allen & Unwin, 1990.

Keogh, Ray. "*Nurlu* Songs from the West Kimberley: An Introduction." *Australian Aboriginal Studies* 1 (1989): 2–11.

Kinsella, John. "The Hybridising of a Poetry: Notes on Modernism and Hybridity—the Colonising Prospect of Modernism and Hybridity as a Means to Closure." *Boundary 2* 26, no. 1 (1999): 156–59.

Mead, Philip. *Networked Language: Culture and History in Australian Poetry*. North Melbourne: Australian Scholarly, 2008.

Minter, Peter. "A Radical Tonic: Lionel Fogarty and Samuel Wagan Watson." *Australian Book Review* 268 (2005): 53.

Muecke, Stephen. "Listening to Paddy Roe: Form and Movement in Narrative Structure." (Lecture). Sydney: University of New South Wales, August 16, 2009.

Roe, Paddy. *Gularabulu: Stories from the West Kimberley*, edited by Stephen Muecke. Fremantle, WA: Fremantle Arts Centre Press, 1983.

Rosenfeld, Andrée. "Structural Convergence in Arrernte Art and Song." In *Many Exchanges: Archaeology, History, Community and the Work of Isabel McBryde*, edited by Ingereth Macfarlane, Mary-Jane Mountain, and Robert Paton, 171–84. Canberra, ACT: Aboriginal History Inc., 2005.

Rothenberg, Jerome. *Pre-Faces & Other Writings*. New York: New Directions, 1981.

Strehlow, T. G. H. *Songs of Central Australia*. Sydney: Angus & Robertson, 1971.

Tedlock, Dennis. "Learning to Listen: Oral History as Poetry." *Boundary 2* 3, no. 3 (1975): 707–28.

# 6: Rites/Rights/Writes of Passage: Identity Construction in Australian Aboriginal Young Adult Fiction

*Jeanine Leane*

A RITE OF PASSAGE is an experience that triggers a significant transformation. During the journey an individual crosses a border or boundary and is transformed in a way that empowers him or her to live in the world differently than before. A genre in Aboriginal writing that often traces a main character's journey from adolescence to adulthood is young adult fiction. Three prolific Aboriginal young adult fiction writers are John Muk Muk Burke, Melissa Lucashenko, and Tara June Winch. This chapter will look at the bildungsroman in Aboriginal writing through the works of these three authors with particular attention to identity construction, belonging, and the search for a sense of place for the young Aboriginal protagonists in late twentieth- and early twenty-first-century Australia. Though the dominant literary canon in Australia still mainly views identity construction in terms of the Enlightenment concept of the individualist, the Aboriginal bildungsroman focuses on belonging and a sense of place as integral and essential parts of identity construction.

Much of the literature that is emerging in the Aboriginal young adult genre centers on cultural as well as individual identity, usually in urban settings where the majority of Australia's Aboriginal population now lives. The characters in Burke's, Lucashenko's, and Winch's narratives demonstrate how contemporary Aboriginal identity is lived in Western contexts, yet this identity still remains distinct from Australian settler culture. The young Aboriginal protagonists in these narratives can be viewed as metaphoric, ethnographic cases, revealing the ongoing struggles and increasing complexity of Aboriginal youth in postcolonial Australia. Issues of stereotyping, institutional and individual racism, and socially deterministic views of Aboriginal cultures and peoples are exposed and confronted through each of these author's works. In all these narratives, the protagonists as adolescents or young adults experience a sense of unbelonging and disconnection from their community, culture, and country. Their transition evolves through their attempts to reconnect, rediscover, and recover their place in the bigger picture as young urban Aboriginals in contemporary

Australia. All of these movements can be read as challenges, negotiations, and crossings of borders in the (re)creation of Aboriginal identities.

Anthropologist Arnold van Gennep coined the phrase "rites of passage" in his seminal work *Les rites de passage* (1909). Van Gennep identifies three stages that characterize a rite of passage: separation, liminality, and incorporation. In the separation stage, people retreat or withdraw from the group with which they were previously associated and begin moving from one place/space or status to another. In the incorporation stage, a transformation has occurred that allows an individual to re-enter and rejoin society, and the rite is completed. The liminal stage is the fluid movement between separation and incorporation, a stage characterized by anxiety, ambiguity, and a state of flux that causes disorientation. It is the liminal stage that is most poignant in this discussion of the Aboriginal bildungsroman, as it is during this stage that the identities of the protagonists are fractured and each one reaches a crisis point that is a catalyst for transformation.

Of particular relevance to this discussion of Aboriginal identity is that all of the main characters are writing an account of themselves through such transitions and discovering, then embracing, certain rights the characters felt they were not entitled to as young Aboriginal Australians. The right to an education, the right to a safe, stable living environment, the right to make one's own decisions about the future, and most importantly the right to belong may be taken for granted by non-Aboriginal Australians and may not be central features of the non-Aboriginal bildungsroman, but they are the rights that the main characters of Burke's, Lucashenko's, and Winch's narratives learn to embrace as part of the transition from the liminal to the incorporation stage of their journey through rites/rights/writes of passage to adulthood, empowerment, and self-actualization.

*Bridge of Triangles* (1994), by John Muk Muk Burke, won the prestigious David Unaipon Award for Aboriginal or Torres Strait authors. Set against the changing social ethos of Australia in the postwar era, Burke's book describes the search for identity and belonging in land, place, and family of the young protagonist Chris Leeton. Burke's opening description of the small country town where Chris was born foregrounds the tension between Australia's first people and the colonists who arrived and made their presence felt in the Wiradjuri lands:[1]

---

[1] The Wiradjuri people are known as the people of the three rivers: the Wambool (also known as the Macquarie River), the Kalari (Lachlan River), and the Murrumbidjeri (Murrumbidgee River). Wiradjuri country is the largest in New South Wales, stretching from the eastern boundary of the Great Dividing Range to the western boundary of Hay and Nyngan. Gunnedah and Albury mark the northern and southern boundaries.

Back in the previous century the townspeople had cleared the land and made their wide street in a grid pattern. The river and the trees, those great solid river gums, were much as they had been forever. Once before the invaders came with their sheep and bags of wheat seed and working men to dig canals, the trees had grown right across the land and kangaroos and emus were plentiful. And people have lived amongst the trees and hunted the plains forever. (3)

The contrast between the traditional homelands of the Wiradjuri people, Chris's people, and colonial imposition is a continuous theme throughout the novel:

Ancient goannas lumbered through what little remained of the bush and the area is still known for its huge bull ants. . . . Chris was born no doubt at that moment the bull ants were streaming over the red earth and the pink and grey parrots were freewheeling against the deep blue sky and the public bar of The Empire was host to those who never questioned their belonging as they drank middies. (3)

Juxtaposed to the violation of the landscape is Chris's sense of unbelonging:

From the beginning he was an exile. He was pushed into the world with its immense fiery sky. The sky was an enormous hill and it seemed he'd just come over the brow and was near the river and the trees to see if he might belong there for a time. The traveller looked at that place and thought pretty early that perhaps he might not belong there. (3–4)

Chris Leeton's journey through the liminal stage of his rite of passage to belonging embodies the complexity and hybrid nature of contemporary Aboriginality. Chris's mother, Sissy, is "Wiradjuri and of the rivers" (4). His father, Jack Leeton, is a dour Irish Protestant who has fallen from favor within his own family because he married an Aboriginal woman who is also Catholic. Chris is thus a hybrid being, the product of both the traditional owners of the country on whose land the town where he was born is built and, in the author's own words, one of the "invaders." This in-between state causes Chris to feel disoriented, anxious, and confused. Chris's Aboriginal relatives—his mother, Aunty Rose, and Granny—no longer live the traditional lifestyle of their ancestors, yet their connections to the land are still strong, as is shown when Sissy warns Jack of the imminent flood that he as a white man cannot sense. Since the British invasion of 1788 and the subsequent occupation of Australia by waves of settlers, Aboriginals have been driven from ancestral lands or banished to the fringes of settlements that have encroached on the network of traditional countries and language groups across the mainland

and surrounding islands. Chris's sense of unbelonging and flux are followed by a desire to reconnect to family and country and to recover lost or unspoken family histories.

Chris's sense of unbelonging pervades the separation stage of his journey through his rites/rights/writes of passage: "he could never really forget his sense of unbelonging" (6). Chris has inherited his dislocation and sense of disconnection from his mother, Sissy, and his grandmother before her, "the Old Granny":

> Sissy's unbelonging to both herself and her people started way back before her birth when the town built its first pub, and named it The Empire, and shearers and cooks needed more than the comforts of grog [alcohol]. Lurching back to quarters in the lonely night-time paddocks . . . it was easy pickings with a bottle of sweet sherry or rum. (26)

The generational sense of unbelonging is clouded in secrecy, and shame heightens the disconnection of the younger generations of Aboriginals: "the Old Granny never told Sissy much of the place where she had been taken as a girl," but we learn that both Sissy and her mother before her "had become the property of uncaring white men" (26).

*Bridge of Triangles* is written from a third-person perspective, and Chris is continually described as a "dreamy" boy or as having "dreamings." Such dreams combine the past, which he does not know but can imagine, and the future, which he longs for as an escape from his sense of unbelonging and disequilibrium of the present. It is these "dreamings" that surface in the narrative and provide Chris with his only tenuous connection to the traditional past of his ancestors.[2] Chris's mother, Sissy, also has "dreamings," "so Sissy lived for a while on her dreamings. Somehow in Sydney with her four kids everything would be better," thus, demonstrating the close connection between mother and son (27).

*Bridge of Triangles* is pervaded by a tension between Aboriginal and non-Aboriginal characters, even though the instance of intermarriage between black and white is high. Nowhere is this more clearly seen than through the flood. After Jack—Sissy's husband and father to her two younger children, Chris and Keith—has an accident and is unable to work or pay the rent on their modest home in the small town, the family moves to a tent on the banks of the river. "The Old Granny," her other daughter, "black Paula," and Sissy know that the river is rising and that a flood is imminent. Jack refuses to listen to Sissy's warning that his family is in danger, and he fails to seek higher ground on the bridge. Throughout

---

[2] The Dreaming is infinite and links the past with the present to determine the future. It is the natural world, especially the land or country to which a person belongs that provides the link between the people and the Dreaming.

the narrative the image of the bridge symbolizes many gaps, chasms, and crossings for Sissy—but most importantly for Chris. The gap between Aboriginal understandings of the land and that of the settlers comes to a climax during the flood:

> Earlier that day, when Sissy had told Jack that the river would flood, her words had been utterly unable to cross that vast gulf between her world and her husband's. . . . Sissy did not curse the river. She cursed the man. Sissy was not one with the river but she understood her mother, and as Sissy would have said, her mother understood the river.
>
> Unlike the man Sissy had an instinct for survival. (55)

The flood is the saturation point for Sissy; afterwards she packs her meager belongings and moves her four children to Sydney to stay with her sister Rose. This physical movement from the country to the city sees Chris cross from the separation stage to the liminal stage of his journey, which is pervaded by further confusion and disorientation as he moves from childhood to adolescence. But Sydney fails to fulfill Sissy's and Chris's dreams of belonging. Aunty Rose's husband, Clarrie, is immediately unwelcoming when the family arrives on the doorstep. Chris's excitement about "a Sydney house with electricity and a T.V." is quickly dashed (66). On Chris's first night in Sydney and "after the grainy disappointment of the T.V.," he is the only person in the house who cannot sleep (68). Chris's restlessness pre-empts his increasing sense of uneasiness in the place where Sissy and he held out so much hope of belonging and freedom (68).

The initial disappointment of Sydney descends into a spiral of hopelessness and despair for the fractured Leeton family. Within weeks Rose's bad-tempered husband, Clarrie, evicts the family from his house, and they are forced to go to an emergency government subsidized housing commission flat on the outskirts of Sydney. As Chris sits in the classroom in the outer suburban school, the only schoolwork he remembers is the teacher drawing a map of Australia on the board and marking where Captain Cook and later Arthur Phillip "had settled the country" (71). In response to this comment, Chris asks, "But what about the people who already lived here?" (71). The teacher's answer only compounds Chris's sense of dislocation and confusion:

> "Well, they didn't really live here. Not properly—not like us. They just moved a little further into the bush. You've got to understand, they just wandered around the place . . ."
>
> Chris concludes by thinking that; . . . something was wrong here, not just in this room but with the whole world . . . this school, this suburb and the whole great sprawling city. (71)

Chris's sense of hopelessness is further compounded by those closest to him: "the boy was being re-formed, like soft clay under the feet of the city: pushed into shapes by others who passed and pressed into his flesh and soul in the darkest of nights" (77). Chris's eldest brother, Joe, falls in with a bad crowd, which has dire consequences. His sister Mary cannot see eye to eye with Sissy and leaves in search of her father, repeating the abusive cycle of her mother and her grandmother as the property of "uncaring white men." The greatest tragedy of the Sydney experience is Aunty Rose's senseless and brutal murder. After this, Sissy is broken and no longer capable of caring for her two remaining sons. After the Department of Welfare intervenes, Chris and his younger brother, Keith, are sent back to the country to live with their father, Jack.

In the final section of the narrative, which completes the end of the liminal stage, Chris is almost broken by his white relatives. As Chris leaves Sydney to return to the country town where he was born and the influence of his white relatives, he notes that he will have "to cross over many bridges under the huge sky with its million lights. To float on black lines like a leaf being carried by a strong and powerful current of a river which flows to the sea" (107). The Leeton family members attempt to force Chris and his brother to live and act like "respectable whites." Chris's father, Jack, is harsh, strict, unaffectionate, and uncommunicative to the extent that Chris wonders "how he would ever get good if he were never allowed to try anything" (113). Granny Leeton insists that the boys be christened for the sake of decency, yet she too shows no affection for her grandsons after this is done. Chris barely manages to pass through this final stage of his journey by "escaping," "surviving," and "dreaming."

Chris's entry into the incorporation stage of his rite of passage is tenuous, but he begins to embrace his right to independence and to re-place himself in a world where he previously felt a sense of exile and loss. As the narrative ends, Chris is beginning another journey. He has made his own decision to go back to Sydney and relocate his mother, who is now his only connection with his Aboriginality. It is his collective identity, not his individuality, that he is seeking: "Christopher Micky, male child of Sissy, Wiradjuri woman and Jack Leeton, Irishman drifted towards his manhood. At the age of fifteen he began his own wanderings" (136).

On one level Chris's growth could be read as being no different than that of any young person from the lowest socioeconomic rung of society and a broken home. However, Burke's work does have an extra layer that relates specifically to Chris finding his place as a young Aboriginal man in postwar Australia. After reading *Bridge of Triangles*, Canadian academic Adam Shoemaker asked, "So what do we do with this? Is *Bridge of Triangles* an existential story of the human condition or is it an overwhelmingly pessimistic literary gestalt? Even more, where and how does Burke place Aboriginality in all of this maelstrom?" (17). Based on his questions, it is clear that Shoemaker needs to consider the sociocultural and historical context in which the narrative is written and the way settler discourse and the Anglo-Western literary canon has positioned and represented Aboriginality in Australia before Aboriginal writers began to represent themselves. Burke responded to Shoemaker's ideas in an interview with Aboriginal author and scholar Anita Heiss that the narrative could not really speak to Shoemaker because he was not an Aboriginal person and could not relate to many of the challenges that being an Aboriginal person in contemporary Australia entails. Ironically, Shoemaker's criticism encapsulates the value of the narrative and is a strong argument for why this work should appear in literary curricula for senior secondary and tertiary students. Shoemaker's metaphor of the "maelstrom" is an excellent description of Burke's main character because he is throughout his liminal stage a turbulent, confused young man thrashing around in the restricted and oppressive space of a nation still governed by an official White Australia Policy as he searches for his Aboriginal identity.[3]

Not only is *Bridge of Triangles* a valuable snapshot of the postwar period from an Aboriginal standpoint but it contains excellent examples of Aboriginal humor, strength, and determination. As scholar Shaobo Xie argues, "Post-colonialism aims to rethink, recuperate and reconstruct racial, ethnic and cultural others," and Burke's bildungsroman, if studied as a work of Aboriginal social and emotional growth towards the formation of an identity that is collective rather than individual, has the potential to open new spaces for readers to see and hear people from a variety of backgrounds and cultural practices (1).

Another significant piece of young adult fiction that focuses on the protagonist's search for identity is Melissa Lucashenko's *Steam Pigs* (1997). Lucashenko's first novel, which is a combination of bildungsroman and autobiography, won her the 1998 Dobbie prize for an Australian woman's first work of fiction. Lucashenko's work, set in the closing decades of the twentieth century, traces the emotional, social, and physical journey of Sue Wilson, the young protagonist. *Steam Pigs* has been widely critiqued by Aboriginal and non-Aboriginal scholars alike. Aboriginal scholars Anita Heiss and Peter Minter identify "the nexus between the literary and the political as a persistent and characteristic element in Aboriginal writing" (2). In Lucashenko's work Heiss and Minter identify Sue's personal journey as political, as it elicits both institutional and individual racism, stereotyping, inequalities that exist in Australia

---

[3] The term *White Australia Policy* comprises of various historical policies that intentionally restricted nonwhite immigration to Australia. From its origins at Federation in 1901, the policies were progressively dismantled between 1949 and 1973. These policies effectively allowed for the privileging of British immigrants for much of the twentieth century.

today, and socially deterministic views of Aboriginality still embedded in contemporary Australian society (2). For non-Aboriginal scholars Ken Gelder and Paul Salzman, *Steam Pigs* is simultaneously "conservative and transgressive" (61). Sue's transgression according to Gelder and Salzman is her metaphorical and physical movement and the fact that her journey follows, to some extent, an Anglo-European trajectory to empowerment and self-actualization.

As a young, fair-skinned Aboriginal woman, Sue Wilson is desperate to begin her journey and escape the small town where she grew up. Her mother, Annette, was raised to be ashamed of her Aboriginal heritage, and Sue was raised knowing that she "had a bit of Aboriginal blood" (9). Consequently, when Sue leaves home she is ambivalent about whether to be proud of her Aboriginal heritage (9). Sue's leaving home and her ambivalence about her identity mark the separation stage and the beginning of the journey through her rites/rights/writes of passage. As Sue moves through the sometimes bleak, sometimes dangerous, sometimes humorous liminal stage, she gives a detached account of herself as a young Aboriginal woman in transition, en route to the incorporation stage: "very young. Along with most poor girls her age, she would have gone to extraordinary lengths to be admitted to the Mythic world of work" (2). It is while Sue works in a bar in a working-class outer suburb of Brisbane that she meets Roger, a young Murri man, who is an Aboriginal Studies student at a local university.[4] Roger is also fair skinned, but, unlike Sue, he is secure in his Aboriginal identity. He tells Sue, "Where I come from we just say we're all Aboriginal, eh? None of that half-caste, quarter-caste bullshit. Like I've got Scots and Irish too, I don't deny that but my heart's with the blackfellas" (21).

As Sue enters the liminal stage of her rite of passage, a journey that forms the bulk of the narrative, Roger teaches her about Aboriginal culture and history. Sue admits that she had "no clue" about her Aboriginal history and culture until "Roger woke her up" (52–54). However, as Roger's dependence on drugs and alcohol increases, he becomes increasingly abusive. Despite the abusive relationship, Sue finds herself, near the end of the novel, secure enough in her Aboriginal identity to leave Roger and pursue a different path to independence, liberation, and reincorporation. When Sue leaves Roger, she seeks refuge with two gay white feminists whom she encountered initially through self-defense classes. The white feminists act as a catalyst for Sue by providing examples of choice and the right to safety, security, education, and good health. The impetus to embrace the same rights and to access the same privileges as settler Australians comes from within the character of Sue.

---

[4] The Murri are Indigenous Australians who occupy most of the state that is now called Queensland.

As the narrative draws to a close, Sue embarks on a formal education at university. Her rite of passage, however, was already completed before she entered the realm of formal university education, as she had already journeyed through separation and withdrawal, confusion, alienation, and disorientation to incorporation, recovery, and rediscovery. *Steam Pigs* ends with Sue finding her sense of place and belonging in Brisbane:

> The Murri girl saw the city through different more confident eyes, saw for the first time the possibility of claiming it as her own, a part of her psyche. . . . It was Yuggera country[5]—shining towers of wealth or no—and that meant she had a connection to work from. No matter what monied artefacts they put on the surface, her belonging roots reached deep into the soil anchoring her like an old rivergum. (239–40)

Non-Aboriginal critic Nathanael O'Reilly is critical of Sue's escape and subsequent empowerment influenced by liberal, Euro-Australian social movements, such as feminism:

> The fact that Sue is "saved" and enlightened by liberal, educated urban whites, rather than her fellow Indigenous Australians sends a disconcerting message about the relationship between Indigenous and non-Indigenous Australians. Ultimately, *Steam Pigs* suggests that the solutions for Indigenous social problems are to be provided by university educated whites, a relationship that perpetuates the colonialist relationship between non-Indigenous and Indigenous Australians. (10)

But why do feminism, tertiary education, and inner-city living compromise Sue's Aboriginal identity? And why does Sue's impetus to embrace social movements such as feminism attract criticism from literary scholars such as O'Reilly, Gelder, and Salzman?

By constructing Sue as a representation of contemporary Aboriginality, Lucashenko breaks free from what Michel Foucault called the "Western order of things." Settler discourse and the previous representations of Aboriginals in the Euro-Australian literary canon have relegated Aboriginals to victim or deficit spaces. Sue refuses to continue to be a victim or to feel inferior to non-Aboriginal Australians. Her physical journey to the inner city and to university and her emotional and intellectual journey to reconnect with her Aboriginal heritage, while embracing social movements of empowerment such as feminism, make her rite of passage complete. Sue's empowerment through education and social mobility challenges the existing "colonist relationship" between non-Aboriginal

---

[5] Yuggera people are the traditional owners of the land where the city of Brisbane is built.

and Aboriginal Australians, as Sue does not conform to the Aboriginal stereotypes. While Sue's trajectory may be a well-worn path for many settler Australians, freedom of movement, access to education, and the ability and means to control one's destiny were systematically denied to Aboriginals until late into the twentieth century. Sue's movements physically, intellectually, and metaphorically break new ground and challenge existing colonial relationships and stereotypes; in this way, the narrative is neither conservative as Gelder and Salzman suggest nor disconcerting as O'Reilly contends. Sue emerges at the end of the novel as an agent of her own destiny.

As with the two previous works, *Swallow the Air* (2006), Tara June Winch's award-winning debut novel (2004 David Unaipon Award), revolves around a physical and metaphorical journey. The narrative, set in early twenty-first-century Australia and told through the voice of the protagonist, May Gibson, explores modern Australian society from an Aboriginal perspective. In structure, Winch's work differs from that of Burke's or Lucashenko's in that it is a short story cycle.[6] American literary scholar James Nagel points out that the origins of the short story cycle are "patently multicultural, deriving, perhaps, both from ethnic cross-fertilisation . . . and from a shared legacy reaching back to ancient oral traditions" (492). Nagel also argues that from the 1990s onwards the short story cycle "became the genre of choice for emerging writers from a variety of ethnic and economic backgrounds" (492). In her article "Identity in Community and Ethnic Short Story Cycles," Spanish scholar R. G. Davis suggests that ethnic writers find the short story cycle useful as "a metaphor for the fragmentation and multiplicity" that "highlights the subjectivity of experience and understanding and allows multiple impressionistic perspectives and fragmentation of linear history" (4). Fragmentation and multiplicity are important themes in Winch's narrative.

The Gibson family and its history are fragmented because of the colonial legacies of the past. In an attempt to fill these gaps in her family history and establish connections to her country, May experiments during her liminal phase with different ways of being. Many of the episodes in *Swallow the Air* introduce new characters that May encounters on her journey to belong and to piece together what it means to be a young Aboriginal woman in today's Australia. Other characters, such as the elderly Aboriginal matriarch Joyce, "Aunty," and May's brother Billy, appear and reappear throughout.

The death of May's mother, which is revealed at the beginning of the novel, allows readers a glimpse of May's character and how she and those

---

[6] A short story cycle is a literary work composed of shorter texts that though individually complete and autonomous are interrelated in a coherent whole according to one or more organizing principle(s) (Dunn and Morris, xiii).

closest to her choose to cope with the loss of a loved one. May Gibson is fifteen when her mother commits suicide. She and her brother Billy are taken in by Aunty, their kindly, but vulnerable, friend. Billy's and May's response to loss takes them on different paths. Billy takes a dangerous, destructive path, fuelled by anger and substances. May goes her own way to search for her identity. The death of her mother and the subsequent circumstances that arise while Billy and May are living with Aunty launch May into the separation stage of her journey through her rites of passage. Along the way, May writes an account of herself in a voice that is a mixture of childish innocence, disillusion, and resilience.

May's sense of belonging to Aboriginal society and culture is connected to the stories her mother has told her. She tells her readers, "I felt Aboriginal because Mum made me proud to be, told me I got magic and courage from Gundyarri, the spirit man. . . . I felt I belonged but when Mum left I stopped *being* Aboriginal. I stopped feeling like I belonged. Anywhere" (97; italics in the original). Telling and retelling family and traditional stories is a central theme in Winch's narrative. These stories reinforce the legacy of ancient oral traditions that connect contemporary Aboriginal culture to the past. A clear example of this is the story "Cloud Busting," in which May retells a story her mother told her about her grandmother, whom she never met, but whose memory is an integral part of May's identity.

The context of the relationships between black and white Australians, both past and present, is the key to understanding the characters in *Swallow the Air*. As May loses her sense of belonging, she enters the turbulent and chaotic liminal stage of her journey. She describes her Aunty's house as a "place of grog [alcohol] and fists" where she cannot stay (53). May drifts into drugs and crime with other young aimless Aboriginal characters who also feel that they do not belong. Like Burke's and Lucashenko's protagonists, May has inherited a collective identity from the previous generation, where the mistreatment of Aborigines was sanctioned through government policies. Readers learn from May that her mother was a "beaten person" (88) and that most of her siblings were forcibly removed to missions (23). While, officially, May no longer lives in this era of discrimination, mistreatment of Aboriginals still continues, and a substantial part of May's journey is centered on her still bearing her mother's sense of grief and loss, as well as dealing with her own sadness over the loss of her mother and later her close friend, Johnny. It is important to read the anger, substance abuse, and crime on the part of some of the Aboriginal characters that Winch constructs as part of a generational response to institutionalized racism and mistreatment, rather than innate dysfunctional behavior on the part of Aboriginals, as has been suggested in the discourses of health and education recently.

As May drifts, teetering on the brink of a destructive path, she gravitates to "the Block" in inner city Redfern.[7] It is here that she meets and is saved from a bleak future by an elderly Aboriginal matriarch, Joyce. Joyce's presence and influence on May reinforces the continuing importance of elders in Aboriginal society. Joyce tells May the history of Redfern, which differs dramatically from the official, recorded history of the area, and this Aboriginal standpoint on a certain place, combined with Joyce's nonstandard English interspersed with some Aboriginal words, highlights the continued importance of narrative by Aboriginal elders to educate younger generations. While Joyce is not highly educated in a formal sense, she has wisdom that she bestows on May and that cannot be taught in Western-style classrooms. Joyce discourages May from trying to find her sense of belonging from "the Block" and encourages her to search for her Aboriginal relatives and her white father. Joyce tells May, "You got people that you gotta find, things you gotta learn" (104).

Despite May's initial sense of isolation from her Aboriginal heritage and her overwhelming sense of unbelonging as she begins her search, she is further nourished and educated by Aboriginal elders she meets while on her journey. Through these encounters Winch brings to the forefront the continuing tradition of Aboriginal youth being taught and influenced by their elders. A moving and evocative example of this is seen through May's meeting with an older Aboriginal woman, Isabelle (Issy), who spends her time between the Aboriginal Tent Embassy in Canberra and her homelands in New South Wales. May introduces Issy to the reader as a woman of dignity and as worthy of respect. The introduction also continues the theme of colonial imposition: "The church gave her the name Isabelle. Her mother gave her the name Galing, which means water dreaming. She is an elder, and that means she has responsibility to protect what belongs to her people. To teach" (145). Issy takes up a saltbush branch and "draws" the philosophy of Aboriginal Dreaming on the ground, once again continuing a practice that predates the colonial invasion. She tells May that everything is sacred, inside the circle and outside the circle; she says that we should look after both areas the same: "She takes the branch again and outlines the circle twice, each circle a little bigger than the other, and then she draws smaller circles from the first circle inwards. She makes another circle the same, next to it and joins the two with a short line. She says that we need to come back. Listen" (147). Issy tells May that if she wants to find her Aboriginal relatives, the Gibsons,

---

[7] By the 1940s a large Aboriginal population had established itself in Redfern, Sydney, and the area was the location of a number of civil rights movements and protests as well as the birthplace of a number of important Aboriginal services that now exist nationally, such as the Aboriginal Medical Service and the Aboriginal Legal Service.

she must follow the Lachlan River, the Dreaming name for which is Bila (meaning river) snake. At the time, May does not fully understand the second circular representation that Issy has drawn in the dust, but she nevertheless senses the power of the elder woman and takes her advice.

In May's quest to belong and find her identity, she takes an actual and a metaphorical journey. Old Issy's circles in the dust are symbolic of May's journey, which begins and ends in exactly the same place. As May completes this circle, she enters the incorporation stage of her rites of passage and recovers and rediscovers her rightful place as a young Aboriginal woman in contemporary Australia. The physical journey takes May from Wollongong on Australia's east coast, where she was born and later loses her mother, to Darwin, in the Northern Territory, in search of her father; to Redfern in inner-city Sydney; to Lake Cowal, the Lachlan River, and Euabalong Mission in central New South Wales; and finally, transformed and secure, May completes the circle of her journey and her rite of passage when she returns to Wollongong. The metaphorical journey is May's social and emotional growth, which is ultimately enhanced by those she meets on the way. More importantly, May's journey through the liminal stage of her rites of passage from unbelonging to belonging is contributed to, and enabled by, both Aboriginal and non-Aboriginal characters. As Australian scholar Gillian Dooley notes, "May finds kindness among white male truckies as well as crowded Indigenous city households and illegal immigrants" (16). These influences reflect the fluid and hybrid nature of contemporary Aboriginality and also that of contemporary Australia.

Some of the chapters in *Swallow the Air* are retrospectives or, as Australian writer and scholar of autobiography Molly Travers describes, "flashback chapters" that describe memories of May's mother, the Dreaming stories from her country, and family narratives told to her by her mother. Linear time is fragmented as Winch explores formative episodes in May's life and the lives of significant others she encounters as she is driven to piece together her ruptured past in order to be whole and belong in the present. As May journeys through the liminal stage, these memories are the only legacy she has left from her broken family and Aboriginal heritage (3). May's "flashbacks" are interspersed with her often chaotic and restless present. She draws on these memories that connect her, however precariously at times, to her mother's Aboriginality. They are a source of emotional nourishment that sustains her through what seems, at times, an unsure future in her quest to belong.

As May's journey is about to end, she meets two significant Aboriginal men who further connect her to her culture. The first is an elderly man, Graham, whom May describes as having "the blackest skin I'd ever seen" (167). Graham wears a checked cowboy shirt and an Akubra hat, and he tells May he loves the city. Travers reads Graham's attire as "symbols of loss of Aboriginal identity," but Graham's interaction with May suggests otherwise (5). He tells May of the removal of blacks from traditional lands to the missions in 1947 and the subsequent ill treatment of Aboriginal children at the hands of the church. He attributes the violence and substance abuse of some Aboriginals today to whites: "those governments just put another number, nother cross on the list. Lockin up bloody young fellas, why do they have prisons? So they don't have to think about it, about people's problems. . . . They still tryin to do it, kill us fellas, that always been the plan. . . . Bloody millenniums come and gone and they still can't treat our people right" (171). Cousin Percy Gibson is the second significant Aboriginal man that May encounters. Travers describes Percy as "the one Aboriginal we see who has made it into the white lifestyle, drinking lime juice instead of beer, and eager to get off to that middle class occupation: golf" (6). Consequently, Travers reads Percy as having "made it" because he conforms to "white middle-class" definitions of success, and, as with Graham, the inference is that Percy's ability to access settler privilege constitutes a loss of culture. Travers' comment evidences the stereotypical and negative images that some settler Australians still hold towards Aboriginals, as her reference to Percy not drinking alcohol implies that most Aboriginals do. It also demonstrates that some settler Australians expect Aboriginals to act in certain ways that conform to the settlers' expectations of what it means to be Aboriginal.

Such expectations are often at odds with the reality of being Aboriginal in late twentieth- and early twenty-first-century Australia. The mark of authenticity for Aboriginals as far as many settlers are concerned is that they reside in communities in remote parts of the country, have very dark skin, speak an Aboriginal language, and practice a precolonial lifestyle. Colonialism has made life difficult for most Aboriginals, but Aboriginal culture has survived and evolved in other spaces and places as the journeys of the aforementioned protagonists demonstrate. Many young Aboriginals in Australia today are bicultural. This is not a deficit, and it does not make a person "less Aboriginal." What Travers reads as Percy's success from a settler perspective has come at great cost, as Percy laments to May that their family's history is fragmented and that when he was growing up he was forced to "act white": "There's a big missing hole between this place and the place, that people, that something you're looking for . . . *we weren't allowed to be Aboriginal*" (181).

While the Aboriginal relatives May follows to the Bila snake may not be as welcoming as she hoped, the meeting does help her place herself as an Aboriginal Australian and reclaim and recover that sense of belonging that she lost when she lost her mother. May reconsiders old Issy's drawing in the sand with newfound knowledge gained from her journey:

And it all makes sense to me now. Issy's drawing in the sand, boundaries between the land and the water, *us*. . . . This land *is* belonging,
all of it for all of us.

     . . . to Joyce . . . to Charlie, to Gary, to Johnny, to Issy, to Percy,
to Billy, to Aunty, to my nannas, to their great nannas' neighbours.
They belong to the spirits. To people I will never even know. I give
them to my mother. (183)

May is incorporated into and re-enters Aboriginal society. She is strength-
ened by a collective history and identity that she has discovered, and her
metaphorical and physical journeys are complete. May's growth is evident in her closing reflection in the final chapter when she returns to
Wollongong where her journey began: "this place still owns us, still owns
our history, my brother's and my own, Aunty's too. Mum's. They are
part of this place; I know now." (194).

Burke, Lucashenko, and Winch all present different formation experiences in their novels, but common threads run through each. Each
protagonist experiences separation, a sense of disequilibrium, and unbelonging. All three novels are works of social realism with the common
themes of a search for identity, the undertaking of physical and emotional
journeys, social and emotional growth towards adulthood, and finding
a sense of place. Memories, dreams, circles, and flashbacks are recurring
motifs in each of the characters' movements from unbelonging to belonging. Through the characters' journeys to belong and understand their
place as young Aboriginals in Australian society, readers are offered alternative perspectives to many of Australia's national metanarrative, such as
"the land of opportunity" or "a nation founded in peace." The three protagonists are agentic black subjects who respond to and challenge previous literary stereotyping and misrepresentation of Aboriginal characters in
Australia's literary landscape.

While the liminal stages of the main characters' rites of passage occur
in a variety of ways, their re-entry to the sociocultural group from which
they previously felt estranged involves more than a quest to discover and
embrace individuality. For the young Aboriginal Australians Chris, Sue,
and May, this quest involves an exploration of the hybrid and fluid nature
of contemporary Aboriginality, an understanding and acceptance of their
sense of being in relation to collective family history, and a sense of place
where they now belong.

Published Aboriginal literature in Australia has had a short but
intense history, with nascent beginnings in the mid-1960s and a blos-
soming in the post-Mabo era of the early 1990s to the present. The
Aboriginal literary canon has emerged with a different sound and voice
than the Anglo-Australian canon that dominated the Australian literary
landscape. This body of literature needs to be read through a theoretical

lens that acknowledges the sociocultural and historical contexts in which Aboriginal authors live and construct their narratives. The three works discussed and others like them in the growing Aboriginal literary canon serve as a counterdiscourse to the colonial positioning of Aboriginals as primitive, exotic, lazy, simple, and isolated. They offer an alternative read beyond the Anglo-Australian literary canon, and they develop critical literacy skills that challenge essentialist views of Aboriginals and examine existing power structures and the ideologies inherent in language written from different cultural perspectives.

# Works Cited

Burke, John Muk Muk. *Bridge of Triangles*. St. Lucia: University of Queensland Press, 1994.

Davis, Rocío. "Identity and Community in Ethnic Short Story Cycles." *Ethnicity and the American Short Story*, ed. Julie Brown, 3–23. New York: Garland, 1997.

Dooley, Gillian. Review of *Swallow the Air*, by Tara June Winch. *Adelaide Review*, February 16, 2007, 16.

Dunn, Maggie, and Ann Morris. *The Composite Novel: The Short Story Cycle in Transition*. New York: Twayne, 1995.

Elliot, Tim. "Interview: Anita Heiss." *Sydney Morning Herald*, April 7, 2012.

Gelder, Ken, and Paul Salzman. *After the Celebration: Australian Fiction 1989–2007*. Carlton, VIC: University of Melbourne Press, 2009.

Foucault, Michel. *The Order of Things: An Archaeology of Human Sciences*, translator anonymous. London: Tavistock, 1970.

Heiss, Anita. *Dhuuluu-Yala to Talk Straight*. Canberra, ACT: Aboriginal Studies Press, 2003.

Heiss, Anita, and Peter Minter, eds. *Anthology of Australian Aboriginal Literature*. Montreal: McGill-Queen's University Press, 2008.

Kennedy, Gerald, ed. *Modern American Short Story Sequences: Composite Fictions and Fictive Communities*. New York: Cambridge University Press, 1995.

Lucashenko, Melissa. *Steam Pigs*. St. Lucia: University of Queensland Press, 1997.

Nagel, James. *The Contemporary American Short Story Cycle*. Baton Rouge: Louisiana State University Press, 2001.

O'Reilly, Nathanael. "Exploring Indigenous Identity in Suburbia: Melissa Lucashenko's *Steam Pigs*." *Journal for the Association of the Studies of Australian Literature* 10 (2010): 1–13.

Shoemaker, Adam. "A Bridge Too Far." *Australian Book Review* 165 (1994): 16–17.

Travers, Molly. "Swallow the Air by Tara June Winch." *CAE Book Groups* (2007): 3–15.

Van Gennup, Arnold. *The Rites of Passage*. Translated by Monika B. Vizedom and Gabrielle L. Caffee. 1909. Reprint, Chicago: University of Chicago Press, 1960.

Winch, Tara June. *Swallow the Air*. St. Lucia: University of Queensland Press, 2006.

Xie, Shaobo. "Rethinking the Identity of Cultural Otherness: The Discourse of Difference as an Unfinished Project." In *Voice of the Other: Children's Literature and the Postcolonial Context*, ed. Roderick McGillis, 1–16. New York: Garland, 2000.

# 7: Humor in Contemporary Aboriginal Adult Fiction

*Paula Anca Farca*

DEPICTIONS OF RACE and gender stereotypes abound in various areas of Australian Aboriginal literature. This literature usually addresses the writers' responses to the injustice done to Aboriginal people by whites and the blatant racism that creeps into Australian society even today. Given the seriousness of these depictions, Aboriginal writers have seldom employed humor, making it a rather unexplored field in Aboriginal literature and criticism. Recently, though, an increasing number of Aboriginal authors have addressed issues of social injustice and racism by creating humorous situations that help readers recognize white Australians' immoral behavior. Memoirs by Kenny Laughton (*Not Quite Men, No Longer Boys* [1999]), Robert Lowe (*The Mish* [2002]), and Mabel Edmund (*No Regrets* [1995]), novels by Mudrooroo (*Doctor Wooreddy's Prescription for Enduring the Ending of the World* [1999], *Doin Wildcat* [1988]), poetry by Samuel Wagan Watson (*Of Muse, Meandering, and Midnight* [2012]), and plays by Kevin Gilbert (*The Cherry Pickers* [1988]) and Jack Davis (*No Sugar* [1986], *The Dreamers* [1996]) are some of the genres in which Aboriginal authors have used humor. Leon Rappoport, a critic who writes on humor and stereotypes, praises those who address "sexual, racial, and other forbidden topics . . . by situating them in the context of humor, [because] the tensions that are aroused can be released as laughter" (50). Triggering an instant and natural reaction from readers, humor attracts a wide variety of audiences to Aboriginal literature because it presents the absurd and vicious nature of stereotypes, teaches lessons about the creativity of Aboriginal people, and suggests that hope and optimism characterize Aboriginal life.

Contemporary female Aboriginal novelists, such as Vivienne Cleven, Gayle Kennedy, Marie Munkara, and Anita Heiss, investigate more closely than any male writer the lives of minorities, especially Aboriginal women, teenagers, children, and homosexuals. More than that, each author pushes an Aboriginal and non-Aboriginal audience to consider forms of discrimination other than racial. Novels such as Cleven's *Bitin' Back* (2001), Munkara's *Every Secret Thing* (2009), Kennedy's *Me, Antman and*

*Fleabag* (2007), all winners of the David Unaipon Award, and Heiss's *Not Meeting Mr. Right* (2007), use humor to address gender discrimination, homophobia, cross-dressing, gender relationships, governmental policies toward Aboriginal veterans, proselytism, and the long-term impact of Christian indoctrination. These women writers employ humor to counter a tradition that viewed Aboriginals as dehumanized and inferior. This is achieved by creating empowered Aboriginal characters that critique these harmful labels by "talking back" to those who ridicule them. The comic stories, exaggerated events, and funny conversations between characters underscore the effectiveness of humor to critique the harsh social and political tensions of contemporary Aboriginal existence. Though it does not make the social problems these novels address disappear, humor raises awareness of these issues, and it potentially breaks down barriers inside and outside the Aboriginal community.

Set in Mandamooka, a small town in Australia, Vivienne Cleven's *Bitin' Back* brings together issues such as homophobia, drug trafficking, cross-dressing, and discrimination against women, and Aboriginals and exposes the prejudices that exist today, particularly in country towns. Despite the gravity of her subject matter, Cleven addresses these issues in a humorous, relatable, and straightforward fashion. In narrating her protagonist's experiences, Cleven reveals the community's representations of masculinity and femininity and ridicules assumptions about race, ethnicity, and gender. As a rule, the inhabitants of Mandamooka reject or render as inferior anyone who is not white and heterosexual; women are also considered powerless, sexual objects who are subjected to preconceived notions of physical beauty. Cleven employs irony and parody to entertain readers while critiquing what she describes. Humor helps Cleven analyze the conflicts among characters in an optimistic light, allowing readers to accept the differences between people and rethink their hostile preconceptions. At the same time, humor has a parodic quality of subverting the situations, a rhetorical device that Cleven employs with hilarious scenes to criticize the absurdity of racism and stereotypes.

Cleven filters the events of the novel through Mavis Dooley, an Indigenous bingo-playing mother who struggles to make a living and provide her son, Nevil, the local football star, with a decent life in the poor rural community. Despite the many obstacles Mavis faces, she uses humor as a way to deal positively with the situation around her. Mavis is feisty enough to counteract the town's gossip and sensitive enough to accept what is happening to her own family. When Nevil starts wearing women's clothes and makeup and announces he is the famous West Indian–born writer Jean Rhys, Mavis is shocked, but she tries to convince herself and the rest of the town that her son is not homosexual. Despite her best efforts, she endures difficult experiences throughout the story to save her son from the ridicule of an old-fashioned and obtuse community. Cleven describes the tensions between whites and Aboriginals that often manifest in verbal abuse and lead to discrimination; she suggests that humor through its irony and parody can be a coping mechanism for Aboriginals to deal with such acute discrimination.

From the beginning of the novel, Mavis reveals an identifiable humanity as she assesses the changes her son undergoes. When Mavis comes to the realization that her son may be homosexual, she thinks to herself: "*one of em homos. Well, they don't call em that any more. Gay, that's the word people use. Jesus Christ! Can ya wake up gay?*" (Cleven, 6; italics in original). In reality, Mavis's comments uncover her fear that her son could indeed be a homosexual and a cross-dresser. After Mavis refuses to believe that her son is writer Jean Rhys, she reacts the only way she knows how, namely by making a joke to her son about race and gender: "Yeah, if you're not Nevil then call me a white woman!" (2). Her joke reveals that she understands her reality well enough to know she is definitely not a privileged white woman; ergo, her son, Nevil, is not Jean Rhys.

Despite her conservative views, Mavis tries to cope with Nevil's new identity by framing her son's unprecedented transformation within familiar contexts and memories of people who supposedly crossed genders and races. Mavis's inner thoughts uncover her charming humor, harmless spontaneity, and continuous efforts to be a good mother to Nevil. Before she judges her son too harshly, Mavis weighs the situation:

> *Ya got white fellas* [men] *sayin they black. I just dunno what's racin round in they heads. Cos, when ya black, well, things get a bit tricky like. See now, if ya got a white fella* [man] *then paint him black n let the man loose on the world I reckon he won't last long. Yep, be fucked from go. But when ya got a black fella sayin he's a woman—a white woman at that! Well, the ol dice just rolls n another direction. Ain't no one gonna let the man . . . boy get away whit that! This here is dangerous business.* (5; italics in the original)

Making sense of her son's cross-dressing in relation to similar metamorphoses, Mavis explains that a white man who paints his face black cannot resist dealing with the realities of Aboriginals, given his upbringing and education. His "downfall" has nothing to do with the rejection of the black community but with his inability to cope with the harsh lives of Aboriginals. But if Nevil, an Aboriginal man, suddenly decides to become a white woman, then the white community will be outraged and will consider this transformation a personal affront. Despite white society's resistance, such transformation could potentially subvert traditional gender and racial depictions of both Aboriginals and whites. Thus, Nevil's cross-dressing could be viewed as a victory for Aboriginals, as he has found a way to parody the rigid gender codes of white society.

Mavis's later story about a young Aboriginal girl whose skin was so white that the government officials decide to separate her from her family places Nevil's transformation in the middle of white society's racial fears. The story of the young girl's forced removal reminds audiences of the Stolen Generation. As before, Mavis uses humor to critique past government actions. The story's humorous twist involves the girl's skin darkening as she grows older and the inability of white society to accept her black skin to the point where the officials send her back to her Aboriginal family:

> *She* [Phyllis Swan] *were parted from her own mob* [family] *by em government wankers* [jerks]*; they reckon she too white for the others, eh. Too white, load a goon* [Aboriginal] . . . *When she growed up a bit more her skin turned up real charcoal like . . . Black as Harry's arse. The wankers say: she too black for us, send the girl back. So she go to her mob. They didn't want her. The whites didn't want her. She was sorta stuck in the middle like.* (6; italics in the original)

Mavis's humor and verbosity turn a sad story about an Aboriginal child, who is rejected by both white and Aboriginal society, into a funny story about the government's questionable choices. The look of Phyllis's skin results in her being tossed back and forth between two races, ethnicities, and cultures, and the fact that she is not welcome in either community reflects the stereotypical and superficial thinking of both races. Phyllis, thus, shares her fate with Jean Rhys's protagonist Antoinette from *Wide Sargasso Sea*, whose skin is too white for the Afro-Caribbean populations on the island and too dark for the English. These examples show that this small Australian community is not ready for Nevil's dramatic changes, yet Mavis's inner narration is so amusing and effective that it criticizes the stereotypes formulated by both whites and Aboriginals.

The inhabitants of the town, including police officers, associate Aboriginals with what they consider the worst activity, and they automatically accuse Nevil and Trevor, Nevil's friend from the city, of drug trafficking and inappropriate sexual behavior. Mavis disagrees with Nevil's cross-dressing because it contradicts her belief system, so she tries to cure his supposed homosexuality by helping him regain his masculine side. Nevil's uncle Booty, a strong supporter of patriarchy, organizes what he considers to be manly activities, such as pig hunting and boxing matches, that will divert Nevil from his desire to dress as a woman and rekindle strengths such as aggressiveness and machismo. Booty's insistence that Nevil attend his football practice and match so that he could once again be the star of the town illustrates his efforts to restore the boy's masculinity. Booty's exaggerated gestures hide his anxieties about homosexuality and his fear that Nevil's status in the community will be lost forever. Both Booty and Mavis think that Nevil will become less of a man if he dresses like a woman and starts going out with men. Homosexuality is an inconceivable concept for the traditional community of Mandamooka.

Nevil's sexuality is not the only issue Cleven addresses in *Bitin' Back*. In the novel female beauty—white and Aboriginal—is discussed. Most of the novel's characters apply racist concepts to feminine beauty and agree that white women are more appealing than Aboriginal women; however, when these concepts are further analyzed, readers can see humor being used to deflect pain and promote optimism. Mavis describes herself as fat and common and recognizes that although Dotty Reedman, her greatest enemy, is mean, she is a sexy white woman. Dotty competes with Mavis in each aspect of their lives: bingo, motherhood, physical beauty, success, and Terry Thompson's attention. Reinforcing this limited framework, Mavis perpetuates the stereotype that white people are physically attractive and black people are ugly.[1] Mavis, who is jealous of Dotty's looks and forward behavior, watches her flirt with Terry, an Aboriginal man, who also courts Mavis: "She's all tarted up. Dirty blonde hair high as an ant hill. Mini-skirt. . . . Face painted up. . . . Blood-red lips, blue eyeshada, rust-colour cheeks . . . n eyelashes so long they look like they gonna sweep the floor" (95). Mavis compares Dotty's appealing look with her own appearance and concludes: "*A woman just can't win. . . . Yep, was never beautiful by any means. A scrubber. Bush pig* [ugly woman] . . . *real pretty, pretty as a punch in the face . . . plain, fat, whit gooby lips, fuzzy hair like a pot scourer, a boxer's nose, thin black moustache on me top lip n skin*" (95; italics in the original). Mavis's self-description reinforces white feminine beauty and degrades Aboriginal beauty. While Mavis's humor and endearing self-description expose her vulnerability in front of a social and political system that perpetuates stereotypes, they also provide her a response to these realities with a certain degree of optimism.

Cleven addresses women's issues further by focusing on women's social status in contemporary society. In *Bitin' Back* Cleven highlights the low social status of Aboriginal women within local communities today. An

---

[1] Michael Dodson describes the cruel realities of Aboriginals today and their relationship with white Australians and the dominant culture and argues that the Aboriginals are subservient to the people of Anglo-European descent: "because Aboriginality has been defined as a relation, Indigenous peoples have rarely come into a genuine relationship with non-Indigenous peoples, because a relationship requires two, not just one and its mirror" (37). Since white Australians want to recognize themselves in *everybody else* living in *their* country, they dismiss people who look, talk, and live differently from them. The three authors under discussion do not describe Aboriginals who have lost their identities altogether, but the pressures of the dominant culture are so acute that they accept the labels given to them. Many Indigenous characters in Cleven's novel, including Mavis, feel less beautiful, less powerful, and less successful than their Anglo-European neighbors and acquaintances.

episode in a local bar involving Mavis, her best friend, Gwen Hinch, and Darryl Kane, Gwen's former lover, reveals just how susceptible Aboriginal women are to gossip and attacks from white men and women. After her affair with the married Darryl ended, Gwen suffers the consequences of the wicked gossip and rumors spread by him. Darryl, an adulterer, manages to maintain his position of an honorable white man while Gwen as an Aboriginal woman does not benefit from the same privileges and is considered sexually promiscuous. Even more, when Mavis and Gwen confront Darryl's wife about the affair, she confesses that her husband "doesn't do *that* with . . . black women" (98–99, emphasis mine). Clearly, Samantha Kane ignores her husband's adultery because she considers Aboriginal women inferior; however, Mavis knows how to "bite back" and get her revenge on Gwen. After Darryl struggles to separate Gwen and Samantha, who start a catfight, Mavis beats Darryl and humiliates him in front of the whole bar by showing everyone that a woman—particularly an Aboriginal woman—can be physically stronger than a man, Aboriginal or non-Aboriginal. The stereotype that white men are invincible is further shaken when readers discover that Darryl, not Trevor, is the drug dealer chased by the police.

With its colorful characters and engaging dialogue, *Bitin' Back* educates and scolds, entertains and raises awareness, and challenges and expands the genre of Aboriginal women's writing. Cleven takes a chance and addresses homophobia and gender stereotypes in a humorous new light. She reverses some of these stereotypes and criticizes others by creating comical moments that deconstruct and parody themselves. Even the secret around Nevil's supposed homosexuality, which sets the whole novel in motion, leaves room for further parodies. Readers discover that Nevil's transformation into Jean Rhys and her protagonist Antoinette is part of an experiment and research for his first novel rather than an identity crisis; Nevil's fiction alludes to individuals like Mavis who are trapped in repressive environments. Cleven's novel ends with a metafictional touch, promising a continuation of Mavis's story through Nevil's novel and his protagonist Lucinda Lawrey.

Cleven does not stand alone in her effective use of humor to tackle stereotypical images of Aboriginals. Marie Munkara sets her first novel, *Every Secret Thing*, on an Indigenous mission in the Tiwi Islands and focuses on the hilarious discrepancies between the "mission mob" and the "bush mob" in order to reveal disturbing differences between the two cultures. Confessing in an interview that she "didn't actually set out to make it [the novel] funny . . . [but just] sarcastic," Munkara directs her cutting irony toward Catholic priests and missionaries with the specific intent to ridicule them (quoted in Gosford). From light episodes such as the Aboriginal children's questioning why black angels do not exist, why Eve did not eat the snake instead of the apple, or why a baby's skin turns darker every day, readers then move to serious issues such as proselytism, the priests' violent sexual abuse geared especially toward Aboriginal women, and the introduction of alcohol to the bush mob. The series of issues presented to the reader paint the priests and nuns not as God's messengers sent to bring civilization to Aboriginals but as violent savages who seek to wipe out Aboriginal identity and culture. Their mission, Munkara shows, becomes a locus in which they release their own sins and frustrations. The second mission featured in the novel, ironically named the Garden of Eden, where half-caste children, the products of the priests' sins and wild urges, are sent, is another form of aggressive colonialism. While the subject matter of Munkara's novel uncovers colonial tensions and cruel abuses, the playful and sarcastic manner in which these troublesome issues are delivered proves effective. Humor attracts various audiences to the novel and provides a venue for Aboriginal characters to challenge the forced indoctrination carried out by white missionaries.

The first sentence of the novel, "It had been a shit day for Sister Annunciata and Sister Clavie" sets the sarcastic tone of Munkara's humorous account (1). The author offers the perspectives of the nuns first, indicating that the missionaries impose control, but she counters this initial stance by showing that trouble can occur rapidly in paradise. The nuns' turmoil is caused by several Aboriginal boys, conveniently renamed Matthew, Mark, Luke, and John, who run away to the bush camp, and by Ignatius, who is not allowed to use the toilet and, thus, releases his noxious fumes on purpose, just minutes before his Most Distinguished, the Bishop, arrives at the mission. From the start, readers understand that the incompatibility of Christian doctrine and Aboriginal spirituality is a source of friction between the two cultures. Moreover, the imposition of a foreign religious system on Indigenous people is meant to destabilize their cultural bonds and shake the trust in their identity and culture. This incompatibility is obvious when representatives of the two cultures comment on one another both publicly and privately. The missionaries, who regard the bush mob as uneducated savages, try to impose English as an official language, because they view Aboriginal language as "gibberish" (2) and believe that the children's reluctance to learn English and become immersed in the Bible relates to how "the tympanic membranes in the bush mob's ears were tuned to another frequency" (6). The teachings of the nuns and priests are so ineffective that Aboriginal children interpret and deconstruct Catholicism in simple terms: "you could murder or rape and pillage, do what you liked, but if you sucked up to his Godliness's arse and showed even a modicum of repentance your slate would be wiped clean" (9).

The sad irony is that the priests and nuns understand and practice Catholicism by following *ad literam* the simplistic conjecture of Aboriginal children. Not only do the priests rape young Aboriginal women and girls and force pregnancies on them but many of the missionaries also turn to Catholicism for the wrong reasons. The missionaries think their immoral behavior toward Aboriginals, whom they believe to be illiterate, animal-like people, is justified and will be forgiven. Brother Michael tries to cure "the lascivious thoughts that were already threatening to consume him" at the sight of little boys' black bodies by watching Brother Brian have sex with Noah, the gardener (16). Described as a bully and misogynist when he was a young adult, Brother Neil rapes Aboriginal women who "weren't anything more than a handy receptacle for men's penises" (42). Wuninga, also called Mary Magdalene, gives birth to a pale baby girl and, when asked who the white father might be, she responds that she is, like Mary, entitled to an Immaculate Conception. Sister Annunciata, who was once named Mira Finkelstein, converts from Judaism to Catholicism because of a failed romance and because of the striking similarities between the two faiths, including the strict dress code, the love of a man named Jesus, and the aversion of both faiths to homosexuality. Although Munkara's sarcasm is pungent when she refers to the sins of missionaries, she does not spare the bush mob either and describes the patriarchal structure of Aboriginal families and the men's tendencies to keep harems.

The Aboriginal people have few weapons at their disposal to challenge, postpone, or deter the impending destruction of their families, their communities, and ultimately their culture, but they use humor to poke fun at the missionaries whenever possible. When anthropologist Colvin Curry, whom the bush mob nicknamed Wurruwatake (Rat), compiles a book on Aboriginal culture and phrases, Pwomiga, who says his real name is Ponkiwutjumayubruguduwayu, feeds Curry lies and incorrect words. Pwomiga tells Wurruwatake that the name for spear is *timurarra* (penis), that the wind is called *dhooroo* (fart), and that Sister Jerome is cooking *kundiri* (shit). Unaware of Pwomiga's sarcasm, naïve Wurruwatake repeats the greeting *Awana juruliwa* (Hello, pubic hair) while the bush mob can barely hold in their laughter. These examples indicate that, with humor and wit, Aboriginals can keep their culture alive outside of the colonizers' destructive expansions. Humor alone, however, cannot stop the physical and mental abuse that Christian missionaries inflicted on Aboriginals.

Like Cleven and Munkara, Gayle Kennedy explores the alternative ways, such as humor and laughter, through which Aboriginals express their identity, subvert the stereotypes thrown their way, and challenge a tradition that silenced them or viewed them as inferior. *Me, Antman and Fleabag* is a collection of episodic tales that feature a sympathetic narrator who is never named, the narrator's partner (Antman), and their pet dog (Fleabag). The book introduces readers to a variety of Aboriginal characters, including funny parents, aunts, uncles, cousins, friends, and acquaintances. The narrator and her cheerful companions attend weddings and family reunions, visit friends, make new friends, and tell stories about their everyday reality. Kennedy has her protagonists pack up the car, turn up the country music, and embark on entertaining journeys that illustrate with humor and warmth some of the prejudices against contemporary Aboriginals. As a mere witness to hilarious or serious events and as someone who does not engage in direct scolding or criticism of others, the narrator responds kindly to what she sees around her and teaches valuable lessons about love, family, leisure, traveling, and laughter. Positive attitudes and ironic, yet humorous, responses to certain discriminatory behaviors or stereotypical portrayals of Aboriginals help bridge gaps between races and cultures and heal the scars of colonialism.

Several of the narrator's stories focus on relationships and interactions among white Australians and Aboriginals, and the stories reveal both unresolved tensions between the groups and unexpected, but hopeful, resolutions to conflict. Some critics believe that humor empowers Aboriginals in their relationships with white people. Scholar Eva Gruber contends that when audiences laugh "with Native characters, narrators, or authors *at* stereotypical or restrictive images of 'Indians' . . . they subconsciously subscribe to new conceptualizations of Nativeness and new perspectives on Native-White relations" (2). Thus, it could be argued that humor is a subversive tool for indigenous people to redefine their relationships to white culture and individuals. In addition, humor empowers indigenous writers to create original and witty forms of self-expression.

In *Me, Antman and Fleabag*, the author creates humorous situations that redefine relationships between whites and Aboriginals. An interracial wedding, an event that in essence proves that numerous contemporary families have moved away from racial prejudice and embraced social change, is still an occasion for incisive comments from both Aboriginals and whites. When an elderly white woman voices that she had concerns about "Gretchen marryin an Aboriginal at first, . . . [but that he has] turned out to be such a lovely boy" especially "if you closed your eyes you would think you were talking to a white man," Aunt Sugar responds acidly: "Yeh, I don't know how, but sometime we fluke a good one" (Kennedy, 80–81). The stereotypical description provided in the novel shows that even today many members of the non-Indigenous community view the Indigenous as less intelligent, educated, attractive, or valuable to the community. The stereotype that most Aboriginals are alcoholics and drug addicts is also reflected in the novel. The white elderly lady is surprised at Aunt Sugar's good looks at her age, given "all the violence and the alcohol and the drugs and whatnot" that Aboriginals are supposedly suffering from or are exposed to (81). Aunty's sarcastic response, "I only sniff unleaded petrol," which triggers roaring outbursts of laughter and the embarrassment of the elderly lady, constitutes an efficient way to subvert and parody such stereotypical descriptions of Aboriginals (81).

Another interracial marriage is a perfect occasion for the narrator to further explore the intricacies of black-white relationships. While Antman's Aunty Bess and Uncle Vic are happily married, their first encounter uncovered the terrible abuse to which Aboriginal women were subjected. Exhibiting gentlemanly behavior, Vic saves Bess, a young Koori girl, from being raped and possibly murdered by his white friends and threatens them with a gun. Vic and Bess's love story with an unusual happy ending also reveals the long-term violent effects of colonialism. Bess sums up some of these effects when she says, "They were white, we was black, end of story. Who do you reckon the cops believed?" (27–28). Bess has no immediate power to change the beliefs of the white society at the time, but she takes smaller steps to influence the attitudes of several white individuals. Understanding that friendship, kindness, and forgiveness are values that transcend race and ethnicity, she forgives Big Jim, one of the white men who tried to rape her, and befriends him over the years.

In a touching story titled "Grandfather's Medals," Kennedy's narrator delves into larger issues such as the direct involvement of Aboriginals in political, national, and international affairs. Though "blackfullas didn't have to go, a lot of em . . . [including the narrator's grandfather] reckoned it was their country, they had to keep it safe," and they decided to fight in the Second World War (60). Grandfather George returns home a war hero, decorated with medals for his imprisonment in Japan. While the government takes advantage of the Aboriginal people's patriotism and willingness to die in the war, it does not guarantee veterans any special rights upon their return home. A humiliating episode, in which Grandfather is not allowed to celebrate with his war mates and is thrown out of a public bar, speaks of the injustices perpetuated by the government and his white friends who do not intervene. Years later, the family's sadness is partially soothed when relatives discover in a public park a big plaque with Grandfather's name engraved in gold.

In addition to stories about black-white relationships, the narrator tells other stories that cover a wide array of experiences, including various connections among Aboriginal people. In several cases, Kennedy exposes situations in which Aboriginals make fun of themselves and their own people and culture. Like Cleven and Munkara, Kennedy shows that these ironic self-descriptions are not damaging but instead expose the Aboriginals' creativity and contagious humor along with their freedom, power, and confidence in their own self-worth and the potentialities of Aboriginal culture. Kennedy's unnamed narrator recounts a story of Aunt Pearlie, a supporter of white people, culture, and language, who, wanting to appear eloquent, always corrects Aboriginal people's speech and grammar. As Aunt Pearlie preaches that they are not "blackfullas," but "Aborigs," she exhibits a rather poor command of the English language (39). Aunt Pearlie's linguistic errors, including "Old Mrs Mac died from remonia last year" or "I'd better get a couple of reels of white cotting, please" (44), have the narrator and Antman falling down on the grass, laughing so hard that the clueless aunt feels the need to admonish them: "It's behaviour like that gives the rest of us Aboriginal people a bad name" (45). While Aunt Pearlie poses as an educated woman, the narrator's parents reveal the spontaneity and unpretentiousness of other Aboriginals. Ma and Dad do not hesitate to make fun of elaborate dishes during their vacation. When Ma sees cherry tomatoes for the first time, her reaction is disarmingly funny: "Look at the size of these fuckin tomatoes, will ya? . . . Ya think they could serve up some decent size tomatoes" (36–37). With this short reply, Ma shows that she is an honest and unsophisticated Aboriginal woman who is unafraid to voice her own opinions.

Through the sympathetic filter of the narrator and her partner, Antman, Kennedy puts together a series of brief stories that might originally appear to be simplistic but are in fact multilayered and compelling fragments of contemporary Aboriginal reality. The protagonists enjoy the company of friends and relatives whether they are white or Aboriginal and prove that increased amounts of kindness, joy, love, and laughs are more important and effective in changing attitudes vis-à-vis Aboriginals than hatred and bitterness.

In her chick lit novel, *Not Meeting Mr. Right*, widely read author Anita Heiss also shows that laughter and joy can accompany any endeavor no matter how strenuous. Having confessed to tackling serious matters such as the Stolen Generations and the politics of Indigenous identity in her other work, Heiss adds that "I also want to write with humour and make people laugh. And sometimes, I just want to lie on the beach, read, escape, and smile, so I wrote a book that I'd like to read, in the hope that women everywhere will chuckle and nod in agreement over how very hard it can be to meet a decent man!" ("Why"). In her easy-to-read novel, Heiss creates a dating guide full of relatable experiences about the endless trials, countless disappointments, and high expectations of Alice Aigner, a history professor in search of the perfect man. Alice's episodic experiences are humorous because her idea of a perfect partner does not fit the men she meets.

An avid serial dater, Alice has a surprising change of heart after she attends her ten-year school reunion and hears her classmates' tired stories on marriages, children, and mortgages. She vows to marry the perfect man before her thirtieth birthday and prove that a woman can have it all: that is, a mind of her own, a successful career, a wonderful husband, and well-behaved children. To achieve these goals, Alice and her friends Peta, Dannie, and Liza, who are the Aboriginal versions of the *Sex and the City* gals, elaborate ten criteria Alice's future husband must meet:

1. Must be single, straight, and wanting to be in a relationship
2. Must be good to his mother and like children
3. Must love his job (don't want him whingeing every night about his day)
4. Must only be addicted to me (not alcohol or narcotics, and he must not smoke)
5. Must think I am the most gorgeous woman on the planet
6. Must be a non-racist, non-fascist, non-homophobic believer in something, preferably himself
7. Must be punctual (although I am allowed to be on Koori time)
8. Must be romantic and be able to show affection in public
9. Must be financially secure and debt-free (mortgage will be acceptable)
10. He must be loyal, faithful, sincere, chivalrous, witty, competent, responsible and a good communicator (i.e., he must be a good listener). (Heiss, 37)

Confident in her looks, charm, and intellectual acumen, Alice is understandably picky about her selection, yet her high standards and her constant judgment of the men she meets inevitably lead to undesirable results. At the end of the novel, Alice does not have a husband but a handful of frustrating albeit humorous experiences.

Alice's tireless quest to find the perfect man reveals some entertaining situations. She does not choose athletic Daniel because he "checks out" other women. During a blind date, which Alice calls "possibly the worst date ever," her date, Jim, an actor, leaves her at the bar because he sees a good-looking woman across the room. Another date, Renan, whom Alice describes as "drop-dead-make-you-scream-inside-gorgeous," fails to make the grade because his career goals include moonwalking and hula dancing (77). Other men also fail to meet Alice's criteria: Charlie's face is scarred, Philip is what Alice calls "Mr Dick Fiddler" (112), and Malcolm has the *"he's just not that into you"* syndrome (132; italics in the original). Alice is happy when she dates Paul, an accomplished Koori engineer with a mysterious past, but he leaves her—not because Alice finds out he is an ex-convict but because she dared to confess she loved him.

Alice's dating debacle continues with partners who disapprove of her Aboriginal identity, and these dates become opportunities for Heiss to present a dark humor uncovering cultural and ethnic conflicts. Alice's Koori identity becomes a source of tension for some men who refuse to date her because she is Aboriginal. When Rod sees Alice's photo featuring an Aboriginal flag in the background, he stops calling her. Pondering whether she should have sent a different photo, Alice realizes that she cannot date a man who does not accept who she is.

Other encounters between Alice and her white dates reveal certain tensions and misunderstandings resulting from a lack of awareness and knowledge of the Aboriginal sensibility. Alice dismisses David because he sees her as an "exotic other" and a prized possession. When David introduces her, "This is Alice, she's Wiradjuri," Alice is quick to respond, "This is David, he's my own personal anthropologist" (34). The exchange between Alice and David is funny because Alice subtly lets David know why she finds his remark offensive. While Alice is proud of her Aboriginal identity, she does not want to be paraded as an ethnic curiosity. In another moment from the novel, Alice reveals her serious side when she offers lessons on Aboriginal identity outside of her history classes. During a heated exchange with a date who claims to be Aboriginal because he found out his great-great-grandmother was Koori, Alice explains that identity goes beyond skin color or book knowledge. She believes that "Aboriginality is spiritual, and it's a lived experience—not something you *find* by accident and then attach its name to yourself. I'm sick of white people deciding they're Black so they have some sense of belonging, or worse still, so they can exploit our culture" (165). Alice contends that Aboriginality is neither an attitude nor a label but a sum of lived experiences and inherited knowledge.

Despite countless attempts, Alice does not find the perfect husband; instead, she goes through a series of experiences that help her ground her needs in the context of the real world. Better, though, Alice does not get discouraged by her inability to marry a perfect man and mostly enjoys these experiences. She ends up dating "Gary-the-Garbo" (garbage collector), otherwise known as the Shirt Guy, who despite his nicknames is a nice, down-to-earth man. Alice's hilarious conversations with friends and dates during her dating dilemmas and her contagious optimism contribute to the novel's readability.

By employing humor, irony, parody, and sarcasm, Aboriginal writers such as Vivienne Cleven, Marie Munkara, Gayle Kennedy, and Anita Heiss enable their characters to respond to gender, racial, and ethnic stereotypes that provide audiences with a renewed understanding of the physical and psychological damage that these stereotypes can cause. Instead of chastising or punishing their characters and audiences with continual gloomy accounts of Aboriginal existence, these authors use "bitin'" humor to laugh with them, create understanding, and promote social change. These contemporary Indigenous writers and numerous others demonstrate that Aboriginals find themselves in control of their narratives and crafts and in charge of producing their own humor.

# Works Cited

Cleven, Vivienne. *Bitin' Back*. St. Lucia: University of Queensland Press, 2001.

Dodson, Michael. "The End in the Beginning: (De)fining Aboriginality." In *Blacklines: Contemporary Critical Writing by Indigenous Australians*, ed. Michele Grossman, 25–42. Carlton, VIC: Melbourne University Press, 2003.

Gosford, Bob. "*Every Secret Thing*—Interview with Marie Munkara, Part 1." *The Northern Myth* (blog). October 21, 2009. *Crikey.com.au*. Private Media Pty. Ltd. Accessed July 11, 2012. http://blogs.crikey.com.au/northern/2009/10/21/every-secret-thing-interview-with-marie-munkara-part-1/.

Gruber, Eva. *Humor in Contemporary Native North American Literature: Reimagining Nativeness*. Rochester, NY: Camden House, 2008.

Heiss, Anita. *Not Meeting Mr. Right*. Sydney: Bantam, 2007.

———. "Why I Wrote *Not Meeting Mr. Right*." 2008. Girl.com.au. Trellian Limited. Accessed June 1, 2012. http://www.girl.com.au/not-meeting-mr-right.htm.

Kennedy, Gayle. *Me, Antman and Fleabag*. St. Lucia: University of Queensland Press, 2007.

Munkara, Marie. *Every Secret Thing*. St. Lucia: University of Queensland Press, 2009.

Rappoport, Leon. *Punchlines: The Case for Racial, Ethnic, & Gender Humor*. Westport: Praeger, 2005.

# 8: White Shadows: The Gothic Tradition in Australian Aboriginal Literature

*Katrin Althans*

THE DISCUSSION OF a Gothic tradition in Australian Aboriginal literature is highly controversial. First, there is the debate over the European origin and colonial legacies of the Gothic; second, there is the exploitation of Aboriginal culture in (Western) Gothic fiction; third, there is the argument that Aboriginal cultural beliefs should not be mistaken for the Gothic. Concerning the European origin of and the abuse of Aboriginal customs in Gothic fiction, one can say that Aboriginal authors engage critically with the Gothic and enter into a state of creative resistance. Combined with elements of Aboriginal tradition and culture, the European Gothic in this creative resistance mutates into an Aboriginal Gothic as a way to negotiate issues of Aboriginal cultural strength and identity. Ranging from the reversal of colonial binaries to the Gothic realities of everyday life, contemporary Aboriginal literature emphasizes the subversive and transgressive qualities that lie at the heart of the Gothic. To understand the uneasy relationship of Australian Aboriginal literature with the Gothic, it is necessary to first explore the Gothic's place in literary and cultural history. Let us therefore start with an overview of the Gothic and the shadows it brings.

The Gothic, as scholar Fred Botting tellingly characterizes it, "shadows" the dominant literary movements in any given time from the eighteenth century to the present (1). Gothic has been the dark double to rationalism, realism, and modernity by concentrating on the irrational, the supernatural, and the past. The Gothic transgresses the laws society has set and instead revels in unlawful excess and concealed desires. It haunts the bright side of the Enlightenment as a phantom forever banned to the darkness beyond. Like a true shadow, however, the Gothic needs a corporeal body to attach itself to and whose predominance it can constantly question—and that it constantly tries to corrupt. Yet, in doing so the Gothic reinforces the very boundaries it attempts to transgress and assures society of its moral values and superiority. As the home to society's dark other, it provides a counterdiscursive space in which cultural anxieties can be played out. But sometimes the cultural anxieties that lurk in the Gothic shadows reach the other side and society is faced with what it has kept hidden.

It is not only because of the Gothic's ghostlike existence and its uncanny attachment to the self that it is best described in terms of shadows; it is also because of its subject matter. Although the Gothic is rather elusive when it comes to generic classifications, it is a literary tradition that very much depends on formulaic conventions. Despite its emphasis on transgression, the Gothic has imposed upon itself the limitations of night, darkness, and gloom. It is replete with stock characters, settings, and themes that suggest darkness and decay, and the first description of a Gothic atmosphere that comes to mind is more often than not "gloomy and mysterious" (Botting, 1). In the wake of imperialism, this metaphoric darkness soon gave way to actual blackness in Gothic literature, black devils, and bloodthirsty savages. When it comes to the Gothic tradition in Aboriginal literature, however, those dark shadows literally pale. In order to appreciate the many shapes the Gothic in Aboriginal literature takes, it is necessary to consider the discursive peculiarities of the Gothic and to rewind to the eighteenth century before fast-forwarding to contemporary Aboriginal literature.

## A Brief Survey of Gothic Origins

The Gothic is an inherently European literary tradition that in the course of its history successfully discarded any restrictions in terms of either genre or mode. Even though it may be classified as a mode whose origins are to be found in an exhausted genre, as genre theorists John Frow and Alastair Fowler state, its dual status as both noun and adjective suggests that the Gothic successfully sidesteps any limitations other than those of its own making (Frow, 66; Fowler, 109). On the one hand, the Gothic as a mode maintains the stock elements of the original Gothic romance, which it applies to various other genres. On the other hand, the Gothic, when considered as genre, allows for identifying different strands within the Gothic tradition itself. Such an ambiguous understanding of the Gothic is particularly suited for explaining the Gothic tradition in contemporary Aboriginal literature. The Gothic captures the different ways Aboriginal writers engage with it, using it as a tool to both Gothicize the experience of colonialism and to reclaim their cultural identity. In order to fully grasp the role the Gothic plays in Australian Aboriginal literature, it is important to briefly trace its origins.

Firmly rooted in eighteenth-century Europe and its ideologies and zeitgeist, the Gothic developed as a counterdiscourse to the Enlightenment and rationality. Early precursors are the works of the so-called Graveyard Poets, whose poetry was characterized by an obsession with death, night, and gloom, as well as Edmund Burke's treatise on the aesthetic principles of the sublime and beautiful, *A Philosophical Enquiry into the Origin of our Ideas of the Sublime and Beautiful* (1757). Here, Burke emphasizes that the sublime rather than the beautiful produces the "strongest emotion which the mind is capable of" and that "whatever is in any sort terrible, or is conversant about terrible objects, or operates in a manner analogous to terror, is a source of the *sublime*" (36). He does, however, add a caveat that will become particularly relevant in the context of Aboriginal literature: "When danger or pain press too nearly, they are incapable of giving any delight, and are simply terrible" (36). Combining the themes of the one with the ideas of the other, the Gothic romance emerged in 1764 in the form of *The Castle of Otranto* by Horace Walpole. In his attempt "to blend two kinds of romance," as is famously stated in the preface to the second edition, Walpole created the easily recognizable pattern of the pursued heroine who is trapped in subterranean passages underneath medieval castles and is at the mercy of the villainous aristocrat (9). Spatially and temporally set at some distance from Walpole's native England, *The Castle of Otranto* takes its readers to medieval Italy, the dark and pre-enlightened Middle Ages of superstition and feudal despotism, an era from which the Gothic derives its name. The supernatural occurrences and terrors the characters face are thus removed from the homely situation of an eighteenth-century English audience. Here again the schizophrenic quality of the Gothic—its double nature of submission and subversion—shows, as current political and social concerns are referred to under the guise of autocratic rule, whereas at the same time the readership is assured of its own moral values. The unfamiliar and distant world thus created in *The Castle of Otranto* provided the model for future Gothic novels in setting, style, and structure. The aristocratic villain plots the downfall of the rightful ruler and devises a sinister scheme to usurp power, including the desecration of the virgin damsel in distress. This plot can only be thwarted by the brave deeds of the young hero, which leads to the inevitable restoration of order. Usually, Gothic novels take place in gloomy mansions, ruined abbeys, or impenetrable forests. Supernatural monsters such as vampires, ghosts, or werewolves have become stock ingredients of Gothic fiction, and nowadays the mad scientist, the mass murderer, or the evil twin are as famous as the early usurpers of power. Similarly, Gothic locations have changed and spread, from the superstitious landscapes of Catholic Europe to the psyche of the madman, and they now span the whole world and even further, into outer space. Albeit in altered form, the forbidding atmospheres of fright and terror are still as menacing to a contemporary audience as they were more than two hundred years ago. The Gothic has invaded our everyday life, and today is omnipresent, a fact that features rather disturbingly in contemporary Aboriginal literature.

# The Gothic in Australia

The Gothic shadowed British society at home, but it also shadowed the expansion of the British Empire abroad. Wherever the empire went, the Gothic followed, quick to embrace and adapt to local conventions. Quite a new strand in Gothic fiction, imperial Gothic, emerged as a consequence of the colonization of new lands, and with it came the introduction of strange and exotic monsters and villains such as Haitian zombies, murderous Indian thugs, or wendigos, those cannibalistic spirits of Algonquian belief. Once again, the Gothic had succeeded in placing a distance between its locale and its audience, thus legitimizing colonial supremacy. Even when those alien perils invaded the very heart of the empire in what is known as tales of reverse colonization, they were eventually securely averted (Arata, 623). The colonies, however, developed their own, distinct variants of colonial Gothic fiction, and Australia was no exception. In fact, its antipodean position, inhospitable landscape, and convict legacy seemingly made Australia a particularly apt Gothic setting. According to one of the leading scholars of Australian Gothic, Gerry Turcotte, Australian Gothic "turned to the specifications of the domestic landscape and voice to articulate the fear and exhilaration of the colonial condition[:] . . . the anxieties of the convict system, the terrors of isolated stations at the mercy of vagrants and nature, the fear of starvation or of becoming lost in the bush" ("Australian Gothic," 12). Quite recently, examples of this colonial Australian Gothic have been resurrected in a number of anthologies, *The Anthology of Colonial Australian Gothic Fiction* (2007), edited by Ken Gelder and Rachael Weaver, as well as the trilogy *Australian Gothic* (2007), *Australian Nightmares* (2008), and *Australian Hauntings* (2011), edited by James Doig. Where Gelder and Weaver write of "a restaging of European and American Gothic tropes" ("Colonial Australian Gothic," 3), Doig gives examples of how exactly the traditional Gothic has been molded to fit the Australian context: "the haunted house is no longer a rambling manor, but an abandoned shanty or rundown homestead; the English wood, shadowy lair of ancient evils and creatures from folklore, becomes the oppressively hot, fly-infested bush; and the wind-swept moor is the empty, endless Australian outback with its blood-red sands and emaciated myall trees" ("Introduction," 8). But apart from genuinely Australian settings, situations, and atmospheres, the examples chosen for these anthologies also recall the dark undercurrent of the colonial endeavor in Australia. Mary Gaunt's "The Lost White Woman" (1916), for example, is the Gothic retelling of one of the most legendary captivity narratives in Australian culture, that of "The White Woman of Gippsland." Here, it is not the fear of getting lost in the bush that creates Gothic thrills but the horrible deaths to which white people are subjected at the hands of bloodthirsty black savages.

Aboriginal people, devoid of any language except "uncouth yabbering," appear as "horrible savages" who "butcher" the unsuspecting white cast-aways under cover of night (224–25). Furthermore, Gaunt adds a spectral quality to her description of the Aboriginal attackers when she writes of "those black figures, with skeletons marked on them in white" (224). As Gelder and Weaver point out, this "turning . . . Aboriginal figures into deathly apparitions" also figures quite prominently in other colonial Gothic stories ("Colonial Australian Gothic," 9). They link this preoccupation with a ghostly Aboriginal presence to the Gothic trope of the return of the repressed, which plays a major role in Freud's reflections on the uncanny (Freud, 363). Ernest Favenc's "Doomed" (1899), in particular, seems to justify this point of view. In this story it is the violence of five colonial set-tlers against an Aboriginal woman and her baby that is responsible for con-juring the phantom of the woman at the hour of each of the men's "violent deaths" (114). This ambiguous obsession with Australia's Aboriginal peo-ple is, however, not limited to colonial Gothic fiction; it also plays a crucial role in postcolonial Gothic fiction, especially since the Mabo decision and the ensuing native title legislation, as Gelder and cultural geographer Jane Jacobs have shown.[1] It is the return of the repressed in Freudian terms, in which the uncanny is literally unsettling "not because it is *un*familiar but rather because it is *all-too* familiar," that is played out in contempo-rary Australian Gothic literature by Anglo-Celtic authors (Althans, 17). In its uneasy treatment of the ghostly Aboriginal absence, this contemporary Australian Gothic does not much differ from its colonial predecessor.

## The Gothic in Aboriginal Literature

Because of its genuinely European and colonial history, quite another kind of schizophrenia is at work when it comes to the Gothic tradition in con-temporary Aboriginal literature. Although the Gothic is certainly not the first example that comes to mind when thinking of Aboriginal literature, Aboriginal authors, who both loathe and love the Gothic, have engaged with it in numerous ways, including copying the Gothicizing at work in

---

[1] In the landmark case Mabo v. Queensland [No. 2] of 1992, the judges held that, prior to 1788, the Aboriginal peoples of Australia had a right to the land based on the principle of native title. This decision overruled the long-established legal fiction of *terra nullius*, which characterized Australia as having been uninhabited when the first English settlers arrived. The Native Title Act, which put into writ-ing what the judges in the Mabo decision had declared to be the prerequisites of native title, was passed in 1993. This legislation, which grants Aboriginal people access to, e.g., sacred sites as long as native title has not been extinguished, has led to widespread insecurity among the Australian people and is under constant scrutiny. Because of lobbying by many non-Aboriginals, the scope of native title has since then been severely limited by amendments and further court decisions.

colonial Gothic, revising the colonial encounter, and, finally, transforming the original Gothic into a tool to express the strength of Aboriginal culture and identity. This appropriation, however, places Aboriginal writers in an ideological struggle. On the one hand, Aboriginal rewritings allegedly center on European origins. On the other hand, Aboriginal authors want to free themselves from aesthetic constraints imposed upon them by European literature—paradoxically with the aid of one of the most disabling discourses of colonial history, the Gothic. While such writers try to use the subversive potential of the Gothic, they are nevertheless caught in its narrations of colonial submission. To argue in favor of the Gothic tradition in Aboriginal literature in terms of the "writing-back" paradigm made famous in the writings of postcolonial scholars Bill Ashcroft, Gareth Griffiths, and Helen Tiffin would mean acknowledging neither the creative potential of Aboriginal authors nor their complex engagement with Aboriginal culture. If all intertextual relations to Gothic works or the Gothic tradition itself were left aside, though, that would mean ignoring a central issue of Aboriginal Gothic. Similarly, assessing Gothic instances in Aboriginal literature only in terms of Maban, which is a parallel and specifically Indigenous reality, as author and scholar Mudrooroo does in his article "Gothic Imagination," removes it from any literary history and context and places it in an imagined precolonial void. Therefore, both extremes deny the Gothic tradition its proper place within Aboriginal literature, one focusing too much on its European origin, the other disregarding its European heritage completely. Instead, Aboriginal Gothic needs to be read in terms of a negotiation with the Gothic as well as with Maban reality to write about the contemporary situation of Aboriginal people in Australia.

## Copying the Colonial Gothic

The very first example of the Gothic in Aboriginal literature is that of the European Gothic being used to tell Aboriginal stories, as, for example, is the case with the Australian Broadcasting Corporation's *Dust Echoes* website, where "we [the Wugularr Community] are telling our stories to you in a way you can understand, to help you see, hear and know" (Lewis). Presented as short animated movies, some of the stories remind a white audience of fairy tales, others of surreal dream sequences, and still others of traditional Gothic stories. Of the twelve Dreamtime stories collected on the *Dust Echoes* website, especially the two introducing the man-eating beast Namorrodor, "Namorrodor" and "The Curse," make use of traditional Gothic imagery and sounds. Set during the night and full of the eerie soundscape of nightly groans and growls, both stories make ample use of darkness and gloom, except for the ominous shooting star signaling the arrival of Namorrodor. The setting evoked in the first of the two stories, centering entirely on the titular beast, seems to be taken straight from a Gothic novel of the eighteenth century. It features a dark night with a full moon, which suddenly turns into the menacing blinking yellow eye of Namorrodor, and a cave that does not betray any sign of being in Australia but that could also be part of any European mountain range. Special emphasis is put on the appearance of Namorrodor itself, a strange coal-black creature, "a flying serpent . . . [that] has claws and a head like a kangaroo or horse" ("Namorrodor—Original Story").

In the second of the two stories, in which Namorrodor enters the body of a small baby, the Gothic effect of the baby's turning into Namorrodor, its mouth sprouting the hideous teeth and terrifying eyes of the beast, is dwelled upon for two seconds at the end of the video. Following the credits, after the screen has blacked out and no sound is audible, a close-up of the baby in Namorrodor-shape suddenly reappears. The baby, appearing for less than two seconds, lashes out at the audience at the same time as a piercing shriek is heard. Then, everything blacks out again. Even though these are traditional stories from the Wugularr Community in Arnhem Land, they nevertheless are rendered in recognizable Gothic terms to make a white audience understand the cautionary background of the Namorrodor tales.

Another illustration of the Gothic as an adequate literary mode used by Aboriginal authors is the short story "The Little Red Man," by Raymond Gates. "The Little Red Man" is part of a collection of Australian vampire stories. Its starting point is not a tale of a classical European vampire but rather the Aboriginal legend of the Yara Ma Tha Who. The only example of a vampire-like being in Australia (Melton, 25), the Yara Ma Tha Who is described by David Unaipon, one of the earliest Aboriginal writers acknowledged by white people, as "a queer little red man" (217) who sucks the blood from his victims and swallows them whole, each time reducing the victim in height, until, after the third time, the victim also becomes a Yara Ma Tha Who (218–19). Although remotely resembling the vampire of European lore in its actions, this uniquely Australian creature lacks all the grandeur and sexual connotations of its Western counterpart and is "neither oversexed sociopath, nor emotional teenager" (Gates, 395). The original story by Unaipon and its rewriting by Gates are included in collections of Australian Gothic fiction, *Macabre: A Journey through Australia's Darkest Fears* (2010) and *Dead Red Heart* (2011), respectively. Whereas including Unaipon's story in *Macabre* can be regarded as an effort by editors Angela Challis and Marty Young to compile a comprehensive collection of Australian Gothic literature, there is more to Gates's "The Little Red Man" in terms of Aboriginal Gothic. This story combines classical patterns of Australian hitch-hiking horror with Aboriginal culture and shows that Maban reality, of which the Yara Ma Tha Who is a part, invades white Australia with a Gothic insistence.

Still, both the Namorrodor stories and "The Little Red Man" are Gothic retellings of Aboriginal stories, thus maintaining the Gothicization of Aboriginal culture that was prevalent in colonial Gothic fiction.

Another way of imitating the structures at work in colonial Gothic fiction, one that is more conscious of being written within a European tradition and with an Aboriginal goal in mind, is the reversal of conventional Gothic patterns. It is first and foremost the figure of the Gothic villain that is taken up by Aboriginal authors, the villain who returns to his beginnings as the usurper of power. Texts by Mudrooroo, whose Aboriginal identity has been a much-contested issue because he identified as Aboriginal without actually being descended from Aboriginal people, have had a strong influence on the perception of the Gothic in Aboriginal literature.[2] In his vampire trilogy, *The Undying* (1998), *Underground* (1999), and *The Promised Land* (2000), there is a white female vampire, Amelia Fraser, who in Draculean fashion invades Australia and infects its Aboriginal population with her disease. Together with Captain Torrens, who turns into a savage polar werebear (a variant of the more traditional werewolf) at the full of the moon, she ravages the Australian landscape and destroys Aboriginal culture and heritage by literally sucking the Aboriginal protagonist George dry of his identity. Whereas Amelia is responsible for the loss of *cultural* identity among the small band of Aboriginal people battling her, Captain Torrens unleashes some of the most gruesome ferocities against their *corporeal* identity:

> The shattered tops of the masts of the brigantine had been buried in the sand and then a spar had been lashed between them, tied securely so that it would remain firm under the weight and thrashings of ten human beings. Then, in order for the murderers to do their work without overly stretching, a long narrow trench had been dug underneath. Nooses had been tied at intervals along the spar and through these the heads of the unfortunate victims had been thrust. Then, from the marks along the edge of the trench, their feet had been kicked away from under them and they had swung out into space, choking at the end of the ropes. Some of them, I saw, had tried to swing back to the side of the trench and thus lessen the terrible agony, but their feet had been kicked away by heavy ghost boots. I stared at the twisted faces with the swollen tongues alive with flies. They protruded like diseased slugs from mouths wide open, gasping

---

[2] During his career as a writer, Mudrooroo first changed his name from his birth name Colin Johnson to Mudrooroo Narogin, then to Mudrooroo Nyoongah, and finally shortened his *nom de plume* to Mudrooroo. Even though the charges brought up against his Aboriginal identity also include his name, I will refer to him as Mudrooroo throughout the text, as that is the name under which his work is published to date.

for air, wide open to force through a final breath which was blocked by the constricting rope. I stared. I could smell the blood congealed in dead veins. I inhaled a stronger stench and glanced down from the faces to a further horror: each corpse had been slashed across the stomach, had been hacked open by a blunt instrument, for the wounds were not clean cuts and seemingly had been prolonged to add to the agony of the suffocating victims. I saw how the blood had flown out along with the intestines which bulged and oozed harsh fluids and odours. (*Undying*, 104–5)

Quite self-reflexively, Torrens refers to his actions as a "Gothic scene" (*Undying*, 124). Here, the label of Gothic is applied in a strictly European sense and reserved for strictly European characters and their usurpation of power in Australia. Unlike any Gothic novel of European origin, however, no restoration of order occurs. The vampiric infection of the Aboriginal people continues in the shape of assimilation even when white brutality and its annihilating force are banned to the depths of the ocean, but not completely destroyed, in a bone-pointing ritual combined with traditional Gothic remedies against were-animals (*Undying*, 177–79).

The Gothicization of whites, however, already started with Mudrooroo's earlier works *Doctor Wooreddy's Prescription for Enduring the Ending of the World* (1983) and *Master of the Ghost Dreaming* (1991), the latter being both a rewriting of the former and a prequel to Mudrooroo's vampire trilogy. A Gothic atmosphere is evoked right at the beginning of *Master of the Ghost Dreaming*, a text that throughout the narrative quite frequently returns to images of darkness, death, and nightmares. In the course of the novels, the appellation of the whites especially shows an increased reversal of Gothic roles. What begins as the Aboriginal term *num* in *Doctor Wooreddy* is, as a gesture towards the submission of Aboriginal peoples and their culture, used only in its titular English form *ghosts* in *Master of the Ghost Dreaming* (10). In Mudrooroo's vampire trilogy, then, the whites are once more renamed *num*, but they also acquire the title of *Moma*, "devil" (*Undying*, 18, 42).

It is not only the return to the primordial Gothic villain that constitutes a reversal of Gothic roles but also the reversal of other characters that challenges the mechanics of black savages pursuing white maidens and being killed by white heroes. There no longer is a white damsel in distress but a black woman, and she is not chased by a bloodthirsty black and rescued just in time; she is actually raped and tortured by white men until she is released through death. This is, for example, the case in *The Kadaitcha Sung* by Murri writer and political activist Sam Watson, in which the white legal system as represented by the honorable Justice Jones brutally abuses a black woman. The setting in which she is raped, however, again resembles that of traditional Gothic sceneries, as it happens in the labyrinthine basement of an old Queenslander-turned-fortress, complete with subterranean passages:

> The gin gave an agonised gasp and died. . . .
> There were two men with her, one white and the other black, and she was lying belly down across a narrow bed. Sambo's fingers were still buried in her throat. He had strangled her while holding her head between his thighs. . . . Mr Justice Jones was naked, lying on her back, his penis buried in her anus and his arms wrapped around her.
> . . . With a series of short, angry thrusts, the white man climaxed. He closed his eyes as the waves of ecstasy washed over him.
> "Whoo!" He rolled off the empty envelope of flesh. . . . "She was a good one! The best I've had for a while . . ."
> Each of the basement rooms was set up in a similar fashion. . . .
> (221–22)

A similar approach to colonial atrocities is taken by Kamilaroi writer Philip McLaren in his *Sweet Water—Stolen Land* (1993). Although *Sweet Water* centers on solving a brutal murder and is, thus, like McLaren's crime thriller *Scream Black Murder* (1995), not primarily concerned with the Gothic, the novel also contains Gothic descriptions of white people and of the actual Myall Creek Massacre of 1838, in which twenty-eight Aboriginal people were brutally murdered and subsequently burned. When Karl Maresch, the story's conventional murderer, remembers his father "covered in blood . . . [and with] contorted facial muscles, the salivating mouth, the wide eyes" (157), it seems he is drawing a picture of himself and other whites, a picture of a bestial monster. At the same time, the account of the Myall Creek Massacre evokes pictures of Nazis rounding up Jews like cattle before they are slaughtered (119–22). Such a reversal of Gothic roles, however, still remains trapped within the very same binaries colonial Gothic has set up.

## Reclaiming Identity through the Gothic

A second strand of the Gothic tradition in Aboriginal literature frees itself from the restraints of its colonial heritage and reclaims Aboriginal identity through the use of Gothic characteristics. Here, the ambiguity of the Gothic is played out in full force, along with the struggle between European ideas of the Gothic and Aboriginal perceptions of Maban reality. Once again, Sam Watson's *The Kadaitcha Sung* is an apt illustration of the way in which a European audience's awareness and expectations of the Gothic are subverted. The Kadaitcha, an avenger of unlawful deaths (Watson, "I Say This to You," 590), has often served as a means to supply Gothic horror in popular fiction, as in movies like *Kadaicha* [sic] and *The Min-Min* or in an episode of the 1970s Australian mystery TV series *The*

*Evil Touch* entitled "Kadaitcha Country." In *The Kadaicha Sung*, the titular character is, at first, invested with the very same Gothic traits. Tommy, the young Kadaitcha in Watson's novel, is seemingly presented as a menacing figure who regularly conjures black magic, as evidenced in his presiding over the trial of Tea-Pot: "Tommy waved his fingers underneath his jaw and a red glow lit his face. . . . Tommy's voice was dead, lacking all human quality. His eyes were black scars, empty of life" (117). At the same time, Watson states, Tommy acts as "the most powerful figure within traditional Aboriginal society" ("I Say This to You," 590). The ensuing dilemma of the schizophrenic status of the Kadaitcha in the novel can, as Mudrooroo does in an article, be tackled by considering it as an instance of Maban reality that "does not correspond with European reality" ("Gothic Imagination"). He does, however, concede that this reality "does approximate the *Gothic* to some extent" ("Gothic Imagination"). Indeed, *The Kadaitcha Sung* is written within a history of Gothic literature and clearly shows Gothic traits, but it also asks its readers to abandon their generic security and consider the meaning of the Gothic itself. If the Gothic is perceived in the shape of Maban reality, it loses part of its crucial power of "othering." Thus, it no longer confines the "other" to the shadows, but it empowers it and lets it reclaim its identity as the self. Therefore, the description of the Kadaitcha in Watson's novel is as much Maban as it is Gothic, as it is appropriate to serve the other. It thus works within traditional Gothic patterns only to bring forth Aboriginal culture from the shadows.

*The Boundary* (2011), the first novel by lawyer Nicole Watson (Sam Watson's daughter), works in much the same way as its literary (and literal) parent. Although classified as crime fiction, the novel also makes frequent use of a Maban reality clad in Gothic clothing. To begin with, the cover art depicting Brisbane's skyline at night in the background and a prominent red feather in the foreground recalls *The Kadaitcha Sung*. The narrative tells of a tribal spirit called Red Feathers, who takes revenge on the people responsible for a failed native title claim. In the end, however, the reader is left in doubt as to the identity of the murderer and is left hovering in midair between a rational and a supernatural explanation, Miranda (one of the novel's main characters) or Red Feathers, respectively. This makes *The Boundary* a prime example of both how the Gothic and its relation to Maban reality is used to strengthen Murri perspectives and also of how one of structuralist critic Tzvetan Todorov's conditions of the fantastic is fulfilled.[3]

Other instances of how the Gothic caters to Maban reality can be found in the writings of Noongar author Kim Scott, who twice won the Miles Franklin Literary Award for his novels. In Scott's novel *Benang:*

---

[3] One of the conditions of the fantastic for Todorov is "to hesitate between a natural and a supernatural explanation of the events described" (33).

*From the Heart* (1999), the protagonist Harley needs to "come back from the dead" in order to be able to fully acknowledge his Noongar heritage (163). Harley is the result of careful planning on the part of his white grandfather, a mad scientist in Gothic terms: he is "the first white man born," and he has to become one of the undead to live out his Noongar culture. In an act of translational defiance, Harley in this situation only refers to himself in Noongar words, "I may well be djanak, or djangha" and leaves the reader in doubt over his actual state of being (163). Scott's short story "Asleep" (2006) also presents the reader with a seemingly creepy creature, Naatj. Again, at no point is this Noongar word translated, nor is the actual creature revealed. All the reader learns is that it has red eyes and that it ranks among a variety of monsters from Aboriginal lore (307, 310). While Naatj is the example of a Gothic monster, it at the same time represents the Noongar people and thus also subverts classical Gothic conceptions and belies the dichotomy of self and other.

## Ghosts of the Past

It is not only the Gothic mode in its structural entirety that is appropriated by Aboriginal authors but also the European genre of the ghost story, especially its obsession with the return of the repressed. Examples of novels where hauntings, ghosts, phantoms, and other forms of trauma play an important role include Murri writer Melissa Lucashenko's young adult novel *Killing Darcy* (1998), Kamilaroi writer Vivienne Cleven's *Her Sister's Eye* (2002), and award-winning Waanyi author Alexis Wright's *Plains of Promise* (1997). Unlike their European equivalents, however, the ghosts conjured in these novels are not the unresting souls of the long dead who wish to take revenge for their deaths; instead, they represent a repressed memory that manifests itself as the shadows of colonial history.

A case in point is Lucashenko's *Killing Darcy*, which centers on a mysterious camera that takes pictures of the past. The subdued memories of the colonial past with its dispossessing relationship between white settlers and Aboriginal people are literally pictured in the novel. There is a haunting feeling evoked throughout the text, and a terrible secret is hinted at through the pictures. Even though the secret is not what the juvenile protagonist Darcy Mango expected all along—that a young Aboriginal boy had been killed by his own father—the ghost in the photo had to be banished for Darcy to reclaim his own identity and find his family. Here, the ghost was properly exorcized and laid to rest, but the traumas the ghosts hide in both Cleven's *Her Sister's Eye* and Wright's *Plains of Promise* go much deeper.

In Cleven's *Her Sister's Eye*, it is the trauma of Raymond Gee, who has buried a terrible childhood memory, which is expressed in Gothic terms. Raymond returns to Mundra, a small country town in rural

Queensland in which he grew up, as Archie Corella. He has no memory but an ill foreboding of ever having set foot there before. Raymond also does not remember his true name or his history. Instead, he is portrayed as a Gothic wanderer, but his proverbial guilt turns out to be a memory too hideous to remember and expel safely: as a child he had witnessed the murder of his little sister, Belle, at the hands of the town's white patriarch. In the end, Raymond cannot live with the memory he has uncovered, and he drowns himself in the river that literally divides the town's white and black communities. His trauma, however, has been the trauma of the whole Aboriginal community of Mundra, who are, unlike Raymond/Archie, strong enough as a community to survive the memory and keep it alive through storytelling.

Similarly, Wright's *Plains of Promise* centers on a personal trauma: that of Ivy Koopundi's sexual and psychological abuse. Koopundi's trauma is handed down through the generations, but it is also the epitome of the shared trauma of the Stolen Generation. The trauma presented in the novel is set against more traditional ghost stories of a European style, that of a husband returning as a niggling terrier (187) and that of an urban legend of a ghost car in the Gulf country (247–48), stories that sharply contrast with the traumatic experience of the novel's Aboriginal characters in white institutions. Thus, European ghost stories are deprived of their ability to cause shivering and terror, as it is the reality of past and contemporary Aboriginal experience that results in truly blood-chilling ghosts. When those ghosts are unearthed rather than exorcized, the truth they illuminate turns the dark shadows of the Gothic white as a sheet.

## Gothic Realities

What Gerry Turcotte observes as the transition from colonial to post-colonial Gothic—that "the Gothic became less a streamlined experience in terror and more of an ongoing descent into nightmare"—is equally true for the development of the Gothic tradition in Aboriginal literature (*Peripheral Fear*, 236). The Gothic realities of Aboriginal existence are threateningly close to home and demand a reconsideration of basic Gothic assumptions. There is, for example, the Gothic reality of white historiography, which is depicted in Scott's *Benang* as the conflict between written records and oral testimony. The novel's preoccupation with anything written as opposed to the stories told to Harley at the campfires by his Noongar uncles paves the way for a gory counternarrative to the narrative told on, literally, white paper (183–87). Then there are the Aboriginal deaths in custody in Watson's *The Kadaitcha Sung* that once more Gothicize the common law legal system of Australia and its representatives. All these instances ultimately deny Gothic fiction any right to exist at all as *fiction*.

This complexity is also pointedly expressed in Cleven's *Her Sister's Eye*, in which two Gothic storylines intersect. There is the traditional tale of the heroine locked up in a mansion at the mercy of the Gothic villain. This tale focuses on the most prominent white family of Mundra and is resolved accordingly, as Caroline Drysdale, the not-so-innocent damsel in distress, lives to see her happily-ever-after. The Aboriginal equivalent to this is the story of the Gothic wanderer Raymond, who is finally confronted with, and overwhelmed by, his long-repressed memories. For him, there is no happy ending and no restoration of order, but a mental and corporeal breakdown. Although the Gothic here does not come in easily recognizable shapes such as vampires, were-animals, or other monsters, it nevertheless shares with its first kith and kin a blood-curdling and spine-chilling sensation. Yet instead of this sensation resulting from a delightful experience of remote terror, it emanates from the realization that the horrors actually are not removed from reality but are being repeated every day.

# Conclusion

The Gothic is a literary mode with a tradition reaching back to the eighteenth century and a history of ever-changing faces. Most of these faces hail from the dark underworlds, but the Gothic's relation to darkness has also taken on quite literally dark faces, that of the black savages from the colonies. In contemporary Aboriginal literature, the Gothic nevertheless reveals its subversive potential and challenges established binaries of the traditional Gothic. Through its association with Aboriginal culture, the Gothic of European origins is "usurp[ed], devour[ed], and finally transform[ed]" (Althans, 183). Resembling a shattered mirror of its original self, it surfaces in several different forms, including an imitation of colonial Gothic patterns, a reversal of conventional Gothic roles, a strengthening of Aboriginal culture and identity, and the expression of Gothic realities. Like the European Gothic that has always taken dark shadows as its beginning, the Gothic tradition in Aboriginal literature turns to the many white shadows Australian history has attached to the life and experience of its Aboriginal peoples.

# Works Cited

Althans, Katrin. *Darkness Subverted: Aboriginal Gothic in Black Australian Literature and Film.* Göttingen: V & R Unipress, 2010.
Arata, Stephen D. "The Occidental Tourist: *Dracula* and the Anxiety of Reverse Colonization." *Victorian Studies* 44 (1990): 621–45.
Ashcroft, Bill, Gareth Griffiths, and Helen Tiffin. *The Empire Writes Back: Theory and Practice in Post-Colonial Literatures.* 2nd ed. London: Routledge-Taylor & Francis, 2002.

Botting, Fred. *Gothic*. London: Routledge-Taylor & Francis, 1996.

Burke, Edmund. *A Philosophical Enquiry into the Origins of Our Ideas of the Sublime and Beautiful*. 1757. Reprint, Oxford: Oxford University Press, 1990.

Challis, Angela, and Marty Young, eds. *Macabre: A Journey through Australia's Darkest Fears*. Edgewater: Brimstone Press, 2010.

Cleven, Vivienne. *Her Sister's Eye*. St. Lucia: University of Queensland Press, 2002.

"The Curse." In *Dust Echoes*.

Doig, James, ed. *Australian Gothic: An Anthology of Australian Supernatural Fiction 1867–1939*. Mandurah, WA: Equilibrium Books, 2007.

———, ed. *Australian Hauntings: Colonial Supernatural Fiction*. Mandurah, WA: Equilibrium Books, 2011.

———, ed. *Australian Nightmares: More Australian Tales of Terror and the Supernatural*. Mandurah, WA: Equilibrium Books, 2008.

———. Introduction to Doig, *Australian Gothic*, 5–8.

*Dust Echoes: Ancient Stories, New Voices*. ABC, 2007. Accessed May 25, 2012. http://www.abc.net.au/dustechoes/.

Farr, Russell B., ed. *Dead Red Heart: Australian Vampire Stories*. Greenwood, WA: Ticonderoga, 2011.

Favenc, Ernest. "Doomed." 1899. In Gelder and Weaver, *Anthology*, 113–15.

Fowler, Alastair. *Kinds of Literature: An Introduction to the Theory of Genres and Modes*. Oxford: Clarendon Press, 1982.

Freud, Sigmund. "The 'Uncanny.'" 1919. In *Art and Literature: Jensen's Gradiva, Leonardo da Vinci and Other Works*, edited by Albert Dickson, 335–76. London: Penguin, 1990.

Frow, John. *Genre*. London: Routledge-Taylor & Francis, 2005.

Gates, Raymond. "The Little Red Man." In Farr, *Dead Red Heart*, 379–95.

Gaunt, Mary. "The Lost White Woman." 1916. In Gelder and Weaver, *Anthology*, 223–30.

Gelder, Ken, and Jane M. Jacobs. *Uncanny Australia: Sacredness and Identity in a Postcolonial Nation*. Carlton, VIC: Melbourne University Press, 1998.

Gelder, Ken, and Rachael Weaver. *The Anthology of Colonial Australian Gothic Fiction*. Carlton, VIC: Melbourne University Press, 2007.

———, eds. "The Colonial Australian Gothic." Introduction to Gelder and Weaver, *Anthology*, 1–9.

Lucashenko, Melissa. *Killing Darcy*. St. Lucia: University of Queensland Press, 1998.

McLaren, Philip. *Scream Black Murder*. Sydney: Harper Collins, 1995.

———. *Sweet Water—Stolen Land*. St. Lucia: University of Queensland Press, 1993.

Melton, J. G. *The Vampire Book: The Encyclopedia of the Undead*. Farmington Hills, MI: Visible Ink Press, 1999.

Mudrooroo. *Doctor Wooreddy's Prescription for Enduring the Ending of the World*. 1983. Reprint, Melbourne: Hyland House, 1998.

————. "Gothic Imagination or Maban Reality?" Review of *Darkness Subverted: Aboriginal Gothic in Black Australian Literature and Film*, by Katrin Althans. *Australian Women's Book Review* 22, no. 2 (2010): n.p. Accessed December 16, 2011. http://www.emsah.uq.edu.au/awsr/new_site/awbr_archive/150/mudrooroo.html.

————. *Master of the Ghost Dreaming*. North Ryde, NSW: Angus & Robertson-Harper Collins, 1991.

————. *The Promised Land*. Sydney: Angus & Robertson-Harper Collins, 2000.

————. *Underground*. Sydney: Angus & Robertson-Harper Collins, 1999.

————. *The Undying*. Sydney: Angus & Robertson-Harper Collins, 1998.

"Namorrodor—Original Story." In *Dust Echoes*.

Scott, Kim. "Asleep." In *The Best Australian Stories 2006*, edited by Robert Drewe, 304–13. Melbourne: Black Inc. Agenda, 2006.

————. *Benang: From the Heart*. Fremantle, WA: Fremantle Arts Centre Press, 1999.

Todorov, Tzvetan. *The Fantastic: A Structural Approach to a Literary Genre*. Cleveland, OH: The Press of Case Western Reserve University, 1973.

Turcotte, Gerry. "Australian Gothic." In *The Handbook of the Gothic*, edited by Marie Mulvey-Roberts, 277–87. 2nd ed. Basingstoke, UK: Palgrave Macmillan, 2009.

————. *Peripheral Fear: Transformations of the Gothic in Canadian and Australian Fiction*. Brussels: Peter Lang, 2009.

Unaipon, David. "Yara Ma Tha Who." 1924/1925. In *Legendary Tales of the Australian Aborigines*, edited by Stephen Muecke and Adam Shoemaker, 217–19. Carlton, VIC: Melbourne University Press, 2006.

Walpole, Horace. *The Castle of Otranto*. Edited by Michael Gamer. London: Penguin, 2001.

Watson, Nicole. *The Boundary*. St. Lucia: University of Queensland Press, 2011.

Watson, Sam. "'I Say This to You': Sam Watson Talks to Meanjin." *Meanjin* 53, no. 4 (1994): 589–96.

————. *The Kadaitcha Sung*. Ringwood, VIC: Penguin Books Australia, 1990.

Wright, Alexis. *Plains of Promise*. St. Lucia: University of Queensland Press, 1997.

# 9: Bold, Black, and Brilliant: Aboriginal Australian Drama

*Maryrose Casey*

PERFORMANCE, AS AN embodied encounter, between people of different cultures occupies a crucial position within the processes of recognition and misrecognition of the other. In the context of colonized peoples, dramas written for performance in effect act as a map for representations and communication. In Australia, performance has been a pivotal point of encounter between Aboriginal and non-Aboriginal people. Historical Aboriginal cultures are probably the most performance based in the world. Explicitly choreographed performances marked every aspect of social, political, and spiritual life, ranging from judicial, religious, diplomatic, and pedagogical practices to hundreds of genres of performances for entertainment. These performances combined dialogue, poetry, mime, song, dance, musical accompaniment, and visual art. As a central and striking feature of Aboriginal cultures, these practices were a crucial point of cross-cultural exchange from the first European colonial settlements in the late eighteenth century.

Throughout the nineteenth century Aboriginal people created and performed shows for the European settlers for a variety of reasons, including proclaiming Aboriginal sovereignty of the land, communicating their culture to the settlers, and engaging with the settler economy. Examples of the creation and performance of these shows are numerous. In his 1865 publication, *The Aborigines of Australia*, Gideon Lang recounted a performance text from the early 1840s (28–29). Lang, a settler who migrated to Australia in 1841, brought together various accounts of a diplomatic event that occurred in Queensland: Bussamarai, a leader of the Mandandanji people, invited the leading settlers to watch a performance that was intended to communicate their fate if they did not leave the area. Though the performance did not have the intended effect and was followed by a period of fighting over the following ten years between Aboriginal people and settlers, the record reveals practices of narrative, costume, and performance styles.[1] Lang describes the performance as

---

[1] See Patrick Collins, *Goodbye Bussamarai: The Mandandanji Land War, Southern Queensland 1842–1952* (Brisbane: University of Queensland Press, 2002).

divided into three main scenes or acts. In the opening sequence, performers imitated "a herd of cattle, feeding out of the forest, camping on the
plain, the black performers were painted accordingly" (28). In the second scene, an Aboriginal hunting party "was seen creeping towards the
cattle," finally spearing two. The hunters then skinned the cows and prepared the meat for carrying away. The third scene

> commenced with the sound of horses galloping through the tim-
> ber, followed by the appearance of a party of whites on horseback,
> remarkably well got up. The face was painted whity-brown [*sic*],
> with an imitation of a cabbage tree hat; the bodies were painted,
> some blue and others red, to represent the shirts: below the waist
> was a resemblance to moleskin trousers, the legs being covered
> with reeds tied all around, to imitate the hide leggings worn in that
> district [by white men] as a protection against the brigelow scrub.
> These manufactured whites at once wheeled to the right, fired, and
> drove the blacks before them! The latter soon rallied, however, and
> a desperate fight ensued, the blacks extending their flanks and driv-
> ing back the whites. The fictitious whites bit the cartridges, put on
> the caps, and went through all forms of loading, firing and wheeling
> their horses, assisting each other . . . with an exactness that proved
> personal observation. The native spectators groaned whenever a
> blackfellow fell, but cheered lustily when a white bit the dust; and
> at length after the ground had been fought over and over again, the
> whites were ignominiously driven from the field, amidst the frantic
> delight of the natives. (28–29)

In the twentieth and twenty-first centuries, Aboriginal drama has
continued to fill a number of important functions. When Aboriginal playwrights began to claim ongoing space on the main stages of Australian
and international theaters, their first challenge was to break the silence
that surrounded their history and survival. As W. E. H. Stanner argued
in his 1968 book, *After the Dreaming*, there was a "Great Australian
Silence" that had written Aboriginal people out of Australian history in
the twentieth century (25). Aboriginal writers faced a number of obstacles to break that silence. They needed to make space for their stories to
be heard, and they needed to persuade white audiences of the veracity
of their stories. In the context of assimilationist narratives that presumed
Aboriginal people who lived in urban or rural environments had no position to speak from, they also had to establish that they were the ones with
the knowledge and ability to tell their stories.

Aboriginal writers such as Oodgeroo Noonuccal, Hyllus Marsh, Kevin
Gilbert, Robert Merritt, Gerry Bostock, Jack Davis, and Eva Johnson
set out to tell their people's stories and counter negative representations
of Aboriginal people. One of the generalizations playwrights sought to

counter was the assumption that all Aboriginal people were of the same group or nation. Across Australia there were at least two hundred different language groups with hundreds of associated dialects. In the aftermath of the destruction wrought by colonization, the Aboriginal peoples of common language groupings whose populations had borne the brunt of violence and death often identify with the general language group name from their region. In Victoria, parts of New South Wales, and parts of Tasmania, the common collective name for the language grouping is Koori. In Queensland, the most commonly recognized grouping is Murri. In southern Western Australia the grouping is Noongar and in South Australia Nunga. In other areas to the north and central Australia where there are larger Aboriginal populations, they identify with their immediate language grouping such as Warlpiri or Pitjantjatjara or Yolngu among many others.

In the 1970s, Koori playwrights Gilbert, Merritt, and Bostock challenged the generalizations about Aboriginal people and the silence around their survival.[2] Their texts present moments of the daily reality and humanity of modern Koori life drawn from the writers' own experiences. They each explore different types of contemporary Indigenous experience. Gilbert's play *The Cherry Pickers* (written in 1968 and published in 1988) was the first play by an Indigenous playwright to achieve any profile within the non-Indigenous mainstream environment. The narrative focuses on the lives and struggles of Aboriginal people working as itinerant farm laborers, seeking work picking fruit. The text offered one of the first examples of Aboriginal people using an Aboriginal English in a drama on Australian stages. This in itself was an important shift. The creation of new languages by colonized peoples such as Aboriginal Australians was often derided within imperial literatures and dramas. Aboriginal Englishes or Kriols were usually represented as a mock, and often mocked, form of pidgin English. Merritt's *The Cake Man* (1977) was the next play to gain critical recognition when it was performed in 1975. Merritt's play is based on mission life. The narrative follows the story of a family, Ruby, Sweet William, and their child Pumpkin Head, as they struggle to survive on a mission. This was followed by Bostock's *Here Comes the Nigger* in 1976. Bostock's play deals with the experience of urban Indigenous Australians. The narrative is about Sam, a young blind Aboriginal man, who is tutored by Odette, a young Euro-Australian woman. The central theme of the narrative is the exploration of the racist attitudes on both the Euro-Australian and Aboriginal sides when the other characters mistakenly assume there is a sexual relationship between the two young people. In all of these plays, political and spiritual issues are important elements.

---

[2] These playwrights and their work are discussed in more detail in Maryrose Casey, *Creating Frames: Contemporary Indigenous Theatre* (Brisbane: University of Queensland Press, 2004).

In the 1980s Noongar writers from Western Australia, such as Jack Davis, brought stories of Australian black-white relations to many audiences for the first time. For example Davis's *Kullark* (1983), first produced in 1979, and using Standard English, southwest Western Australian Aboriginal English, and the Noongar language, sets out to give an overview of the history of the colonization of Aboriginal people by Europeans from first contact to the treatment of Aboriginal returned servicemen after the Second World War. This was followed in the 1980s by other plays, including Davis' trilogy *The First Born*, which consisted of *No Sugar* (1986), *The Dreamers* (1983), and *Barungin* (1989). These three plays follow generations of a Noongar family from the 1930s to the late twentieth century. Productions of these plays and others toured nationally and internationally.

Many of the texts in the 1970s and 1980s focused on telling collective stories about the experiences of Aboriginal people. In the 1990s and 2000s, as well as those focused on collective stories, many texts by Aboriginal writers concentrated on individual experiences. This work explores themes perceived as specifically Aboriginal, such as racism or the impact of racialized government policies, including the removal of children as well as more general themes. Some of this work is written primarily for raising awareness of important issues either with Aboriginal or non-Aboriginal audiences. For example, work such as Jimmy Chi's *Corrugation Road* (1995) focuses on the experience of mental illness as it affects any patient. In Ningali and Kelton Pell's *Solid* (2000) and Odette Best's *True* (2004), attention is focused on the ways in which Aboriginal people relate to each other. Work such as *Ngurrumilmarrmiriyu: Wrong Skin* (2010) created by the Chooky Dancers and elders from Elcho Island sought to make urban Australia aware of the social and economic impact of "the Intervention" on Aboriginal communities.[3] Among the cumulative results of this extensive body of work was the launch in February 2012 of the Australian Script Centre *BlakStage* website to showcase Indigenous Australian theater texts. In April 2012, a national Indigenous Australian playwriting award was announced. Wesley Enoch, the first Aboriginal artist to hold the artistic directorship of a state flagship theater company, Queensland Theatre Company, acknowledged the debt contemporary writers owe the artists who first broke through to wider Australian and international audiences. As Enoch put it, "You don't get people like me . . . without people like them" (quoted in Frew).

---

[3] The Northern Territory National Emergency Response (usually referred to as "the Intervention") is a raft of changes to welfare provisions, law enforcement, land tenure and other measures, introduced by the federal government under John Howard in 2007.

One of the main goals since the 1970s has been to create Aboriginal-controlled theater companies. Over the decades there have been a number of these companies established across Australia. Currently the longest-running company is Ilbijerri Aboriginal and Torres Strait Islander Theatre Co-operative in Melbourne. The company has been responsible for developing and producing some of the most important dramas by Aboriginal Australians over the last two decades since it began in 1990. Notable plays include Jane Harrison's *Stolen* (1997), which tells the stories of a group of children who were forcibly removed from their families by white Australian government policies, and John Harding's *Up the Road* (1997), which explores the different pathways and futures available to young Aboriginal men: despair and death, withdrawal, or government employment. On their website the company proclaims that "Ilbijerri exists to tell Indigenous stories with passion, integrity and humour. The company believes in Black voices telling Black Stories—for all Australians. . . . Exploring a range of complex and controversial issues from a uniquely Aboriginal and Torres Strait Islander perspective, Ilbijerri has sustained one simple ideal when creating new work; Bold, Black and Brilliant." This mission statement could stand as an overall statement for Aboriginal playwrights and their work over the last fifty years.

However, despite writers constantly pushing against the limitations set by expectations and preconceptions of Aboriginal people and producing work within every type of genre, Aboriginal drama is, as the playwright, musician, and filmmaker Richard Frankland argues, still locked into a single genre of "black" (quoted in Litson 19). This compression of everything from tragedy to comedy and dance theater to musicals into one genre is increased by the narrow stereotypes that are understood as authentically Aboriginal. One of the challenges facing Aboriginal people is to break continuing stereotypes that frame "real" Aboriginals as exclusively those living according to traditional Law in remote areas of Australia. These stereotypes continue to hold currency. In 2009 Andrew Bolt, a conservative Australian journalist, published his belief that, for Aboriginal people to be authentic, they must be identifiable by "racial differences you [can] detect with a naked eye." They come "from the bush," practice "real draw-in-the-dirt" art, and "real Aboriginal techniques or traditions."

As I have discussed elsewhere, these terms of recognition operate within an economy of authenticity established in the nineteenth century that located the cultural and embodied "real" Aboriginal people as savage and absent, something from the past, temporally and spatially distant (Casey, 2012, 7). Logically, therefore, Aboriginal people who are physically present and engaging cannot be real Aboriginals because they do not fit within that economy, regardless of cultural heritage and life experience. This results in performances and individuals being located within or excluded from the economy of authenticity. These notions of authenticity continue to inform thinking about Aboriginal identity. Research around land rights cases in the mid-1990s revealed that within the courts, in order for an Aboriginal person to be received as authentic and therefore a credible witness, the claimant had to be very dark skinned, from a remote area, illiterate, with minimal, if any, English skills, and inexperienced in negotiating in a legal context (Walsh, 98). The reality is that more than 75 percent of Aboriginal Australians live in rural and urban contexts with around 24 percent living in remote communities. Unlike Bolt's definition, which is based on external signifiers, the current definition of who is or can identify as Aboriginal or Torres Strait Islander is primarily social. An Indigenous Australian is defined as a person who is a descendent of an Indigenous inhabitant of Australia, identifies as an Aboriginal or Torres Strait Islander, and is recognized as Indigenous by members of an Aboriginal or Torres Strait Islander community.[4]

Conflicting or confused generalizations about who is Aboriginal are further compounded by the lack of social contact between Aboriginal and non-Aboriginal people. This lack of direct experience enables many non-Aboriginal people to think that Aboriginality equates with social problems, such as poverty or alcoholism, and race-specific issues, such as the impact of child removal and the belief that Aboriginal people are all the same. As musician and actor David Page suggests, one of the challenges that confront Aboriginal artists is that "you have to separate yourself from the pigeon hole attitude . . . that is out there in Australia. . . . We are not all 'just' Aboriginal. We don't all come under that banner. The similarity is that we have become these victims of colonisation. That is the similarity. Beyond that, and before that, it was complex and diverse" (personal interview, Sydney, 2007).

The task of contesting these generalized and stereotyped attitudes is not straightforward. Wesley Enoch, a prominent example of the current generation of playwrights, argues that there is pressure on Aboriginal playwrights to conform to audience expectations about the type of material and approaches they use. This pressure, notes Enoch, is in part because as a general rule "you have one show and the audience member sees that in isolation. Then they say, 'that's who you are.' . . . They don't get to see what else you're about or the diversity of our own experience or where we're coming from in our own minds" (personal interview, Melbourne, 2007). On this basis, as an effectively representative example, there is a need to be aware of the image of Aboriginality that will be taken

---

[4] This definition resulted from a High Court decision and is accepted by the Australian Commonwealth Government and its authorities. It is also the definition preferred by most Aboriginal and Torres Strait Islander people. See Marcia Langton, *Well I Heard It on the Radio, and I Saw It on the Television* (Sydney: Australian Film Commission, 1993).

away by audience members who may well never either deal directly with Aboriginal people or see another Aboriginal performance. This pressure is exacerbated by what Enoch sees as

> the need from non-Indigenous Australians in particular, but also Indigenous Australia, for us to have this united face, this front, this political position that calls on us to try and tell this kind of story because this kind of story gives us political traction in the world and gives us some kind of moral authority or whatever. My battle is to say, well if it's the truth let's tell it, if it's interesting let's tell it, if it's a story let's tell it, but let's not tell only one story, let's tell all the multitude of stories and then people can see that we are more complex people than just one face allows. . . . You scratch the surface and realise it's so much more complicated. (personal interview, Melbourne, 2007)

Artists like Enoch recognize a responsibility to represent a people and a history. So, as a writer and director, Enoch negotiates the bind that, as an Indigenous practitioner, his work is received as representing a generalized notion of Indigenous people, but it is his individual Indigenous sensibility that is expressed, not that of a representative Indigenous person. An example of the strategies he has explored to engage with this bind is demonstrated in his direction of Harrison's *Stolen* in the late 1990s. *Stolen* was the result of Ilbijerri commission to create a drama focused on the stories of children removed from their families from 1880s to 1970s, known as the Stolen Generations. These policies dating from the late nineteenth century continued into the 1970s and were the focus of a major Human Rights Commission enquiry in the 1990s. In *Stolen*, Harrison's text offers the impact on the lives of five Aboriginal children of being stolen from their families and institutionalized. In production under Enoch's direction, at the end of the performances of the play, each member of the cast stepped out of character and told his or her own story as an Aboriginal person. Some cast members, like the characters in the play, have tragic stories to tell about the impact of racism and racialized government policies; others do not. This moment confronts the audience's expectations and contests the tendency to generalize all Indigenous people as having the same experiences.

The focus on the differences among individual experiences has been one of the theatrical pathways that many Aboriginal performers and writers have taken in the face of racialized generalizations. The power of an individual telling his or her story has been used by Indigenous performers and writers as an important part of Aboriginal theater practices. Over the last couple of decades, numerous performances have been based on the single performer as storyteller. These texts often use multiple forms including direct address to the audience and incorporating untranslated

Aboriginal languages and Aboriginal Englishes as well as Standard English, song, music, and dance. The experiences and personal journeys in these monodramas are as varied as the individuals who write and perform them. Many of these monodramas are based on autobiographical details of the performer's or writer's life; others combine details from many lives into a representative central character or characters.

The list of highly successful monodramas is extensive and includes, in chronological order, Eva Johnson's *What Do They Call Me?* (1989); Jack Davis' *Wahngin Country* (1992); *Ningali* (1994), by Ningali Lawford with Angela Chaplin and Robyn Archer; *7 Stages of Grieving* (1994), by Wesley Enoch and Deborah Mailman; *Oh My God I'm Black* (1995), devised by Maryanne Sam with Patricia Cornelius and Irine Vela; *Thumbul* (1996), by Tom E Lewis and Mac Gudgeon; *White Baptist Abba Fan* (1997), by Deborah Cheetham; *Box the Pony* (1997), by Leah Purcell with Scott Rankin; *I Don't Want to Play House* (2002), by Tammy Anderson; *Windmill Baby* (2005), by David Milroy; *Gulpilil* (2006), by David Gulpilil with Reg Cribb; *Little Black Bastard* (2006), by Noel Tovey; David Page and Louis Nowra's *Page 8* (2006); Jack Charles and John Romeril's *Jack Charles v The Crown* (2010); and Gary Foley's *Foley* (2011). The rest of this chapter focuses on a range of monodramas representing different types of Aboriginal Australian lives. The writers and performers, through the diversity of these stories, contest the generalizations that are the basis of racism. In the process they promote a deeper and richer understanding of the complexity of Aboriginal experiences and lives. As Hilary Glow argues, monodramas are "notable and distinctive for capturing the particular nature of Indigenous experiences in order to achieve a new set of negotiated meanings between Indigenous and non-Indigenous Australians" (71).

# Black Voices Telling Black Stories: For All Australians

Monodramas fall into three main general categories reflecting the different types of lives and challenges facing Aboriginal people: urban, rural, and remote. The majority of monodramas engage with the diverse experiences of urban life for Aboriginal people. These often focus on particular aspects of the impact of racialized government policies such as those that resulted in the Stolen Generations. Other monodramas focus on the rural experience, particularly life in small country towns. Another grouping engage with the culture clash and tensions experienced by people who were raised or primarily live in remote traditional communities and then make the transition into life in urban environments. Beyond these three main groups, a further small group of monodramas focus on stories from the past that remain untold, such as the slave practices exercised for the benefit of the pastoral industries in the first half of the twentieth century.

## Stories about Urban Lives

The monodramas about urban life from across Australia divide into a number of further categories. Within the monodramas based on fictionalized characters, composite characters drawing on a number of people's biographies and autobiographical texts, these dramas reveal differences in content between work created by older generations who came to adulthood between the 1940s and 1980s and that created by younger people who came to adulthood in the 1990s and 2000s. One of the major contributing factors to this is that most of the older generations endured removal from their families or experienced restriction to reserves and often institutionalization. The younger writers' stories focus more on survival of their families and cultures. Though the monodramas all deal with racialized violence, death, and grief, a commonality is the strong humor through them all.

From Perth, the capital of Western Australia, Jack Davis' *Wahngin Country* (1992) presents the fragile yet resilient human being behind an established stereotype of Aboriginal men: homeless, living in parks, and drinking alcohol excessively. *Wahngin Country* documents that life, based on Davis' knowledge of people in that situation and observations of a park in Perth in the 1970s. It is a fictional story of a man called Michael Pedro Sebastian, a mission-raised Aboriginal in his seventies living on the fringes of urban life, inhabiting a park bench. The monologue is a humorous text that reveals the loss and anger that are part of the legacy of systemic racism and colonialism, as it reveals the self-mocking humor that enables people to survive and continue with some sense of self and dignity. Davis described Sebastian as "a happy go lucky fellow who knows all the scandals around the edges of the park, in the caryard, the delicatessen and the hotel. He's a sticky beak and a scandal monger" (quoted in Laurie, 91). Sebastian raids rubbish bins for food then tidies away the contents, ironically reiterating the popular advertising slogan "Don't rubbish Australia" (91).

In performance the action moves in promenade style from a broken-down old car to where a bench, a rubbish bin, and rusty old sprinkler represent the park. Sebastian punctuates his day by annoying local police, haranguing passers-by, and conversing with neighboring tradespeople who provide him with hot water to resurrect his "born again tea bag." They also supply him with methylated spirits (white lady) that he uses "to hold back the hate and hasten the dying."

A monodrama from the other side of the country, *Little Black Bastard* (2006), by Noel Tovey, is an autobiographical urban Koori story that starts in Melbourne, Victoria. Tovey is slightly younger than Davis, but he is still from the older generations. His story could easily have ended in the same place as the fictional Sebastian. Born in Melbourne, Tovey endured sexual abuse, neglect, poverty, and homelessness throughout his childhood and adolescence in the 1940s and the 1950s. By the age of twelve, he was working as a prostitute. He served a prison sentence when he was seventeen, after the police raided a drag party he attended.

Tovey fled Australia as a young man in 1960 and spent most of his life in England. A dancer, actor, director, and choreographer, for many years he denied his Aboriginality. As he states, "When I went to England, from the time I stepped off the boat until 1990, the word Aboriginal was never mentioned. . . . I'd invent stories about my past and be whatever people wanted me to be" (Tovey quoted in Benedictus). He reconnected with his identity as an Aboriginal man through the process of writing his autobiography, *Little Black Bastard* (2004), and the creation of his one-man show based on the book. Tovey describes the experience of reconnecting with his childhood memories as "unbelievably traumatic." In the text, he acknowledges the trauma and suffering of his childhood and his experiences as an adult in London, and he recalls "his return to Australia and his reconciliation with the country that had never managed to provide him with a home" (Tovey, "Little").

Two other monodramas from Melbourne focus on the autobiographical stories of pioneers of Aboriginal theater in Australia, Jack Charles and Gary Foley. Charles was involved in setting up Nindethana Theatre Company in the early 1970s and in its first production, *Jack Charles Is Up and Fighting* (1972). In the 1970s, Foley was a well-known figure in Aboriginal politics and an actor and occasional playwright. He was involved in *Basically Black* (1972), the first production by the National Black Theatre in Sydney in the early 1970s. In 2010 and 2011 these two men, Charles and Foley, separately devised and performed one-man shows drawing on the stories of their lives as part of the celebration of more than twenty years of theater production by Ilbijerri Aboriginal and Torres Strait Islander Theatre Co-operative in Melbourne. Both men have colorful personal histories and have played important roles in creating the space for Aboriginal drama.

*Jack Charles v The Crown* (2010), though different, has many parallels with Tovey's *Little Black Bastard*. Both are autobiographical, starting from abusive childhoods, but the paths followed from their late teens diverge. Charles's autobiography presents a personal account of the impact of systemic social and political racism that has changed over the years but still has consequences for him. As a member of the Stolen Generations, Charles was removed from his family, told they were dead, and institutionalized; he suffered physical and sexual abuse, homelessness, and heroin addiction; he was a thief and a regular prison inmate. Charles discovered theater in his teens, but even this positive influence was not enough to immediately fulfill the young actor.

Charles is the sole performer in the play, and, through the use of direct address, multimedia, and a trio of musicians, he tells the story of his life and his achievements to date. Not the least of these is his recovery from heroin addiction and dedicating himself to working with young Aboriginal people to save them from the life he led. Though Charles has turned his life around, his record stands against him and prevents him from effectively working to help others. The show is in two parts. In the first part of the play, Charles tells his story through direct address and video images. In the second part of the play, Charles gives a theatricalized address to the High Court, making a formal plea requesting the court lift the restrictions that his past still imposes on his activities and to allow him to legally teach.

In contrast to Charles, Gary Foley sets out to tell a different biography; the untold history of Australia. As Foley states in the Melbourne Festival program, "History will be kind to me as I intend to write it" (quoted in "Melbourne"). A leading Aboriginal political activist from the age of seventeen when he first went to Sydney, Foley was at the center of major political activities, including anti-Apartheid demonstrations in the 1970s, the Aboriginal Tent Embassy in Canberra in 1972 protesting Indigenous land rights, and the ongoing Aboriginal land rights campaigns throughout the 1980s, including the Commonwealth Games protest in 1982 and the protests during the 1988 bicentennial of Australia celebrations. He was involved in the formation of Redfern's Aboriginal Legal Service in Sydney and the Aboriginal Medical Service in Melbourne. Foley was a director of the Aboriginal Health Service (1981), the director of the Aboriginal Arts Board (1983–86) and the Aboriginal Medical Service, Redfern (1988). A man known for his biting wit and humor, his show *Foley* (2011) recounts the history of Aboriginal Australian political activism in the twentieth century in and around his own contribution, presenting, as he informed one journalist, "postmodern Aboriginal storytelling without a dot painting or a Rainbow Serpent in sight" (quoted in Flanagan).

As well as these, there are monodramas from members of younger generations from across the country. One notable example from Brisbane, Queensland, is Wesley Enoch and Deborah Mailman's *7 Stages of Grieving* (1996), a one-woman show delivered direct to the audience. Drawing on their own biographies and those of friends and family members, Enoch and Mailman created "a collective story that merges personal and family history with instances of public grief" (Allen and Pearlman, 26). The title, and a basis of the work, is a parallel between Elizabeth Kubler-Ross's analysis of the five stages of dying—denial and isolation, anger, bargaining, depression, and acceptance—and a division of Aboriginal history into seven stages—the Dreaming, invasion, genocide, protection, assimilation, self-determination, and reconciliation (Enoch, 14). Many of the stories are drawn from real life, such as the death in police custody of the Aboriginal dancer Daniel Yocke and the protests, grief, and outrage that followed. In a series of scenes, the text engages with a myriad of aspects of contemporary Aboriginal life, from urban protest to daily racism in retail outlets and the importance of family. An undercurrent through a number of scenes is a sense of sadness from the lost knowledge and people, a part of the legacy caused by the breach between the past and the present.

Another monodrama from Queensland, David Page's autobiographical one-man show, *Page 8* (2006), written by Page and Louis Nowra, explores a different story again of Aboriginality and urban life. The title plays on Page's position as the eighth of the twelve children. *Page 8* is an urban Murri story about a working-class family living in a housing commission estate in the Brisbane suburb of Mt. Gravatt. The show uses a mixture of storytelling, music, Indigenous traditions and practices, and home movies to tell the interlocking stories of David Page and his extended family. The monodrama narrates the life of an Aboriginal family negotiating systemic racism and getting on with life. *Page 8* tells Page's story from his experiences as a childhood singing star in a white satin jumpsuit in the 1970s to the present as an award-winning musical director and composer for performance and film, an actor, singer, and dancer. In the process, Page demonstrates how the family environment nurtured the artistic talents of its members. The result is a celebration of life and family, because as Page says, "you can't do it on your own."

## Stories about Country Towns

Life in country towns is the basis of *Box the Pony* (1997) another Murri story from Queensland. Written as a collaboration between Leah Purcell and Scott Rankin, the text is a semibiographical work drawing on Purcell's life. The story takes place primarily in Murgon, a country town where Aboriginal people live on the fringes, struggling against poverty and discrimination on a daily basis. In Murgon, as in many other country towns, life for young women follows the same pattern as their mothers', with early pregnancies and alcoholism. The narrative is delivered as direct address to the audience. Within the monodrama, Purcell plays seventeen characters or groups of characters. Song is integral to the narrative, complementing the storytelling. The languages used in the text include traditional Murri languages, Murri English, and Standard English.

The narrative is structured around two stories. One, told in the first person, is the story of the central character, Leah, based on Purcell's life choices, and her flight in her Datsun Sunny car to fame in Sydney. Purcell shares her experiences of wealthy areas of Sydney with a very humorous look at prejudice in cafes and on the streets. The other story, narrated by Purcell, is of Steffie, her friend back in Murgon, the life Purcell might have had. Purcell traces Steffie's story from childhood to her attempted suicide in the Datsun Sunny. The splitting of the narrative into two people allows Purcell to deliver the story once removed, comment on it from the outside, and return to it. The pain and humor of the story is shared between the audience and the central character, allowing the audience the space to recognize Steff's identity. The text illustrates two paths for a young Aboriginal woman: either to be lost to the recurring cycle of poverty and struggle or to escape the rural environment to the larger possibilities of the city.

There are multiple layers of humor in *Box the Pony* that range from that which is immediately accessible to anyone to elements whose humor requires a deeper knowledge of black-white relations. For example, in one scene, Steffie competes in the Miss Murgon Beauty Pageant. While Steffie is giving a speech arguing that racial harmony can exist only if both sides participate, a physical brawl develops in the hall (73–83). The writing is funny and includes obvious levels of humor; however, other elements are also revealed. Gillian Cowlishaw, in an analysis of race relations in Burke (another Australian country town), reveals the ways in which Aboriginal and non-Aboriginal people in rural Australia enact race: Aboriginal people are represented and expected to be loud, aggressive, drunk, and violent, while the white population represents themselves as moderate, controlled, and in authority (20–21). Given the pre-existing roles, there is a lot of playing up to and fulfilling expectations. This scene in *Box the Pony* is one where the different elements of the community act out the racialized role that has been imposed. Those aware of the dynamics in country towns are positioned to appreciate multiple layers in the scenario. This has resonances with traditional Aboriginal performance, where knowledge enabled people to understand layers of meaning within performance texts.

## Stories Negotiating the Transition to Urban Society from Traditional Life

The clash and competition between urban life and the life in remote communities is the focus of some outstanding monodramas from Western Australia and the Northern Territory. *Ningali* (1994), based on Ningali Lawford's life, and *Gulpilil* (2006), in which David Gulpilil shares his life with the audience, both seek to communicate and bridge the gap between cultures and lifestyles that they have experienced. Gulpilil grew up in a remote community under Aboriginal traditional Law, which governed social and spiritual life. He is an initiated man of the Mandalpingu grouping, one of the Yolngu peoples in Arnhem Land in the Northern Territory. His first languages were Yolngu dialects. Before he had extended contact with Euro-Australian culture, he was an accomplished ceremonial dancer, hunter, and tracker. His first contact was at the mission school at Maningrida in northeast Arnhem Land. In the late 1960s, his skill as a dancer brought him to the attention of filmmaker Nicholas Roeg for his film *Walkabout* (1970). The fifteen-year-old Gulpilil was cast to play one of the principal roles in the film. After that, with his newly learned English, he went on to appear in more films and television productions including *Crocodile Dundee* (1986), *The Tracker* (2002), *Ten Canoes* (2006), and *Australia* (2008).

The script of *Gulpilil* was the result of a collaboration with non-Indigenous writer Reg Cribb. Gulpilil told Cribb his stories, Cribb structured them, and then Gulpilil improvised his stories in performance. The development process and Gulpilil's personal performing style resulted in a performance that shifted between a comfortable sharing of yarns with a master storyteller and spontaneous revelations of pain and loss or mischievous humor.

For the last thirty-five years, Gulpilil has maintained an often precarious balance between his life within traditional Law and practices living in a remote community and his work in the film industry. He speaks from a position of cultural strength and knowledge within his community. The show captured moments and life in both the worlds that have shaped and marked him. This included discussion about his skin or totem and its meanings, ceremonial dance, hunting and survival in the far north of Australia, as well as his film experiences, awards, and clashes with the white judicial system. In between these stories, he speaks of regret, disappointment, and bitterness. He tells of the difficulties his fame within non-Indigenous cultures brought him and the problems facing his community and their children. He asks, "What can he do?" He answers this question with his commitment to teach and pass on his culture.

## Stories across Generations

Unfinished business left from often unacknowledged past racialized abuses and practices under colonization continues to leave traces in the present. This includes the slave practices used in and to support the pastoral industries in outback Australia until the 1970s. *Windmill Baby* (2005), by David Milroy, is a monodrama that explores some of this unfinished business. Milroy is a musician, director, and writer. Through one woman's eyes, his text reveals the experience of the rural racism and poverty that imprisoned Aboriginal people, the violence of white people, and the exceptions to the racist cycles of behaviors.

*Windmill Baby* is a highly awarded drama. As well as the Patrick White Award, the most prestigious Australian award for playwrights, *Windmill Baby* was awarded the 2005 Western Australia Equity Award for Best New

Play. In 2006 *Windmill Baby* won the Deadly Award for Best Theatrical Score. The Deadlys are annual awards established to recognize Aboriginal and Torres Strait Islander excellence and achievement. In 2007, Milroy's *Windmill Boy* was the recipient of the Kate Challis RAKA Award for the best Indigenous play of the previous five years.[5]

Set in the contemporary Kimberly, Milroy says that "the story was blending of a number of yarns, legends and oral histories from the Pilbara and Kimberley that had swirled around in my head for many years." According to Milroy, "Many of the characters and stories in *Windmill Baby* including the dog are based on, in some part, real events, people, and animals" ("Director's Notes"). Milroy's monodrama is delivered by Maymay, an old woman who has "unfinished business" (Milroy, *Windmill*, 207). Times have changed over the fifty years of her life from her youth as a station servant washing the Boss's family's clothes by hand. Now she carries a mobile phone while helicopters round up the cattle. However, the old stories and past deaths still need to be acknowledged, and through that acknowledgement their spirits are laid to rest.

The narrative, framed by the deaths of two newborn babies, shares the poignant story of lives and deaths of the Aboriginal people on the station and the tragic outcome of a love affair between an Aboriginal man and a white woman under a racialized colonial system. The lyrical and evocative language, combined with Maymay's earthy pragmatic relationship with the spiritual, demonstrates Milroy's light touch in dealing with strong emotions and pain.

## Conclusion: Indigenous Stories with Passion, Integrity, and Humor

All these monodramas deal with difficult stories sharing the pain and injuries of colonization and racism. The stories affirm life experiences that are both individual to the storytellers and creators and shared with their communities through common experiences. These experiences in turn reveal the political and social context that created the pain and continues to cause harm. Larissa Behrendt's description of *Windmill Baby*, in the introduction to a collection of contemporary Indigenous plays, could stand as a description of all the monodramas discussed here. The writing, notes Behrendt, "chronicles the cruelty of colonisation whilst paying tribute to the way in which wit, music and steely resolve allow Aboriginal people to survive heartbreaking events" (ix). As Ilbijerri proclaims, the work is bold, black, and brilliant, seeking to tell Aboriginal Australian stories to the widest possible audience.

---

[5] Kate Challis, the person for whom the award is named was known in her youth as Ruth Adeney (RAKA is an acronym for the Ruth Adeney Koori Award).

# Works Cited

Allen, Richard James, and Karen Pearlman. *Performing the Unnameable.* Sydney: Currency/Real Time, 1999.

Bolt, Andrew. "White Is the New Black." *Herald Sun*, April 15, 2009.

Casey, Maryrose. "Colonisation, Notions of Authenticity and Aboriginal Australian Performance." *Critical Race and Whiteness Studies* 8, no. 1 (2012): 1–18.

———. *Creating Frames: Contemporary Indigenous Theatre.* Brisbane: University of Queensland Press, 2004.

Collins, Patrick. *Goodbye Bussamarai: The Mandandanji Land War, Southern Queensland 1842–1952.* Brisbane: University of Queensland Press, 2002.

Cowlishaw, Gillian. *Blackfellas Whitefellas and the Hidden Injuries of Race.* Oxford: Blackwell, 2004.

Enoch, Wesley. "Murri Grief." *Dialogue* 27 (1996): 10, 14.

———. Personal interview. Melbourne. 2007.

Flanagan, Martin. "Fire Still Burning for a Champion of the Aboriginal Story." *Age*, October 10, 2011. Accessed February 2012. http://www.theage.com.au/national/melbourne-life/fire-still-burning-for-a-champion-of-the-aboriginal-story-20111009-1lflu.html#ixzz1x5KUCDRb.

Frew, Wendy. "National Playwright Award Aims to Unearth New Indigenous Voices." *Sydney Morning Herald*, April 4, 2012.

Glow, Hilary. "Recent Indigenous Theatre in Australia: The Politics of Autobiography." *International Journal of the Humanities* 4, no. 1 (2006): 71–78.

"Ilbijerri Bold Black and Brilliant." *Ilbijerri Theatre Company Site.* Accessed April 15, 2012. http://ilbijerri.com.au/.

Lang, Gideon. *The Aborigines of Australia.* Melbourne: Wilson and McKinnon. 1865.

Langton, Marcia. *Well I Heard It on the Radio, and I Saw It on the Television: An Essay for the Australian Film Commission on the Politics and Aesthetics of Filmmaking by and about Aboriginal People and Things.* Sydney: Australian Film Commission, 1993.

Laurie, Victoria. "Black Stars Risen in the West." *Bulletin*, February 18, 1992, 91.

Litson, Jo. "Giving Voice to Desperation." *Australian*, February 15, 2002, 19.

"Melbourne Festival Program 2011." *Melbourne International Festival Site.* Accessed May 7, 2012. http://www.melbournefestival.com.au/program/production?id=3960.

Milroy, David. "Director's Notes *Windmill Baby* Program 2005." *Belvoir Theatre Company.* Sydney, 2005.

———. *Windmill Baby.* In *Contemporary Indigenous Plays.* Sydney: Currency Press, 2007.

Page, David. Personal interview. Sydney, 2007.

Purcell, Leah, and Scott Rankin. *Box the Pony*. Sydney: Sceptre/Hodder Headline Australia, 1999.

Ross, Andrew. Personal interview. Perth, 2000.

Stanner, W. E. H. *After the Dreaming*. Sydney, Australian Broadcasting Commission, 1969.

Tovey, Noel. "Little Black Bastard." Belvoir Street Theatre Company. 2005. Accessed 9 May 2009. http://www.belvoir.com.au/310_whatson_upstairs.php?production_id=17.

———. "Tovey or not Tovey." Interview by Luke Benedictus. *The Age* January 16, 2005. Accessed 9 May 2009. http://www.theage.com.au/news/Arts/Tovey-or-not-Tovey/2005/01/14/1105582704727.html.

Walsh, Michael. "Tainted Evidence." In *Language in Evidence*, edited by Diana Eades, 97–124. Sydney: University of New South Wales Press, 1995.

# 10: The Stolen Generations in Feature Film: The Approach of Aboriginal Director Rachel Perkins and Others

*Theodore F. Sheckels*

FOR MOST OF the many years of Australian cinema, Aboriginality, as McFarlane, Mayer, and Bertrand (the editors of *The Oxford Companion to Australian Film* [1999]) note, was a rare subject. Then it emerged in a handful of films, either in negative stereotypical terms, as in Charles Chauvel's *Jedda* (1953), or in positive, mythic terms, as in Nicholas Roeg's *Walkabout* (1971) or Peter Weir's *The Last Wave* (1977). Either way, Aboriginality was filtered through a white consciousness that arguably distorted it. Then, beginning in roughly 1980, there were many films that reflected a white social consciousness insofar as they dealt with the injustices that Aboriginal people had experienced. Simon Wincer's *Quigley* (1990) highlighted nineteenth-century injustices, such as forcing Aboriginals over cliffs to their death; films such as Craig Lahiff's *Black and White* (2002) and Paul Goldman's *Australian Rules* (2002) emphasized more recent injustices in the court of law or the field of sport. But even these films essentialized Aboriginals: they were neither the dangerous figures of *Jedda* nor the spiritual ones of *The Last Wave*; instead, they were essentialized as victims—more so in earlier decades, less so in more recent ones. Other films, frequently ones involving a degree of white-black collaboration, got somewhat beyond essentializing. Bruce Beresford's *The Fringe Dwellers* is an example from the 1980s; Esben Storm's *Deadly* is an example from the 1990s.

What is, of course, missing from this brief history is film created by Aboriginals. This essay will attempt to account for the appearance of Aboriginals behind the camera beginning in the late 1980s. Certainly, Marcia Langton's Australian Film Commission report *Well I Heard It on the Radio and I Saw It on the Television* (1993) resulted in the promotion of the Aboriginal film artist. So did, in the nation's political consciousness, the 1992 High Court *Mabo* decision and the 1997 Human Rights and Equal Opportunity Commission's report, *Bringing Them Home*, on the Stolen Generations. There was more to talk about through film than nineteenth-century murders and twentieth-century courtroom and football corruption—more matters of relevance to Aboriginals were out in the open. The crucial difference, however, once Aboriginals became artists, not just subjects, was the removal of the filtering white consciousness. Removing that filter had a counterintuitive effect, though: rather than prompting more overt depiction of the story of Aboriginals in white Australia, removing the filter resulted in strategic indirection in the telling of that story. This essay explores that strategic indirection.

Peter Fainam's 1985 *Crocodile Dundee* is a film that, despite its popularity outside Australia, many in the nation like to fault, and its take on Aboriginality, although positive, can certainly be criticized. The film, however, did present the Aboriginal attitude toward land accurately. Whereas white Australians focused on ownership, Aboriginals focused on stewardship over land they were part of. Colonial degrees and deeds notwithstanding, they never, in their minds, totally lost this stewardship. Thus, when Aboriginals turn to film, it is less the land issue evoked by the High Court decision in *Mabo v. Queensland (No. 1)* (1988) that they raise and more the Stolen Generations one. The land issue was important, but it was arguably less compelling because stewardship had remained continuous in Aboriginal eyes and because white Australians were willing to engage in discussions about the land—thus, several pieces of parliamentary legislation— but avoided the Stolen Generations issue almost entirely.[1]

The "almost" is illustrated well by Beresford's 1980s film *The Fringe Dwellers*, as much for what it does not say about the Stolen Generations as for what it does. It presents three groups of Aboriginals, all living on the fringes of a white-dominated Australian town. Its focus is on the youngest, who wants to make their way in a white Australia without discrimination. As a counterpoint, the oldest group wants to return to tribal lands and to live as in the past. The truly interesting group, however, is the middle group who exhibits both the anxiety of being torn between two worlds and many of the ill effects (alcohol, gambling) of white influence. Many of this middle group note, very much in passing, their mixed racial status. However, what is interesting is what is not said in the film's

---

[1] A comment might be offered here about Felicity Collins and Therese Davis's 2004 study *Australian Cinema after Mabo* (Cambridge: Cambridge University Press, 2004). Their thesis is that the *Mabo* decision compelled Australians—in particular, filmmakers—to rethink Australian identity. The films Collins and Davis discuss with this thesis in mind are, however, overwhelmingly the works of white Australians. So, it would seem that, if *Mabo* compelled rethinking, it compelled rethinking among white Australians along the subtle and not-so-subtle lines Collins and Davis trace. My point is that such a rethinking was less crucial among Aboriginal filmmakers because the *Mabo* decision did not alter how they viewed the land. Rather, the High Court decision confirmed a view that they had long held and never abandoned. Rethinking, then, was not necessary. What was necessary was the insinuation of the Stolen Generations issue into Australian awareness.

dialogue but is sung in Bob Randall's tune "My Brown-Skin Baby." It is sung at a fringe campfire by a member of the middle group with others, from all three groups, joining in the chorus. Beresford reprises the tune as the film's concluding credits roll, so its significance must have been known to him. Commentators, popular and academic both, however, seemingly missed the song's point, since they failed to discuss the Stolen Generations at all when discussing the film. It is almost as if the issue is not even raised in the film. The song's lyrics, however, tell the story of "a young black mother, her cheeks all wet" and how the "police be taking my baby away," how at a home the child receives "new clothes and a new name," and how, years later, the boy "tried in vain" to find his mother. The story of the Stolen Generations is raised in the film, but so covertly that few noticed.

Phillip Noyce in 2002 discussed the Stolen Generations overtly—and exclusively—in *Rabbit-Proof Fence*; Baz Luhrmann in 2008 discussed the matter as well in *Australia*, blending the issue in with other "epic" Australian stories and a compelling romance.[2] So, in two decades, the white consciousness changes from implying in Beresford's case to confessing in Noyce's and Luhrmann's the story of the Stolen Generations. Noyce's film was, of course, controversial in Australia, with some in the government trying to soften if not suppress its message and some in the media questioning its accuracy. Luhrmann's film was, arguably, less popular in Australia than it might have been because it foregrounded the Stolen Generations story. The white consciousness, as one might expect, seems to have changed more among some Australians than others. But the story, whether accepted or rejected, had become overt in white-directed Australian film.

Aboriginal directors, for whom the story was central, proceeded differently in presenting it. Tracey Moffatt in the late 1980s and Rachel Perkins a decade later proceeded in a manner much less overt than Noyce and Luhrmann. The work of these two women and their place in the emergence of Aboriginal film cannot be stressed enough, so, before considering their strategies in presenting the Stolen Generations story, let us consider briefly who they are.

Moffatt was born in 1960 in Brisbane. Her academic training is in photography, and her works in that form are widely exhibited in and out of Australia. Her three most famous films are *Nice Coloured Girls* (1987), *Night Cries: A Rural Tragedy* (1990), and *Bedevil* (1993). The first two are short films, and the second was nominated at the 1990 Cannes Film Festival for the best short film award and won a comparable award at the Melbourne International Film Festival that same year. In Tom O'Regan's

---

[2] According to Collins and Davis, *Rabbit-Proof Fence* "became *the* film of the Stolen Generation" (133).

*Australian National Cinema*, when he finally turns to "cultural diversity behind the camera," he mentions only Moffatt, about whom he says, "There is no more important figure than the Aboriginal and Islander film-maker Tracey Moffatt" (326). Her work was both groundbreaking and highly experimental insofar as her work in photography leads her to play with the visual images she puts before an audience.

Perkins was born in 1970 in a rural area east of Alice Springs. She received professional training at the Australian Film Television and Radio School in the suburbs of Sydney, but, even before receiving this formal training, she was extensively involved in Indigenous television program and short film development. Before turning director herself, she was both the founder of her own film production company, Blackfella Films, and the executive producer of ABC's Indigenous Programs Unit. As a director, her two most noteworthy full-length films are *Radiance* (1998) and *Bran Nue Dae* (2009), and her two most noteworthy films for television are the documentary *First Australians* (2008) and the musical *One Night the Moon* (2001). Both *Radiance* and *One Night the Moon* were award winning, and in 2002 Perkins received the Australian Film Institute's Byron Kennedy Award for innovative work in film.

Moffatt's preferred form was, as already noted, the short film. In general, Aboriginal artists found openings for their work in this genre and in documentaries as well as in television programming.[3] For all of these media choices, there is an economic explanation: films in these media were less expensive to make than feature-length films, and government support, which did, after Langton's report, increase, covered a higher percentage of the costs. For the short film especially, there is also an artistic explanation: the film artist was less confined by the conventions of Hollywood-style filmmaking.

Moffatt deals with the Stolen Generations story in her short film *Night Cries* (1990). Its cinematography is strikingly atypical, taking the viewer into a surreal scene suggestive of dream- or nightmare-scape. The film's music is strikingly ironic, setting Jimmy Little's happy song "Royal Telephone" against the sad reality of Moffatt's central characters. But what makes this short film especially memorable are its relationship to Moffatt's life, its intertextuality, and its emotional ambiguity.[4]

Moffatt was herself a member of the Stolen Generations: she was ripped from her home and her mother and raised for supposedly better

---

[3] For an account of the largely collaborative work in the documentary tradition, see Tom O'Regan's *Australian National Cinema* (London: Routledge, 1996), 170–75.

[4] For a slightly fuller discussion of this film, see Theodore F. Sheckels, *Celluloid Heroes Down Under: Australian Film, 1970–2000* (Westport, CT: Praeger, 2001), 130–32.

purposes in white society. The middle-aged Aboriginal in the film, then, is very much Moffatt's alter ego. The anger this character projects is Moffatt's anger, so is the tie to white society, presented in the film as the middle-aged woman's tense devotion to her feeble white stepmother. This woman raised her, but, just as the stepmother is stifling her independent adult life by emotionally demanding her care, this woman stifled her Aboriginality throughout all the years since her forced removal from her home and birth mother. The middle-aged woman then has much to resent in the aged white woman for whom she now must care, but she also has a measure of a child's gratitude and devotion. Thus, at the elderly woman's death, the Moffatt alter ego experiences both relief and sadness.

Noyce and Luhrmann, through their white consciousness, will depict the Stolen Generations as victims. The young girls in Noyce's film, who, against all odds, find their way back home after escaping a re-education camp near Perth, and the young boy, Nullah, in Luhrmann's, who dodges both the evil Neil Fletcher and the benevolent stepmother Lady Sarah Ashley, are presented in such a way that how they are acted upon, not how they act, is the central story. Noyce's film does not depict all of white Australia as victimizers, but it comes close in a presentation saved from melodrama and sentimentality by the fact that it represents a true story. Luhrmann's film adds some ambiguity insofar as Lady Ashley is a positive character who saves young Nullah from government forces while refusing to see that the surrogate mother role she gradually adopts is just as destructive of the boy's Aboriginality. The ambiguity is heightened by the boy's positive-feeling devotion to "Missus Boss."[5] This ambiguity, however, lacks the emotional depth seen twenty years earlier in Moffatt's *Night Cries*.

Luhrmann's film and Moffatt's also share intertextuality. Luhrmann evokes Australian films (e.g., *The Overlanders* [1946]) and Hollywood films (e.g., *The Wizard of Oz* [1939]) to achieve a variety of effects. Moffatt centers her attention on just one film: Chauvel's *Jedda*, to which she offers a striking counterpoint. In Chauvel's film, the adopted Aboriginal girl is lured away from her stepmother by a highly sexual Aboriginal male figure. The result is tragic for both the girl and the man Jedda and therein is Chauvel's moral point about the rightness of the Stolen Generations policy and the dangers of Aboriginality. Moffatt asks, what would the girl's story have been like if she had rejected Jedda and stayed with her stepmother? Moffatt offers a disturbing answer, although

---

[5] Of course, his name for her, "Missus Boss," undermines the sentimental mother-child relationship that the film's narrative very much presents. Thus, Luhrmann, having complicated the Stolen Generations story by making the boy complicit in it, undercuts that very complicity by having Nullah address Lady Ashley in terms that reflect the white-Aboriginal power imbalance.

not one without the emotional ambiguity noted above. Moffatt, then, offers viewers a film that is both personal testimony and cultural commentary, implicitly tearing down the film *Jedda*, which put on screen the moral justification many white Australians felt, if not articulated, for the Stolen Generations policy.

Moffatt's *Night Cries* is then an essential document in Aboriginal filmmaking. However, it is limited in its impact by its short length and, thus, its lack of widespread distribution. A decade later, Aboriginal filmmaker Rachel Perkins will take the next step—presenting the Stolen Generations story from the Aboriginal perspective in feature-length films. The major constraint upon Perkins was that, as will be explained, she was not the sole creative force behind her two noteworthy films *Radiance* (1998) and *One Night the Moon* (2001). Nonetheless, Perkins manages to refine what we might term the "indirection" in Moffatt's approach.

Hollywood feature films are direct in offering a narrative. Innovative plotting and unusual perspective can result in the narrative being less than overt. Nonetheless, even if viewers must work somewhat to assemble it, narrative dominates Hollywood feature films. And, despite occasional nods to other feature film traditions (e.g., Paul Cox's more European-style films), Australian cinema is very much in the Hollywood tradition. *Night Cries* runs counter to this tradition because it is a short film. Thus, it foregrounds cinematography and music, letting a narrative emerge in the background. The relationship between the two women develops. That this relationship is an Aboriginal story with historical resonance then arises—perhaps not for all viewers. That this relationship is a counterpoint to a well-known Australian artifact (*Jedda*) then emerges—perhaps for relatively few viewers. Moffatt, then, indirectly makes a political point. Her indirection allows her to make that point without evoking the backlash Noyce and Luhrmann received. That her film is in a medium not widely viewed limits this rhetorical advantage, however.

Perkins stumbles upon the opportunity to be indirect within the Hollywood feature film genre in *Radiance*, for the indirect telling of the Stolen Generations story is already in the Louis Nowra play on which the film is based. The play and film both foreground the story of what viewers presume are three sisters. They have reassembled in Queensland upon the occasion of their mother's death. One sister, Mae, had stayed with her mother to her senile end while the other two had roamed. The older sister, Cressy, had become a world-renowned opera singer; the younger, Nona, had lived a wild life in Sydney. The expected narrative, then, involves the relationships among these three, since not surprisingly Mae rather resents that she has had to surrender her dreams to be the mother's caretaker. Subordinate to that narrative is a seemingly extraneous one concerning the island off the coast that the mother spent her dying days staring at. The island was Aboriginal land once; it was seized by white Australians and, later, sold to a Japanese corporation for a resort. Nona wants to spread the mother's ashes on the island to reclaim symbolically the land of their ancestors.

The question of the fate of the mother's ashes is one that the film raises; another is the fate of the beachfront cottage she and Mae had been living in. The cottage was supposedly a residence the mother's former boyfriend, Harry, had given her to keep her quiet about their affair. But the gift proved to be a loan: Harry wants it back now. We never meet Harry, but we see his house when an angry Mae goes there after the mother's funeral to toss the flowers the unseen man sent at his door. Our suspicion that Harry is a white man has been aroused by now, and we soon come to suspect that all of the men in the mother's life, the different fathers of the three sisters, were also white men. Thus, we begin to grasp that the sisters are all of mixed descent.

As the sisters talk about their lives, we discover more. We discover that authorities had taken Cressy and Mae away from their mother and put them in schools in Brisbane. We discover that Nona was not stolen away because the mother successfully hid her when the authorities came. We also discover that Nona's mother was really Cressy, raped by one of the mother's boyfriends when she was not even yet a teenager. Although the film—and Nowra's play—focuses on the relationships among the three women and its trajectory is toward the purging of their mutual resentments, making them truly "sisters" again, these interpersonal feelings are not the only ones purged in the fire Mae and Cressy set to burn the cottage down. Also purged is the evil associated with the dwelling: the sexual abuse of Aboriginal women by white men and the kidnapping of the resulting mixed-descent children.[6]

*Radiance* is a very political film. It alludes to the confiscation of Aboriginal land; it alludes to how white men sexually used the black women in remote areas such as the Queensland canefields; it alludes to how mixed-descent children were stolen away from their homes and mothers by government officials; it even indicts the Christianity that white Australians hid behind and imposed on Aboriginal peoples.[7] The film also celebrates violent revolution against all of the above. Those viewing the film, however, would probably not initially categorize the film as "political." Rather, they would point to the foregrounded narrative of

---

[6] The Stolen Generations policy primarily affected mixed-descent children; however, in many cases, kidnapping authorities were only guessing about a child's racial background based on his or her appearance. Thus, a particular kidnapped child might have Aboriginal parents (and, perhaps, a more distant white ancestor). Also, the policy varied from state to state.

[7] Striking in both the film and in the play's stage directions is the picture of Jesus on the cottage wall. The picture is shown in flames along with the rest of the cottage, sharing the cottage's symbolic fate.

the three sisters, especially the late twist in the narrative that transforms the eldest and the youngest from sisters to mother and child. Beneath the surface of this human drama, however, playwright Nowra and director Perkins insinuate several Aboriginal stories, especially that of the Stolen Generations and the sexual exploitation of Aboriginal women that created the mixed-descent children in the first place.

The effect of this indirection is at least twofold. First, it arguably prevents a backlash against the film—or the decision by white Australians viewers to simply ignore it. The matters raised in the film's background were controversial ones. Noyce and Luhrmann, protected by international reputations as well as by their skin color, would be assailed for their "black armband" view of Australia's not-that-distant past. One can only imagine how Perkins's effort would have been received if the political message in the film had been overt, not indirect. Second, the indirection allows the controversial, uncomfortable message to sink gradually into the minds and consciences of white viewers. A frontal assault is, as military and rhetorical strategists both know, often ineffective. Not only is there a potential backlash but there is the strong likelihood of rejection. The filmic analogy to a military sneak attack would be indirection—gradually insinuating a controversial message in a manner that makes rejection less likely.

Perhaps as a matter of strategy, the film never says that Harry is white; it never says that the fathers of Cressy, Mae, and Nona were white. Furthermore, although we know authorities took the older girls away from their mother, we do not know for certain whether their removal was because they were thought to be of mixed racial descent. Perhaps they were removed because the mother was deemed unfit, something for which there is some evidence in both her early promiscuous behavior with men and her later socially unacceptable actions, which, for all we know, may have begun long before she became elderly and ill. So, if a white viewer wanted to, he or she could process the film's narrative without recognizing at all what it undoubtedly says about the Stolen Generations. But, even in such a case, the political message might be insinuated into the viewer's mind, especially if others, in conversation about the film, suggested that the abusive males were white and the three supposed sisters of mixed descent.

In the case of *One Night the Moon*, Perkins was not working with an adapted screenplay. Her constraint in this case was that she was brought into the creative team behind the fifty-seven-minute telefilm rather late in the process. As Richard Pascal describes the creative process, the idea for the film was composer Mairead Hannan's. It was inspired by watching Michael Riley's 1997 documentary film *Black Tracker*, in which Riley presented the true story of his grandfather. Hannan brought Aboriginal activist singer-songwriter Kevin Carmody and singer-songwriter Paul Kelly into the team and wanted Riley to direct. Riley demurred, and so

Perkins was asked. Despite her joining the team after certain decisions had been made (e.g., the basic storyline, the heavy use of music), Perkins was able to affect the shape of the finished film. Not surprisingly, given her work in *Radiance*, Perkins wanted to deal more with the mother-child relationship in the film. Somewhat surprisingly, Perkins wanted to pare the dialogue even farther, relying on cinematography and music more than already planned. Perkins, perhaps, saw in the film the possibility of merging the narratively-driven Hollywood feature film with the more artistic short film genre.

Another genre, one related to plot, is also relevant. As Pascal notes, there are many Australian film narratives that deal with a child lost in the outback. Thus, viewers of *One Night the Moon* undoubtedly began processing the film as another such story: charmed by a bedtime story, lured by the moon's bright light, a young outback farm girl wanders away from her home. Father and mother organize a search, but the father bans the black tracker Albert (Alex Riley in real life) from the party because of his race. The plot follows the true story the screenplay is based on. The search party makes mistake after mistake, while the black tracker, who could have led the group to the lost girl, looks on.

The mother finally turns to the tracker in secret. They form a search party of two and find the girl, who is already dead. They bring the body back, and the father is forced to confront the fact that his racism had resulted in his making the decision that had prevented her safe rescue. The father then commits suicide, leading to a highly emotional concluding burial scene of daughter and father.

*One Night the Moon* is neither a musical nor an opera, but it has elements of both, as well as cinematography more typical of a short film, such as Moffatt's *Night Cries*, than a Hollywood-style feature film. These characteristics compel reading patterns other than those used when viewing a Hollywood motion picture. One looks to the photography for signals of mood and theme; one listens to music and songs for clues as to the film's surface and deep tensions.

The film uses stark whites to highlight young Emily's innocence at the narrative's beginning. Then, the film fades into sad blues, probably enhanced by the use of a filter. The sky becomes increasingly ominous as the story progresses, and the film's early fades to black emerge as an ominous editing technique when used after the girl's body is discovered and as the father shoots himself. Perhaps most curious is the symbolic use of a gate at the front of the outback home. It stands without fences on either side; yet, the white inhabitants still use it. They have, then, placed a barrier where there really isn't one, and it affects their behavior—entering and exiting through the gate, even though doing so is absurdly unnecessary. The filmmaker shows us the gate increasingly as the film progresses, visually stressing that it is not just a gate.

Although the music throughout the film is a revealing aural text, four songs are quite striking. Early, the father and the tracker sing an alternating duet "This Land is Mine." The father sings the title lyrics; the tracker sings "is me" instead, establishing their contrasting views of the land. Later, an unseen source sings a Dylan-esque folksong that talks about an ideal world in which there is racial justice and equality. The song's lyrics contrast with the tracker's 1932 reality, which is what the screen depicts at that point. Still later, the mother and the tracker sing an alternating duet "Unfinished Business," where the song's reference is deliberately ambiguous. Does it speak about finding young Emily? Does it speak about the unspecified indignities the Aboriginal tracker has faced? Finally, there is the song "Once I Knew" that sandwiches the film. It is sung by the father. Between its first sounding and its last, we come to understand his shocked state of mind, having had all of his certainties about life knocked out of him by the events depicted in the film.

Reading a film through its visual images is not unusual; reading a film through its music is not unusual when the film is a musical. This film, however, is uncomfortably a musical. When we first see the father, we do not expect him to start singing.[8] We are surprised by song at other points: the convention of singing that we accept in a musical is jarring in such a realistic and tragic film. The discomfort we feel seems intended by the filmmakers: we are supposed to feel uneasy as we watch the film's story unfold.

It unfolds largely as a flashback from what we know to be a tragic moment for the mother and father to its causes. What is the nature of this tragedy? We find an answer on the surface—a dead child. We also find a deeper answer—the father's racial pride and the father's fear, almost pathological, of losing authority and control, tragic flaws certainly as profound as those that characterize Greek tragedy.

In keeping with the genre of tragedy, we expect some sense of uplifting in the end. We get it in the Christian spiritual sung by an Aboriginal woman at the funeral. Black and white stand side by side at the funeral, and as a black woman sings a song from the white religious tradition, all seem to tilt their eyes heavenward.

But why does the woman sing? There has, of course, been a tragic death. Furthermore, all in the community, regardless of status, can share in the feelings evoked by the tragedy. Of course, they share to different degrees, and one would think that one who is disempowered in the film's world because she is an Aboriginal would not sing so movingly at a white girl's death, especially when racist stupidity played a role in it. Those paying close attention to the film's images know a possible reason she sings

---

[8] Here, the reactions of Australians, who know Paul Kelly as a singer, and non-Australians, who largely do not, may differ.

as strongly as she does. At the film's beginning, we see her, the tracker (who is her spouse), and a child walking along the road; in a flashback— what we are led to believe is in the tracker's mind—we see the family at a happy community gathering. We note also, if attentive, that the child has a lighter complexion than the tracker or his spouse. But, in the bulk of the film, there is no such Aboriginal (or part-Aboriginal) child. The attentive viewers should ask, "Where has she gone?"

We are left to guess that the singing Aboriginal woman had a child, perhaps a mixed-descent child with a white man. The tracker then may be her father, may be her stepfather. This child, perhaps, was kidnapped away from the mother (and the father or stepfather) by authorities. The singing Aboriginal women therefore share the white mother's grief, especially since both had lost daughters because of Australia's racism. The Stolen Generations policy cost the one her child; the father's racist banning of the black tracker cost the other her child. The back-white bond we feel in the film's final scene is, thus, perhaps, deeper than we initially realize. Remember that one of Perkins's major contributions to the team effort was to shift the story away from a focus on the father to a focus on the mother-child bond. This shift, one might argue, sets up the parallel between the two mothers that insinuates the Stolen Generations matter into a film that is more ostensibly about a lost child and a scorned tracker. *One Night the Moon*, then, raises the issue of discriminatory behavior and, through the song "This Land is Mine," the issue of land rights. The film also insinuates the more troubling, more silenced issue of the Stolen Generations.

*One Night the Moon* is a film about a child lost in the outback; *One Night the Moon* is a film about a black tracker, this time one scorned. In being both of these types of film, Perkins's work situates itself in territory familiar to Australian film viewers. As noted earlier, there have been many films (as well as novels) about lost children. As of late, as Felicity Collins and Therese Davis note, there have been a slew of films depicting black trackers. Situating a film in a familiar genre not only actuates frames of interpretation but creates comfort, for the tension of not knowing how to read the film can dissipate once one recognizes its kind.

Just as *Radiance* immerses viewers in many plots other than the one that raises the most volatile issues, *One Night the Moon* situates viewers in familiar genres, keeping the most volatile issues at bay. The strategy of indirection or insinuation is identical. Rather than court backlash or rejection, the filmmaker suggests the core issue that she wants film viewers to recognize and reflect upon. Both films also give reluctant viewers an "out." Just as viewers can read *Radiance* as having nothing to do with the Stolen Generations, viewers can readily miss the Stolen Generations issue raised in *One Night the Moon*. For example, Pascal, in his otherwise insightful commentary on the film in *The Cinema of Australia and New Zealand* (2007), fails to note how the singing Aboriginal woman's story might parallel that of the white farm woman insofar as they have both lost a daughter. He attends to the film's racism as presented through the father but misses what is insinuated through the images in the film and the images not in the film.

*One Night the Moon* also immerses viewers in the trappings of experimentation. Its photography invites comment as does both the music in general and in specific songs. As noted earlier, the very fact that characters who in the formal realism tradition would be highly unlikely to burst into song do so in the film also invites comment: why is the director—or the team of filmmakers—choosing to use the conventions of the musical or, maybe, the opera in a film that is far removed from the standard fare of either?

John Schilb in the book *Rhetorical Refusals* (2007) talks about a variety of works of various artistic kinds that refuse to conform to the expectations of their genre. The immediate effect of refusing is discomfort. Beyond that, the artist, regardless of media, may wish to stage a variety of effects. Schilb highlights many. One he does not dwell upon is subterfuge—that is, using a genre or kind to evoke expectations with the hope that those expectations will distract the audience, temporarily, from some other point that the work is making. In both *Radiance* and *One Night the Moon*, Rachel Perkins (in concert with others) seems to be proceeding in just this manner. Believing that the Stolen Generations represent the crime or sin against Aboriginals that white Australia must face but (largely) will not face, she insinuates messages about the racist policy into films in such a way that they strike the viewer later, when the formation of other interpretations has provided a buffer to soften the impact.

Strategic indirection is then a strategy used by the two most noteworthy Aboriginal directors, Tracey Moffatt and Rachel Perkins, to raise the issue that they believe must be raised by artists within the nation and confronted by white Australia. The Australian Labor Party's victory in 2008 and Prime Minister Kevin Rudd's government's almost immediate issuance of an apology for the Stolen Generations policy represent a milestone in Australia. Perhaps, after this apology, strategic indirection will be less necessary for Aboriginal filmmakers who want to talk not about land or about white law versus Aboriginal law—matters that can be conveniently abstracted—but about sexual exploitation that gave rise to mixed-descent Aboriginals and a policy that denied these men and women home, family, and culture. There are suggestions in Aboriginal filmmaking (e.g., Ivan Sen's *Beneath Clouds* [2002]) that other such issues can now be raised. There are, however, suggestions in how the Rudd government's action was criticized in some quarters and in how Luhrmann's film was received that an indirection that insinuates rather than overt political commentary may remain a necessary strategy for Aboriginal filmmakers who wish to lead a multicultural Australian nation beyond its past injustices.

# Works Cited

Collins, Felicity, and Therese Davis. *Australian Cinema after Mabo.* Cambridge: Cambridge University Press, 2004.

Langton, Marcia. *Well I Heard It on the Radio and Saw It on the Television: An Essay for the Australian Film Commission on the Politics and Aesthetics of Filmmaking by and about Aboriginal People and Things.* Sydney: Australian Film Commission, 1993.

McFarlane, Brian, Geoff Mayer, and Ian Bertrand, eds. *The Oxford Companion to Australian Film.* Melbourne: Oxford University Press, 1999.

O'Regan, Tom. *Australian National Cinema.* London: Routledge, 1996.

Pascal, Richard. "*One Night the Moon*: Rachel Perkins, Australia, 2001." In *The Cinema of Australia and New Zealand*, edited by Geoff Mayer and Keith Beattie, 212–21. London: Wallflower Press, 2007.

Schilb, John. *Rhetorical Refusals: Defying Audience's Expectations.* Carbondale: Southern Illinois University Press, 2007.

Sheckels, Theodore F. *Celluloid Heroes Down Under: Australian Film, 1970–2000.* Westport, CT: Praeger, 2001.

# 11: A History of Popular Indigenous Music

*Andrew King*

> *We're talking about building bridges, and*
> *there's nothing like music to unite people.*
>
> —Mandawuy Yunupingu[1]

SINCE THE INVENTION OF recording technologies like the phonograph in the late 1800s, Indigenous music has been performed and recorded across Australia for a wide range of audiences. In the early twentieth century, for instance, music was recorded by anthropologists keen to capture the sounds of a culture that was believed to be in rapid decline (Thomas). Individual performers were not considered important in these recordings; their music was produced for scientific posterity rather than popular pleasure. And even though Aboriginal participation in local music festivals, touring vaudeville shows, and community gatherings was well documented throughout the twentieth century, it was not until the 1950s that Indigenous "pop stars" began to sell records for mass consumption (Dunbar-Hall and Gibson). Yet, with the persistence of recording artists like Jimmy Little over the past sixty years, Indigenous musicians have steadily gained prominence in Australia's mainstream. This has been particularly true of the past twenty years, especially since the Sydney Olympics, where promotional strategies have brought about a new popular pride in musical achievements, based upon a celebrated history of diverse sounds and voices.

Throughout this history, different Indigenous artists have negotiated changing degrees of non-Indigenous criticism, patronage, and recognition. In an attempt to capture these social and cultural changes, this chapter's history of popular Indigenous music has been broken down into four loose-fitting phases—the first emerges with the careers of Georgia Lee, Jimmy Little, and Harold Blair in the 1950s and 1960s. The commercial success of these early performers hinged upon the negotiation of prevailing ideas about their Aboriginality, which at the time centered on

---

[1] *Epigraph:* Mandawuy Yunupingu, quoted in Fabinyi et al., *Tribal Voice*, videorecording, Mushroom Pictures (Bendigo, VIC: Video Education Australia, 1994).

white policies of assimilation. A second period begins with the rock bands of the 1970s and 1980s like No Fixed Address and Warumpi Band; these bands incorporated Indigenous themes into their lyrics for the first time, promoting Aboriginality as a commercially central product. As demand for Indigenous music grew in the early 1990s, artists like Yothu Yindi and Christine Anu became popular exponents of "world music," where promotion and sales were directed to both domestic and international audiences. Today, performers like Shakaya (R&B), Local Knowledge (rap), and Troy Cassar-Daley (country), illustrate a further proliferation of musical styles in the mainstream, some borrowing from overseas trends.

## The Moomba Music Festival and Beyond: Commercial Aboriginal Music in the 1950s and 1960s

Though Aboriginal participation in local festivals and community gatherings was well documented before the 1950s, there were very few opportunities for Aboriginal participation in more mainstream venues or media (Dunbar-Hall and Gibson). Even during the 1950s and 1960s, a time of unprecedented expansion in popular musical tastes and markets, only a handful of Indigenous musicians managed to gain any kind of national attention. The earliest festival to showcase popular Indigenous musicians was the Melbourne Moomba music festival, a carnival-style show first developed from the performances of an all-Indigenous cast in 1951. The first festival was called "An Aboriginal Moomba: Out of the Dark" and, as a prototype for contemporary festivals like The Deadlys, featured the most prominent Aboriginal singers of the day. The first half of the program entertained audiences with corroborees, ornate displays of ancient myths, and Dreamtime stories, while the show-stopping finale consisted of a cabaret act with jazz singer Georgia Lee and opera star Harold Blair (Kleinert). Quite notably these two singers gained popularity both in Australia and overseas during the 1950s and, like their successor Jimmy Little, even starred in television dramas. Amid often condescending public debate about Aboriginal issues at the time, all three singers were promoted as highly talented performers, even though their Aboriginality was mostly spoken about by the non-Indigenous in the media.

As the Moomba festival's main attraction, Georgia Lee was one of the earliest popular Indigenous singers in Australia. Although Lee received acclaim for her performances in Australia, it was no coincidence that she first attracted notoriety performing for largely nonlocal audiences—American troops, who were stationed in Queensland during the war and who brought their own insatiable taste for jazz to Australia. Lee later found success in the clubs of Melbourne and Sydney, even becoming the first female artist to record an LP, but she encountered much greater demand from English audiences when she performed across the country and at upmarket West End venues. Her success in Australia ironically drew attention to some of the local prejudices producers had against Indigenous performers. As one newspaper editor mentioned upon her return, "It took an Englishman to tell us yesterday what a treasure we have in our midst in the Australian aborigine" ("Introducing"). In the mid-1950s, Lee's jazz style and exoticized looks were promoted to attract a more cosmopolitan listener. Her image and style connected her with black American performers, and she later toured the country with the globally famous Nat King Cole. As a black Australian woman, Lee was exotic, and as a jazz singer she was promoted with a sexual allure—as a star feature, for instance, one headline claimed how she made the "white men coo-ee [the] blacks" at the Moomba ("Introducing").

While tenor Harold Blair followed a similar career trajectory to Georgia Lee's, returning from overseas to greater domestic recognition, his profile generated more public debate about his Aboriginality. As an opera singer, Blair's talent garnered praise from critics and aficionados of the genre, as well as standing ovations from local crowds during his Australian tours. He moved to the United States in 1950, on the invitation of African American singer Todd Duncan, only to return a year later. But with the experience of performing with African American composers and singers and at community events in New York, Blair became more engaged in public life through Indigenous political advocacy at home. He joined the Aboriginal and Torres Strait Islander Arts Board and stood as a federal Labor Party candidate in 1964, using his respected position in white society to politicize issues such as land and citizenship rights. Though Blair's public image was strong enough to sustain a career outside of singing, his clean-cut persona was often co-opted into more mainstream ideas of Aboriginality. At the height of assimilationist policies in Australia, the singer helped brand the Harold Blair Aboriginal Children's Holiday Project; in later years his association with the Project came under scrutiny, as the organization was implicated in the forcible separation of Aboriginal children from their families. Blair's legacy as an Indigenous advocate remains contentious in that respect, remembered as a vocal supporter of justice and equality for some yet also a symbol of the unjust policies of assimilationism by others. He was often marketed as a model Aboriginal citizen in official government publications, which celebrated his career as proof "that there [was] no limitation to what the Australian aborigine can aspire [to], if he has sufficient aspiration" ("Dream").

Georgia Lee's and Harold Blair's careers as Indigenous singers in the 1950s were somewhat limited by the prevailing discourses of Aboriginality—being seen as an exotic exponent of jazz music and an "ambassador" (however the term has been judged) for Aboriginal people respectively. Without becoming stuck within the promotional limitations of the day, and the burden they placed on Aboriginal singers in particular, Jimmy Little's more enduring career demonstrates a promotion of his Aboriginality that has changed significantly over the years. Little's major record contract with Columbia Records in 1956 helped establish the artist as "Australia's first Indigenous pop star" (Pedersen et al.). In the early years Little was featured regularly on the *Johnny O'Keefe Show* and *Bandstand*, performing his style of harmonious ballads. Much like Harold Blair, Little's image was suave for the day—he was always presented in smart designer suits and impeccably groomed for live appearances, concerts, and album shoots. Compared with Blair's and Lee's careers, however, Little maintained a career in the media throughout the swinging sixties—he produced several top ten hits during the decade, including his 1963 signature tune "Royal Telephone." The following year he was voted by *Everybody's* magazine as Australia's favorite pop star. In 1960 his handsome looks helped secure a role in a Hollywood film, *Shadow of the Boomerang*, as an Indigenous Christian worker fighting for justice against a newly arrived American cowboy. Little also sang the theme song for the movie. In the 1970s, when Aboriginal activism courted media attention, Little was criticized for not being political enough about his Aboriginality. But a big part of his success was a more general characteristic shared by many celebrities, an affability and charisma in interviews and performances.

As the most successful Indigenous singer of the 1960s, Jimmy Little succeeded where no other Indigenous artist had before. Little's profile as an affable pop star, reinforced by publicity surrounding his strong Christian faith, helped the singer withstand often condescending commentaries about his Aboriginality. By describing him as "three-quarter caste" in a 1962 issue of *TV Times*, the magazine claimed that the star "doesn't stress the white blood in him, but neither does he make special capital of being Aboriginal" (quoted in Walker, 38). At a time when Indigenous issues in the media were spoken about in the patronizing guise of white protectionism, Little's gentle style enabled him to record a single like "Give the Coloured Lad a Chance" in 1958, an early protest song about Indigenous working rights (Walker, 35). His career has been complex, to say the least, cutting across television, film, and live performances. Little made a comeback after several film roles in the 1990s, releasing his signature *Yorta Yorta Man* (1995) as an album title. As recognition for his contribution to Australian music, Little's *Messenger* (1999) album featured the singer's unique versions of Paul Kelly, Ed Kuepper, Crowded House, and Warumpi Band songs. Little was later awarded an Order of Australia (AO) for his career in music, and he continues to be celebrated in Indigenous concerts such as The Deadlys and by non-Indigenous singers like Kylie Minogue.

Little's career has been the most enduring of any popular Indigenous performer, but like Lee and Blair before him, his Aboriginality was inescapably connected to a politicized public profile of 1950s and 1960s Australia. As successful performers in the public eye, their Aboriginality had to be talked about—usually in moral terms and in ways that would often position them as spokespeople for Indigenous people collectively (i.e., in films, TV programs, and government publications). Through their music Blair and Lee met with much enthusiasm from overseas audiences, yet public knowledge that they were Indigenous overshadowed ongoing commercial success at home. By contrast, Jimmy Little's longevity has only recently been acclaimed. Little's good looks and genial personality have enabled him to become the only Indigenous performer to record popular music across six decades. With the politics of Aboriginal social movements on the horizon in the 1970s and popular musical styles and cultures being transformed by more masculine forms of rock protest, the 1980s gave rise to a more political form of popular Aboriginal music.

## Beyond the Bush: "Settlement Bands" of the 1980s

'Cause we have survived, the white man's world
And the horror and the torment of it all.
We have survived, the white man's world
And you know, you can't change that.

These lyrics were performed live on Australia's popular music show *Countdown* by the Aboriginal band No Fixed Address in 1982. Before No Fixed Address sang the title song to their album *In My Eyes*, the program's host Molly Meldrum introduced the band as "one of Australia's most controversial groups." Though their image and promotion did not always seek to agitate the status quo, the simple presence and novelty of an all-Indigenous band evoked new ideas about how white audiences could relate to Aboriginal people through music. By drawing upon the musical style and politics of reggae after Bob Marley's successful 1979 Australian tour, No Fixed Address was the first popular Indigenous band to appeal more directly to a mainstream youth demographic interested in the alternative voices of Indigenous people. In the following years, Warumpi Band and Coloured Stone continued to attract fans throughout the 1990s through tours and concerts. Though each band achieved significant popular appeal, their insistence on developing music as an expression of black solidarity, land rights, and social justice became a unique marketing point, one that would endure in decades to come through a number of "anthemic" songs and productions.

The idea that Aboriginal music could be a mainstream form of entertainment is explored in the 1983 documentary *Wrong Side of the Road*, which was a promotional vehicle for the bands No Fixed Address and Us Mob (Lander). The film follows the musicians travelling to, and performing at, live gigs across the South Australian outback. The narrative starts in urban Adelaide (where both bands studied at the Centre for Aboriginal Studies in Music), and combines documentary-style footage of the band members trying to balance work, social life, and a future in music. The film draws attention to the difficulties band members faced performing at white venues, including police harassment at gigs and being denied pay and bookings by landlords. In one scene the group travels kilometers out of town to perform at a country hotel, only to be refused when the landlord tells them, "I've had trouble with Aborigines getting drunk here before." Feelings of injustice are not belabored in the dialogue; instead, the music promotes its own message of resistance. The film, through songs like "Black Man's Rights," which echo Bob Marley's famous "Get Up, Stand Up," also deals with more everyday elements of urban Aboriginal life. The strength of the narrative lies in its presentation of these political issues through ordinary characters, who themselves have a public profile and respect through their music.

*Wrong Side of the Road* brought to light the infusion of black activism with Australian music through a new Indigenous aesthetic. No Fixed Address articulated a protonationalist voice, which in the Australian Indigenous context pushed for greater recognition of Aboriginal sovereignty and land rights. In the decade following the referendum on Indigenous citizenship rights, for instance, the 1970s saw media interest focus on Indigenous issues as a source of conflict within the public sphere. This was evident in news coverage of activists involved in the famous Aboriginal Tent Embassy like Gary Foley who, in the early 1980s, was described as a "terrorist" for raising land rights concerns with politicians (Hawley, 11). The same demands for justice and for recognition of distinctive Indigenous rights were being made through music. No Fixed Address, through an affiliation with the reggae aesthetic, tapped into an international form of black youth culture to attract urban white fans who had not previously considered such Indigenous musical perspectives— either on television or at live concerts. "We Have Survived" has become an anthem from this era and is still performed by the band's lead singer Bart Willoughby at concerts around the country today, is still played on radio stations, and is evoked as the theme for Australia Day, the country's national day of celebration.

Warumpi Band pushed the possibilities of mainstream Aboriginal music further in 1984, when they released the first Aboriginal-language song called "Jailanguru Pakarnu" ("Out from jail"). From Papunya in the Northern Territory, the band was formed in 1982 by a mix of Indigenous musicians, including vocalist George Burarrwanga and Neil Murray, a white schoolteacher from Victoria. Maintaining a lyrical interest in Indigenous issues, their strength in performing both Indigenous and non-Indigenous songs saw their appeal grow among outback communities (Gibson and Dunbar-Hall, 258). Warumpi's aggressive rock style complimented Midnight Oil's political activism, and the two bands worked together on the 1985 "Blackfella-Whitefella" tour, which introduced their music to Aboriginal settlements across the outback (McMillan). A video of the tour captures Midnight Oil travelling and performing with Warumpi Band; each so-called concert was very small scale and impromptu, in dusty settlements with few amenities, but with plenty of locals dancing and having fun. The idea behind the tour according to Neil Murray was to "let the black people know that there's [sic] white people out there that want to understand." The film shows that an ethos of cooperation and mutual understanding between black and white could be achieved through music, promoting Warumpi Band as an icon of Aboriginal reconciliation. Consequently, they became more famous for the tour's namesake single "Blackfella, Whitefella," which was released in 1987 and is widely recognized as Australia's first pop song about Aboriginal reconciliation.

When the Warumpi Band released "My Island Home" in the same year, however, they unknowingly produced a song that would become a more nationally significant anthem as a song about Australia. The single was featured on the band's *Go Bush* album but reached a new popular audience when Christine Anu released her version just eight years later. A celebrated Torres Strait Islander, Anu's career was propelled by the song, which won the Australasian Performing Right Association's Song of the Year in 1995. Despite its author (Neil Murray) being non-Indigenous, "My Island Home" has a strong Indigenous lineage. It was also recorded by the all-female Aboriginal band Tiddas for the Aboriginal film *Radiance* in 1995 and most spectacularly performed again by Christine Anu at the 2000 Sydney Olympics. It is this later version that best illustrates the symbolism of its Indigenous performance as a song that sought to promote—whether successfully or unsuccessfully—Australia to the world as a harmonious and reconciled nation (Barney, 143). For Indigenous people, more aware of the song's Aboriginal history, lyrics about "salt water people" and "holding a long turtle spear" conjure up specific associations with local places and practices (143). Anu's lyrics also proclaim that "My home is Australia," which ties the song more explicitly to a more general sense of place—the nation being seen as a "land bound by sea." Despite different interpretations, the song's promotion as an Indigenous-themed text illustrates the increasing significance that representations of Indigenous music now play within the nation's popular imagery.

It is in this sense that "My Island Home" can be seen as both an anthem about Australia and an affirmation of Indigenous identity. Its promotion has taken on a whole new popular dimension since its inception as a Warumpi Band song in the mid-1980s, during a time when Indigenous music was primarily about seeking political recognition. Music was one of the few receptive media outlets for Indigenous expression in the mainstream at that time.

## Tribal Voice to Mainstream Icons: 1990s World Music

The symbolism of Indigenous music in the mainstream attracted a new level of commercial interest in the early 1990s with Yothu Yindi, arguably one of Australia's most successful bands. When the group released their second album *Tribal Voice*, featuring the award-winning single "Treaty," positive domestic exposure spawned opportunities overseas. The band initially charted new commercial waters in the emerging genre of world music with their combination of rock, dance, and traditional musical styles, singing in both English and Yolngu (Aboriginal) lyrics. The promotion of traditional Yolngu culture widened Yothu Yindi's appeal to more mainstream audiences, without the band disregarding its political focus. The seemingly incongruous idea of a commercially successful Aboriginal band generated the most publicity—it was noted, for instance, that the band would only sign a contract with the American label Hollywood Records after a company executive met with tribal elders back in Arnhem Land (Baker, 12). At the height of their touring success, the band's lead singer, Mandawuy Yunupingu, could be heard in interviews and radio programs in America, Europe, and Australia answering questions about the tribal significance of Yothu Yindi, their lyrics, dances, and performances. These educational values, of teaching white people about Indigenous culture through music, could also be seen in the band's commitment to the Yothu Yindi Foundation and its yearly Garma Festival of Indigenous music. Traditional meanings of Yolngu culture are also communicated through Yothu Yindi's music, explained on the *Tribal Voice* album's cover as representing "a complex and elaborate world view, a sophisticated system of kinship and rich ceremonial and religious behavior. By attributing human qualities to all natural species and elements, Yolngu people live in spiritual harmony with nature. This is communicated in ceremonial song and dance."

Though scholars have suggested that the success of Yothu Yindi in the 1990s relied too heavily upon marketing as an "authentic" and "exotic" Indigenous band, there can be no doubt that the band has retained a strong political focus through their music.[2] For instance, their most famous single, "Treaty," based on the Yolngu's ongoing demands for a

---

[2] Phil Hayward, "Safe, Exotic and Somewhere Else: Yothu Yindi, Treaty and the Mediation of Aboriginality," *Perfect Beat* 1, no. 2 (1993): 33–42; Tony Mitchell, "World Music, Indigenous Music and Music Television in Australia," *Perfect Beat* 1, no. 1 (1992): 1–16.

formal agreement between white and black Australia, reached number eleven in the Australian charts. The Melbourne-based remix group Filthy Lucre's dance version of "Treaty," which promoted the song through an equally successful music video, helped gain the single a top-thirty position for the year (ARIA). The original music video for the single contains footage of former prime minister Bob Hawke visiting the Yolngu, when he famously proclaimed there would be a treaty between black and white Australians. The lyrics capture the disappointment some three years later when Hawke failed to deliver, showing that "promises can disappear, just like writing in the sand." Similar to emerging singers like Archie Roach, whose acclaimed single "Took the Children Away" deals explicitly with the Stolen Generations, Yothu Yindi's profile developed at a time when popular interest in reconciliation became mainstream, even formalized in government legislation through the Aboriginal Reconciliation Act in 1991. Along with a focus on issues of native title, Yothu Yindi's success drew just as much interest in Indigenous culture from overseas as it did from a new political momentum for change in Australia.

Though Christine Anu's career developed during the same decade as Yothu Yindi's, her music and profile has extended beyond the label of world music. Most widely known for her rendition of "My Island Home" and as the first Indigenous female artist to maintain a career in the mainstream, she has also been held up as an ambassador for various Indigenous issues. Early TV appearances, for instance, tended to focus on Anu's Indigenous background, but subsequent work outside of the music industry—as a film and theater actor, dancer, and more recently a TV personality—helped her develop a more sustainable media personality, in keeping with other (non-Indigenous) popular singers. Anu, for instance, has appeared on ABC's popular children's show *Playschool* (2004) and recorded a traditional Torres Strait Islander song, "Taba Naba," with the children's music group The Wiggles on their album, *It's a Wiggly, Wiggly World* (2005). In these instances Anu's Indigenous identity may be signified quite explicitly, particularly if audiences associate her appearance with Jimmy Little's contribution on the same album. Knowledge of her Torres Strait Islander background, however, is not necessary for excitable toddlers and their parents—the target audience for the album—to make sense of her musical identity. In other media appearances, Anu's identity might not even be known—she provides the vocals for the national magazine *Woman's Day*'s advertising jingle, and her single "Talk about Love" was used in Channel Ten's 2003 promotional music. Unlike Mandawuy Yunupingu, and other Indigenous performers before her, Anu's musical career has successfully incorporated a variety of different media roles, some related to her Indigenous identity and others not. Her success in that respect illustrates important changes in the way that Indigenous music has been seen, heard, and promoted throughout the media since the turn of the millennium.

# Black and Deadly: Indigenous Vibes in the 2000s

As Australia's most famous Indigenous performers of the 1990s, Christine Anu and Yothu Yindi were integral to the 2000 Sydney Olympics closing ceremony, an event of unparalleled international magnitude. "My Island Home" and "Treaty" were iconic songs in that respect, helping to promote a new sense of national pride through Indigenous recognition and reconciliation. As an immense spectacle of theater, choreography, and music, the ceremony inadvertently became something of a watershed for Indigenous popular music. Firstly, it demonstrated that Indigenous music in its diversity had a central place in mainstream culture. Such interest has been sustained through events like The Dreaming festival, an annual international festival of Indigenous dance, music, and arts, showcasing national and local performers. In the lead-up to the Olympics festivities, Indigenous culture was also promoted through a series of performing arts festivals, including the first The Dreaming festival in 1997 and culminating in the "Hemispheres" world music concert, which drew large crowds with Christine Anu and Jimmy Little as star performers. But it was through the Olympics opening and closing ceremonies that Indigenous musicians proved their value as main attractions. Secondly, while Anu and Yothu Yindi were cast in somewhat ambassadorial roles as Indigenous singers for the closing ceremony, later concerts allowed for a much broader spectrum of performances, styles, and music. In the early 2000s, and through increasing exposure on television and radio, Indigenous musicians in Australia became associated much less with the world music brand. While emerging rap and hip hop artists maintain an interest in "black" forms of musical expression, Indigenous music as a whole has increasingly been promoted as an inclusive and expansive brand through integrated forms of promotion.

A key element in the promotion of contemporary Indigenous music has been the extent to which different musicians are connected through their public support of each other—through television, concerts, and websites. One of the most visible forms of such integrated cross-promotion has been The Deadlys, an annual award ceremony celebrating Indigenous achievement in the music and entertainment industries. Since it was first televised in the mid-1990s, it has become a major national event, attracting politicians and media personalities from across Australia. Though not exclusively focused on musical achievement, The Deadlys has been a useful platform for the promotion of both established and emerging Indigenous musicians. Over the years the event has featured musicians like Shakaya, Christine Anu, and Jimmy Little, whose songs have been supported by Indigenous choreographies and elaborate stage designs. Building upon the modest achievements of the Aboriginal Moomba of the 1950s, the ceremony also draws upon Indigenous culture and vernacular expression through its music. The term *deadly*, for instance, meaning "very good" in Indigenous vernacular, was self-consciously incorporated into the promotional campaign for the 2010 event, using lyrics from the R&B band The Last Kinection. The song comments upon the disparity between being awarded enormous respect as an Indigenous celebrity in such events on the one hand and experiencing a comparative lack of respect in everyday contexts on the other:

> When you see us on the street
> You don't really want to speak—to us
> You don't know we're black and deadly
> When you see us at a show—all night
> You wanna know us 'cause we're black and deadly.

Supported by the event management and promotions company Vibe Australia, which maintains the long-running website Deadly Vibe is an excellent example of a more integrated form of musical promotion. As an online resource for news about Indigenous music, concerts, tours, interviews with artists, and profiles of bands and singers, the website is a repository of information about the depth and breadth of Indigenous musical achievement. Rather than focusing solely upon emerging talent, Vibe and Deadly Vibe promote a historical sense of Indigenous continuity. The award ceremony frequently pays tribute to past musicians, while the website also details the lives and achievements of a range of contemporary artists. In that respect, the promotion of Indigenous music is seen to be expansive, incorporating successful artists of the past, emerging performers, and more established mainstream talents. A singer like Troy Cassar-Daley, for instance, whose award-winning style of country music is equally celebrated in events like the annual Tamworth Country Music Festival (claimed to be the second-largest country music event in the world) as well as television chat shows where he can be seen talking about his music and Indigenous background. Cassar-Daley is both a mainstream country music star and a successful Indigenous musician, lending his mainstream public profile to support Indigenous events like The Deadlys and the Dreaming.

While Indigenous music is now seen to incorporate many different styles, events like The Deadlys also actively engage emerging Indigenous musicians. One of the most popular performers on The Deadlys has been the R&B band Shakaya, who featured a number of times in the early 2000s after winning awards for Band of the Year and Single of the Year in 2002. Before their breakup in 2006, Shakaya were two young women from Cairns, Queensland, Simone Stacey and Naomi Wenitong, who gained national recognition after releasing their first (self-titled) album in 2002 with Sony and touring in the same year with Destiny's Child and Kylie Minogue. As mainstream artists they have frequently performed at other local and national music festivals, publically lending their support for Indigenous musicians at events like the Dreaming and NAIDOC's (National Aboriginal and Islander Day Observance Committee) week of nationwide community celebrations. In music videos and television appearances, their image is similar to other international R&B bands such as Destiny's Child, Eternal, and TLC. Shakaya cite Destiny's Child—the black female group from Texas who often speak of a shared sense of "sistahood"—as their biggest influence. Shakaya's appeal is also connected to the prior successes of the UK all-girl band Eternal and Irish boy band Westlife in the late 1990s, who were marketed more directly towards a principally female, teen demographic. Like these bands, Shakaya's music is often promoted through television endorsements and the sale of SMS ringtones, while their image informs the latest fashions and hairstyle trends. Though lyrically they are not as politically charged as their Aboriginal hip hop counterparts, their sense of style combines a contemporary black aesthetic that is marketed to both black and white audiences.

As Indigenous rap and hip hop has gained acceptance in the mainstream, a sense of black subcultural expression through Indigenous music has emerged. Much like the appeal reggae had in the early 1980s for Indigenous Australians, black music today is a form of Indigenous self-expression and the basis of a subcultural identity. Indigenous hip hop cultures have adopted practices like scratch or turn-tabling, graffitiing, and certain dress codes, including baseball caps, basketball tops, and sports jackets. Much of the ethos of hip hop comes from its African American political roots, and, through an awareness of the struggle for black justice, US hip hop "constitute[s] a means [of self-expression] by which otherwise silent (silenced) voices could be heard" (Maxwell, 46). Aboriginal hip hop is no different, and it includes artists who hail from around the country, rapping in different dialects and languages, such as Gumbaynggir rapper MC Wire (a.k.a. Will Jarrett); members of the Sydney's South West Syndicate, including Brotha Black (a.k.a. Shannon Williams); the Perth-based band Downsyde; Wilcannia Mob, who take their name from their hometown in rural New South Wales; and the Newcastle outfit Local Knowledge. As a means of localizing their profile, many Aboriginal hip hop artists find themselves actively emphasizing their difference from their US counterparts. MC Wire, for instance, emphasizes the value of vernacular expression and proclaims "I'm a proud Indijinus Hiphopper and my lyrics reflect a New Dreaming."

Once considered the music of a radical underclass, rap and hip hop have now become the music of the mainstream, and Indigenous artists have no doubt contributed to this commercial success in Australia. When Local Knowledge rapped the words "All the Murries, All the Kooris, All the Goories, Can you hear me?" at the national Oz Music Awards in 2006, for instance, Indigenous music engaged mainstream audiences in a more personal way—as if their audience were themselves Indigenous. Through such a "call out" to different Indigenous people around the country, their music asserted a pan-Indigenous connection with local audiences through the mainstream. With the integrated promotion of different Indigenous musical endeavors, artists are no longer limited by the catch-all "Indigenous music" category. Finding examples throughout all manner of musical styles, artists have commanded respect and admiration through a range of public forums—from mainstream commercial appearances, community events, and Indigenous promotions. With Vibe Australia and The Deadlys leading the way, and supported by Indigenous music features in other media, such as the youth radio station triple j and ABC TV, the public support for Indigenous music has grown throughout the past decade.

## Conclusion: Integrated Indigenous Promotion

Since the harsh assimilationist era of the 1950s and 1960s, Indigenous musicians have persisted in taking their musical skills to the concert, pub, or outback stage—even the film and television screen—to entertain black and white audiences. In the early days of pop music, the promotion of particular Indigenous careers was obfuscated by the assimilationist politics of the day. But, as black music entered into the global music industry during the 1980s, Indigenous musicians developed their own forms of political engagement, reaching audiences through national tours and concerts. Christine Anu's and Yothu Yindi's rise in global music markets in the 1990s became a sign of national pride and Indigenous success. Through the continued efforts of contemporary musicians, whose profiles are connected to different genres, styles, festivals, and audiences, definitions of Indigenous music have now become much more difficult to pin down. Such a freeing up of musical categorization shows the extent to which Indigenous music has become a more accepted part of the Australian mainstream.

Yet, in one form or another, Indigenous music has always been part of mainstream Australian culture. It has been through the persistence of performers themselves that their music no longer signifies one single idea or message. No longer are performers' simply silenced or negated as Indigenous spokespeople. As a variegated demographic, musicians themselves bring their own histories and influences to the music they write and perform and in doing so sing about experiences, memories, and knowledge that cross over with mainstream forms of musical expression. The indelible link among performers, their music, and audiences takes place within a context of changing values and attitudes. With greater emphasis placed on the integrated promotion of Indigenous music today, those values and attitudes in the mainstream can only change for the better and thereby change the way we see, hear, and remember ourselves in the music of our cultures.

# Works Cited

ARIA. "ARIA Charts—End of Year Charts—Top 50 Singles 1991." *Australian Record Industry Association.* Accessed May 10, 2011. http://www.aria.com.au/pages/aria-charts-end-of-year-charts-top-50-singles-1991.htm.

Baker, Glenn A. "40,000-Year-Old Culture Surfaces on Aussie Chart." *Billboard* (1992): 1, 12.

Barney, Katelyn. "Celebration or Cover-Up? 'My Island Home,' Australian National Identity and the Spectacle of Sydney 2000." In *Aesthetics and Experience in Music Performance*, edited by Elizabeth Mackinlay, Dennis Collins, and Samantha Owens, 141–50. Newcastle: Cambridge Scholar's Press, 2005.

Council for Aboriginal Reconciliation Act 1991 (127). Accessed March 10, 2011. http://www.austlii.edu.au/au/legis/cth/num_act/cfara1991338/.

"A Dream Came True! Our Singing Ambassador." The Koori History Website: Items of Interest from NSW Aborigines Welfare Board's Magazine *Dawn*. Accessed November 28, 2012. http://www.kooriweb.org/foley/images/history/1960s/dawn/dawn33.html.

Dunbar-Hall, Peter, and Chris Gibson. *Deadly Sounds, Deadly Places: Contemporary Aboriginal Music in Australia.* Sydney: University of New South Wales Press, 2004.

Fabinyi, Martin, Stephen M. Johnson, Mandawuy Yunupingu, John Buck, and Amanda Higgs. *Tribal Voice.* Videorecording. Mushroom Pictures, Bendigo, VIC: Video Education Australia, 1994.

Gibson, Chris, and Peter Dunbar-Hall. "Contemporary Aboriginal Music." In *Sounds of Then, Sounds of Now*, edited by Shane Homan and Tony Mitchell, 253–70. Hobart: ACYS, 2008.

Hawley, Janet. "The Unshakeable Black Conscience." *Age*, September 25, 1981, 11.

Hayward, Philip. "Safe, Exotic and Somewhere Else: Yothu Yindi, Treaty and the Mediation of Aboriginality." *Perfect Beat* 1, no. 2 (1993): 33–42.

"Introducing Miss Georgia Lee." ABC. 1951. Newspaper clippings courtesy of Dulcie Pitt and Karl Neuenfeldt. Accessed March 7, 2013. http://www.abc.net.au/radionational/programs/awaye/introducing-miss-georgia-lee/3671178.

Kleinert, Sylvia. "Bill Onus." *Dictionary of Australian Artists Online.* 2011. Accessed March 10, 2011. http://www.daao.org.au/bio/bill-onus/.

Lander, Ned. *Wrong Side of the Road.* Lindfield, NSW: Australian Film Institute with assistance from the Dept. of Aboriginal Affairs, 1983.

Maxwell, Ian. *Phat Beats, Dope Rhymes: Hip Hop Down Under Comin' Upper, Music/Culture.* Middletown, CT: Wesleyan University Press, 2003.

McMillan, Andrew. *Strict Rules: The Blackfella-Whitefella Tour*. Rev. ed. Nightcliff, NT: Niblock, 2008.

Mitchell, Tony. "World Music, Indigenous Music and Music Television in Australia." *Perfect Beat* 1, no. 1 (1992): 1–16.

Pedersen, Aaron, Sean Kennedy, Frank Haines, Stewart Young, and ABC-TV (Australia). *Jimmy Little's Gentle Journey*. Sydney: ABC TV, 2004.

Thomas, Martin. "Rush to Record: Transmitting the Sound of Aboriginal Culture." *Journal of Australian Studies* 90 (2007): 107–21.

Walker, Clinton. *Buried Country: The Story of Aboriginal Country Music*. Annandale, NSW: Pluto Press, 2000.

# Contributors

KATRIN ALTHANS is working on a postdoctoral project in the field of law and literature and teaches English language and law at the University of Muenster, Germany. She holds a PhD in English Literature and Culture from the University of Bonn, Germany, as well as a German law degree. In 2010, Althans published *Darkness Subverted: Aboriginal Gothic in Black Australian Literature and Film*, which was nominated for the Walter McRae Russell Award. Further publications on the relationship of law and Australian Indigenous writing are forthcoming, as is an essay on the implications of gender and the Gothic in adventure video games.

MARYROSE CASEY is director of the Performance Research Unit in the Centre for Theatre and Performance at Monash University, Melbourne, Australia. She is a cultural historian recognized as a leading expert on Indigenous Australian performance. Her work focuses on race relations, indigeneity, cultural identity, and the politics and reception of cross-cultural performances and public events. Her major publications include *Creating Frames; Contemporary Indigenous Theatre* (University of Queensland Press, 2004), *Transnational Whiteness Matters* (Rowan Littlefield, 2008) coedited with Aileen Moreton-Robinson and Fiona Nicoll, and *Telling Stories: Aboriginal and Torres Strait Islander Performance* (Australian Scholarly Publishing, 2012). She is currently an Australian Research Council Future Fellow working on a comparative study examining cross-cultural performances in Australia and the United States in the long nineteenth century. She is also a Buffalo Bill Historical Centre fellow 2012–13.

DANICA ČERČE is an assistant professor of literatures in English at the University of Ljubljana, Slovenia. Her field of research includes American and Australian literature. She is the author of *Pripovedništo Johna Steinbecka* (2006) and *Reading Steinbeck in Eastern Europe* (2011). Most recently, she has published several articles on Australian Indigenous poetry in the academic journals *Acta Neophilologica*, *JASAL* (*Journal of the Association for the Study of Australian Literature*), *Antipodes*, and *Elope*.

STUART COOKE is a lecturer in creative writing and literary studies at Griffith University, Gold Coast, Australia. He received his PhD from the Center for Research on Social Inclusion, Macquarie University, Sydney. His critical work on Indigenous Australian and Chilean poetry, *Speaking the Earth's Languages: A Theory for Australian-Chilean Postcolonial Poetics*, was published by Rodopi in 2013. He has also published a book of poetry, *Edge Music* (IP, 2011). His essays, poems, and translations have been published widely in Australia, as well as around the world.

PAULA ANCA FARCA is a teaching assistant professor in the Department of Liberal Arts and International Studies at the Colorado School of Mines, Golden, Colorado. Originally from Romania, Farca received her PhD in English literature at Oklahoma State University. Her research focuses on contemporary and postcolonial literature. Along with several published critical essays, Farca has published two books, *Identity in Place: Contemporary Indigenous Fiction by Women Writers in the United States, Canada, Australia, and New Zealand* (2011), and a textbook she coauthored with Cortney Holles and Shira Richman, *A Student's Guide to Nature and Human Values* (2010).

MICHAEL R. GRIFFITHS is INTERACT postdoctoral fellow at the Institute for Comparative Literature and Society at Columbia University. Originally from Australia, Griffiths received his PhD in English at Rice University, Houston, Texas. His research interests include transnational postcolonial studies, Australian literature, animal studies, and critical theory. Griffiths's essay "Biopolitical Correspondences: Settler Nationalism, Thanatopolitics, and the Perils of Hybridity," which was published in *Australian Literary Studies* in 2011, was discussed as an example of the "Best Recent Work in Australian Literary Studies" at the *Indian Association of Australian Studies* Postgraduate Workshop in Calcutta, India, 2012. An analysis of Kim Scott's novel *Benang* recently appeared in Nathanael O'Reilly's edited collection *Postcolonial Issues in Australian Literature* (Cambria Press, 2010). Griffiths's most recent work will appear in *Postcolonial Studies* in 2013.

OLIVER HAAG is a research fellow at the Austrian Research Center for Transcultural Studies, Vienna, Austria. Haag studied history and political science at the University of Vienna. His research interests are in the areas of Indigenous studies, German reception of Indigenous culture, and theories of nation building, with particular interest in Australia and the South Pacific. Haag is the author of academic writings on published Indigenous Australian autobiographies and (Indigenous) Australian literature in German translation. He has published in English- and German-language journals, including *Aboriginal History*, *JASAL (Journal of the Association for the Study of Australian Literature)*, and *Zeitschrift für Genozidforschung (Journal of Genocide Research)*.

MARTINA HORAKOVA is an assistant professor at the Department of English and American Studies at Masaryk University, Czech Republic. Her research interests include Indigenous literatures in Australia and North America, the impact of indigeneity on Central European minority discourse, and the ethics of cross-cultural life-writing narratives and narratives of belonging. She has published articles and chapters in *Contemporary Canadian Literature in English: European Perspectives* (Al. I. Cuza Press, 2012), *Alternatives in Biography* (Masaryk University Press, 2011), *Postcolonial Issues in Australian Literature* (Cambria Press, 2010), and *Central European Journal of Canadian Studies* (2008).

JENNIFER JONES is a lecturer in Indigenous Studies in the School of Historical and European Studies at LaTrobe University, Victoria, Australia. Her current project is titled "Disparate Housewives? Rural Women, Cross-Racial Collaboration and Life Writing in the Country Women's Association of New South Wales, 1956–1996." She has published an array of articles on Indigenous literature as well as one book, *Black Writers, White Editors: Episodes of Collaboration and Compromise in Australian Publishing History* (Australian Scholarly Publishing, 2009). Research for Jones's chapter in this Companion was funded by a grant from the Australian Research Council.

NICHOLAS JOSE is professor of English and creative writing at the University of Adelaide, Australia. He has written widely on Australian and Asian culture. He has published seven novels, two collections of short stories, a book of essays, and two works of nonfiction. He has been a member of the Writing and Society Research Centre, University of Western Sydney, since 2008. He was general editor of the *Macquarie PEN Anthology of Australian Literature* (2009) and visiting chair of Australian studies at Harvard University, 2009–11.

ANDREW KING is an associate lecturer in the school of journalism, media and communication at the Queensland University of Technology (QUT), Australia. King completed his doctorate in philosophy at QUT. His current publications examine how the commercialization of everyday media enables new kinds of interpersonal relationships between members of different communities, paying particular attention to Indigenous representations in Australia and the production of Burmese language media in Myanmar. His publications include articles in *Continuum: Journal of Media and Cultural Studies, Journal of Australian Studies*, and *Australian Journal of Communication*.

JEANINE LEANE belongs to the Wiradjuri nation in southwest New South Wales, Australia. She holds a postdoctoral fellowship at Australian

National University, Canberra. She completed her PhD at the University of Technology, Sydney, and she also held the position of education research fellow at the Australian Institute of Aboriginal and Torres Strait Islander Studies. Her interest in education, diversity, and Indigenous perspectives is strongly grounded in twenty years of teaching at secondary and tertiary levels. In 2010, Leane won the David Unaipon Award for her novel, *Purple Threads. Purple Threads* was also shortlisted for the 2012 Commonwealth Book Prize.

Theodore F. Sheckels is professor of English and Communication Studies at Randolph-Macon College in Ashland, Virginia. He is the author of book-length studies of South African literature, Canadian women writers (*The Political in Margaret Atwood's Fiction*), and Australian film (*Celluloid Heroes Down Under: Australian Cinema, 1970–2000*) as well as several book-length studies on political topics in the communication studies discipline. He has also authored journal essays and book chapters on these literary, film, and communication topics including essays on film adaptations of Peter Carey's fiction and the Australian films of Peter Weir in *Antipodes* and the overview essay on Australian film in *A Companion to Australian Literature Since 1900* (Camden House, 2007). He is the founding editor of the journal *Margaret Atwood Studies* and past president of the American Association of Australasian Literary Studies.

Chern'ee Sutton is a sixteen-year-old, contemporary Indigenous artist with family links to the Kalkadoon people from the Mt. Isa area in Queensland, Australia. She started painting when she was thirteen years old and mostly paints on canvas using acrylic and raised acrylic paints. She is very passionate about her family's culture and history and she wishes to share this culture with the rest of the world. She has paintings on display in Queensland's Parliament House, Queensland's State Library, the Minister for Aboriginal and Torres Strait Islander and Multicultural Affairs' office, and she has worked with several government departments across Queensland.

Belinda Wheeler is an assistant professor of English at Claflin University in Orangeburg, South Carolina. Originally from Australia, Wheeler completed her PhD in English at Southern Illinois University. Her research interests include Australian Aboriginal literature, African American literature, and twentieth-century American literature. She has published chapters on Australian Aboriginal literature in edited collections. Outside of her Australian Aboriginal scholarship, Wheeler has published articles on American modernist poets Lola Ridge and Gwendolyn Bennett in *PMLA* (*Publications of the Modern Language Association of America*). She is currently completing a book on African American poet, artist, editor, columnist, and educator Gwendolyn Bennett (University Press of Mississippi).

# Index

CPSIA information can be obtained
at www.ICGtesting.com
Printed in the USA
LVOW11s1744050418
572435LV00004B/906/P